The German Novel
and the
Affluent Society

The German Novel
and the
Affluent Society

R Hinton Thomas
&
Wilfried van der Will

University of Toronto Press

© 1968

First published in Canada
by University of Toronto Press

Printed in Great Britain by Butler & Tanner Ltd
Frome and London

Contents

Authors' preface

The task we set ourselves was to examine in depth the response of six leading West German novelists to the challenge of their society, limiting ourselves to writers whose literary career belongs predominantly or entirely to the post-war period. In this inquiry, with Gaiser as a significant point of contrast, the problem of identity emerges as of fundamental concern. If not a new problem, it is of outstanding importance in the Contemporary context.

In the works here examined language is a factor of very special importance, and our method has required close preoccupation with it. As a rule we have found it satisfactory to quote in English, generally using our own rendering, but in the case of Günter Grass we have often resorted to the published English versions, and we gratefully acknowledge permission from Martin Secker and Warburg Ltd. to quote from Mr. Ralph Manheim's translations of *The Tin Drum* and *Cat and Mouse*. Where an English rendering would for our purposes have been inadequate, only the German has been given, usually with indication as to its content. Bibliographical material is contained in the notes. As the material is frequently not to be found in books, but in more casual contributions, a formal bibliography would have been disproportionately long or, if selected, inadequately representative.

We have benefited from the stimulus of week-by-week discussions of many of these topics in our undergraduate Seminar on Modern German Literature and especially with the students in the postgraduate M.A. Course in Modern German Studies during the session 1965–6, We must express our gratitude for their help also to Mr. Keith Bullivant and Mr. Paul Botheroyd—and, of course, to Professor Roy Pascal, to whom anyone who works in his Department owes at every turn a debt of a very special order.

Introduction

'Whether the year has been a good one, a moderate one or a poor one from the literary point of view, is decided not by the drama or by lyrical poetry but by the novel.[1] What Michael Georg Conrad wrote in 1885 about France is true of West Germany today. For a time after the war lyrical poetry had a strong claim from this point of view, but during the nineteen-fifties the novel established itself as the genre arousing the greatest critical interest and most easily opening the doors to fame and influence. Writers like Heinrich Böll, Günter Grass, and Uwe Johnson, have reputations on a scale only exceptionally attained by those working mainly in other literary fields. When Wolfgang Koeppen's *Das Treibhaus* appeared in 1953 confident prognostications about the future of the West German novel would have been premature, and the evidence then was not such as to lend weight, as far as West Germany was concerned, to Percy Lubbock's belief over forty years ago 'that the craft of fiction has larger resources than might have been suspected before', that it 'may now be starting upon a fresh life', and that 'there are unheard of experiments to be made'.[2] The appearance, however, in quick succession in 1958 and 1959 of novels so important as Gerd Gaiser's *Schlußball*, Heinrich Böll's *Billard um halbzehn*, Günter Grass's *Die Blechtrommel* and Uwe Johnson's *Mutmaßungen über Jakob* rather changed the situation. Lubbock had pinned great hopes on the 'dramatisation' of the novel through interior monologue, and the history of the novel in West Germany within the last decade or so has lent support to this view rather than to the belief that the death of the narrator signalled the end of the novel.[3]

An initial difficulty after the war — which is why at this stage no novel of comprehensive scope appeared on the seemingly obvious theme of Germany's recent past — was that the language inherited from a society so poisoned as that of Nazi Germany seemed unacceptable as a suitable medium any longer to speak about reality. It had to be subjected to critical scrutiny, and new possibilities had to be explored. Not even the language 'could be used any more, for it had been made impure by Nazism and war-propaganda. First of all it had to be trimmed. Every single "and", every single adjective called for the greatest circumspection.'[4] This was the task undertaken in Gruppe 47 by the so-called *Kahlschlägler*, so nicknamed by analogy with the job of clearing a forest or jungle. The short-term aim was language 'short of breath, and bleak', 'distrustful of long sentences and big words',[5] exemplified in Wolfdietrich Schnurre's story *Das Begräbnis*.[6] Presented at the opening meeting of Gruppe 47, its theme is the burial of God, and its style broken and staccato, without pretension to sustained argument or coherent reflection, disjointed like the language of a chance meeting between people hardly aware of what the others are talking about. The language of the West German novel has meanwhile discovered much more subtle and sophisticated possibilities, but the importance of this prepara-tory development remains, illustrating the relevance in this context of the statement that 'the problem of the modern novel is a language problem, and, if there is a crisis of the novel, it is a crisis of language'.[7] On the related question as to why so significant a stage in the post-war novel in West Germany was not reached till the late nineteen-fifties, this has to do with the advent of the affluent society, the speed of the transformation, the intensified focusing of attention on the present, and the critical and imaginative challenge this new social reality presented.[8] Obviously rich in opportunity and possibilities, it was, however, fraught with problems, some of which were of the same order as those that had confronted writers since the time of Naturalism in the last decades of the nineteenth century.

The Naturalists stood at the beginning of a period in which the representative writers were in the main not to be those who sounded what Gottfried Benn later called the 'seraphic tone'[9] but those in whose work experience was above all analysed and reflected upon. One aspect of this was the rejection by the Naturalists of historical themes for the dissection and scrutiny of contemporary social phenomena, and this at a time when, in the form of sociology, scholarly energy was beginning to be directed in a new way and with a new intensity to the analysis of society under conditions of change which, making traditional assumptions problematical, heightened intellectual curiosity about what society was and the way it functioned. In its revolutionary response to this situation lies, regardless of questions of literary merit or demerit, the deeper significance of German Naturalism. Thus Thomas Mann could describe it as a liberating experience for his generation; thus, too, writers as different as Rilke, Kafka, Mann and Brecht came to owe something to the mental climate that Naturalism helped to create. True, its campaigns now seem dated and melodramatic, but this is partly because there is no longer a significant German writer believing in a frontier to defend against the claims of social experience and sociological insight.

The self-conscious and crude rhetoric in Naturalist circles, under the slogan of *die Moderne*, about the battle to be joined against outdated convention marked the assertion, as far as Germany was concerned, of an important new awareness provoked by the way Germany was abruptly and belatedly being transformed by industry, science and technology. The spokesmen of the 'revolution in literature' were responding not just to the effects of industrial capitalism, which even in Germany was not so very new, but to the sense of having reached a stage at which it was no longer a question of adjustment to the capitalist industrial system, but of confrontation with the qualitatively new reality of advanced industrial society.[10] Just about the same time the shock of this discovery presented Ferdinand Tönnies with his distinction between the organic community of *Gemeinschaft*, and the open society of *Gesellschaft*, the one, as he called it, 'a living organism', the other 'a mechanical aggregate and artifact': 'all intimate, private (*heimlich*) exclusive living together, so we discover, is understood as life in *Gemeinschaft*. *Gesellschaft* is public life—it is the world itself. In *Gemeinschaft* with one's family, one lives from birth on, bound on it in weal and woe. One goes into *Gesellschaft* as one goes into a strange country (*wie in die Fremde*).'[11] The last sentence would exactly describe Rilke's experience when, soon after the turn of the century, he found himself in Paris confronted with a type of society at the opposite extreme to that with which he had been accustomed and the liberating implications of which he can affirm in his *Aufzeichnungen des Malte Laurids Brigge*, but only in his case by counterpointing them against the cosily reassuring imagery of the natural and *heimlich* world, of 'fruit' and 'kernel', of 'mother', 'womb' and 'breast': 'do not imagine that I am suffering disappointment here, but take note of how willingly I surrender what I had expected for reality as it is, even when it is horrible',[12] and he concludes his book with the consummation of the Prodigal Son who rejects his family, and can return to it only as consciously its alienated child, as *der Entfremdete*.

The Naturalists' preoccupation with milieu was one expression of this new degree of alienation in man's relationship to his environment, this confronting him now as a bewildering reality and for this reason in a heightened degree provoking analytical scrutiny. Naturalist and Expressionist drama have in common that in play after play man faces a reality felt as strange and alien, a *fremde Gegenwart*[13]—a disturbing, but also a liberating experience, as Tönnies was quick to recognise. Whereas, he wrote, in the organic world there is no 'dichotomy of cause and effect as, for instance, between the action of a ball striking another and the movement of the other ball', the 'emancipation of individuals from all traditional bonds produced, in addition to egotism and materialism, the victory of that reflective, clear and sober consciousness with which educated people and scholars now try to face things human and divine'.[14]

Thus it is that from about the eighteen-eighties important assumptions long taken for granted are, together with their metaphysical pretensions, abruptly called into question.

The idea of organic continuity, its dignity enhanced by association of nature with divine creation, and lending metaphysical prestige to concepts like 'culture' and 'tradition', faces Rilke's sharp challenge in the *Aufzeichnungen des Malte Laurids Brigge*, 'is it possible that our whole view of history rests on a misunderstanding? Is it possible that the past is false? . . . Yes, it is possible.'[15] The title of Rilke's book is significant, for reasons stated by Elias Canetti. Distinguishing between *Aufzeichnungen* (sketches) and *Tagebücher* (diaries), he says that the latter 'serve to demonstrate the continuity of a life', but in the former 'nothing is anticipated, nothing expected, and the aim is not to complete or to round off. The leaps between the sketches is the important thing; they stem from quite disparate parts of man, aim in different directions at the same time and accentuate the impossibility of reconciling them.'[16] 'The more time passes', it has recently been said, 'the clearer will it be that any genuine tradition in European history becomes a thing of the past, i.e. morally and in practice it will lose its authority', and so the possibility arises that we may have already 'crossed the boundary' to what in a drastic phrase is here called the age of 'post-histoire'.[17]

The second aspect, equally relevant with regard to the present situation of the West German novel, is the assumption that the individual, enjoying the fruits of culture, can at least to some significant degree embrace in his experience totality and unity. The *Sekundenstil* of the Naturalists, reducing narrative to a second-by-second succession of disjointed detail, and the aesthetics of Impressionism, are complementary symptoms of the breakdown of this belief, and Thomas Mann's Devil in *Doktor Faustus* applies the consequence to music, when he says that the 'historical movement of the material of music has turned against the unified work', which has come to 'despise extension in time . . . and leaves it empty'.[18] The distinctive nineteenth-century literary form of the *Novelle*, growing to a climax and unfolding thence to its close, becomes less typical than the fragmentary and often disjointed short story, and the integrated form of five-act drama comes to be increasingly challenged by 'epic' drama, with its sequence of disconnected or loosely connected parts. The principle of unified and unifying narrative runs into difficulties, and the stock of the all-knowing narrator sinks. Rilke struck a very modern note when, in 1905, he wrote to Lou Andreas-Salomé his moving letter about the 'antique painting' he had seen in Paris, a picture of a wanderer 'from distant lands' encountering a woman 'full of hearth and home', a *heimatvolle Frau*: 'But I, Lou, your somehow lost son, I am very far from being able to be a narrator . . . from being able to describe what has overtaken me in the past: what you hear is only the sound of the movement of my feet, ever going forward, ever vanishing on uncertain paths into the distance, I don't know whence or whither.'[19] This corresponds to a passage in Robert Musil's *Der Mann ohne Eigenschaften*: 'and Ulrich now noticed that he had lost this primitive epic sense (*dieses primitiv Epische*) to which private life still clings, though in the public sphere everything has passed beyond the possibility of being narrated (*unzählerisch geworden ist*) and no longer follows a "thread", but spreads out over an infinitely entangled plane (*auf einer unendlich verwobenen Fläche*)'.[20] Both statements, hinting significantly at the image of the labyrinth, are in much the same key as the opening of Peter Weiss's *Das Gespräch der drei Gehenden* ('the men just walked and walked and walked'), while in Grass's *Die Blechtrommel*, the central figure is specifically characterised amongst other things by his 'love of the labyrinthine'.[21]

The third aspect, related to the other two both as cause and effect, is the notion of the unified and unifying experience of reality, which becomes questionable as, against the older idea of organically unified character, the pluralistic society, pressing on the individual contradictory demands and opportunities in different directions at once, establishes the phenomenon of the pluralistic personality. Goethe's insistence on the inescapable identity of selfhood ('So mußt du sein, dir kannst du nicht entfliehen') within an organically evolving pattern of form ('Und keine Macht und keine Zeit zerstückelt geprägte Form, die lebend sich entwickelt') runs up against Nietzsche's assertion that 'each of us contains within himself a sketch of many different people. ... One is richer than one imagines, one carries within one's body the stuff of different persons . . . every character is really a role that is being played',[22] and against Rilke's: 'there are a number of people, but the number of faces is greater, for each individual has several'. Not surprisingly, the *Bildungsroman*, portraying the growth of the individual to wholeness, remains on the literary scene only to be parodied (lovingly it may be, as in Mann's *Der Zauberberg*), mocked (in Grass's *Die Blechtrommel*), or reversed (as in Martin Walser's *Ehen in Philippsburg*), and the German novel comes to derive many of its main preoccupations from the problems of a person's identity, or lack of identity, or different simultaneous identities. Walter Helmut Fritz's *Abweichung* (1965)[23] contains this remark about its central character: 'as so often, he has the sense of being composed of different elements all pulling apart from each other. The difficulty of having unified and consistent impulses, intentions, objectives. Sometimes a balance seems to establish

itself. But what about all the times that this doesn't happen?'
Hans Erich Nossack's remark in 1961 that 'one's own reality is
in the present condition of the world the only reality'[24] could on
this evidence appear as rather too confident a simplification, and
Gottfried Benn's phrase some forty-five years earlier about 'the
age-old swindle of the supposedly unified personality'[25] as more
in line with the pluralistic image of man in most of the novels
that will occupy us in this book, and implicit, for example, in
Hans Magnus Enzensberger's remarks about nationality:[26]

I have never really understood why nations exist. The people who
most enjoy talking about them have been least able to explain them
to me; in fact, they haven't even tried. I refer to those vehement
nationalists and their counterparts, the vehement anti-nationalists.
For about thirty years now, I have been listening to both insisting
that I am a German. I can't quite account for their emphatic tone,
for I don't in the least doubt the truth of what they are saying; and
yet they never seem to tire of bringing up this modest fact again
and again. I can tell from their faces that they feel that they have
proved something, that they have enlightened me about my own
nature, that it is up to me to comfort myself accordingly—i.e. as a
German.
　But how? Ought I to be proud? Ought I to be ashamed? Ought
I to assume responsibility, and if so, for what? Ought I to defend
myself, and if so, against what? I don't know, but when I examine
the faces opposite me I can guess what role has been assigned to me.
It is a role I can neither refuse nor accept. But even by refusing, I
can't rid myself of it. For the other's expression already intimates
his reaction to my reaction: outrage or satisfaction, approval or rage,
at how, *as a German*, I choose to behave.
　My nationality, then, represents something expected of me by
others. Of course, it is only one among many such 'role expectations' (*Rollenerwartungen*): my social status, my family, background,
my age—all call forth in every environment certain *idées fixes*,
designed to form me or to deform me into what I am in the eyes of
others . . . Strangely enough, the more clearcut these ideas are, the
easier it is to shake them off. Nationality, the most abstract and
illusory, is also the most tenacious.

With the claims pressed upon the individual by ideology thus
seen as having only the force of a role to be accepted or rejected,
writers are the more reluctant to be confined within any particular social or political dogma. Thus, while those connected

with Gruppe 47 have criticised the attitudes of East German writers and their adherence to a single and powerful ideology, they have also been readier than many to enter into discussions with them, exposing their attitude to abuse as 'an incredible balancing act between East and West'.[27] Moreover, since writers have ready access to the mass-media, the notion suggests itself that, as a 'militant association of interests', they dominate or even control them, using them for their subversive purposes like some 'vast propaganda machine'[28] and there have been publications wanting to expose the 'disruptive effect of left-wing intellectuals in radio and television'.[29] So in one of his essays Enzensberger ironically imagines himself setting out—in vain, of course—to track down the headquarters of this 'horde of communistic moles', the 'mafia of our literary life'.[30] This parodies the attacks to which the writer is open when, like Günter Eich in 1960, he can remark[31] that power 'has the tendency to make itself absolute, to free itself from its content and become an end in itself', that 'serious attempts are being made to construct the perfectly functioning society'. If, he goes on to say, 'our work is not understood as criticism, as an awkward question and a challenge to power, then we write in vain, then we are positive and decorate the slaughter-house with geraniums'. Eich's stand 'on the side of literature that is opposition' illustrates the point that, where the individual senses society as 'compulsion as the abstract', his protest 'must be directed at the whole, he has no longer any particular objectives'. Two years earlier Max Frisch had talked about 'the element of emigration that unites us all'. Writers, he said, demanded to be allowed 'the unspoken feeling of not belonging', for 'we have become emigrants without leaving our countries'.[32] This is in the spirit of Enzensberger's line about being 'here but absent',[33] and of Walser's remark that the language of the contemporary writer is 'the language of a spectator'.[34] The spirit of this critical reaction to the claims of power and ideology influences writers' views of their own activities as reflected in Gruppe 47. No longer shielded by the dignity and authority of being a 'poet' but now a 'poet without incense',[35] the writer's work exposes itself to open criticism in discussions in which, after completing his reading, he agrees not to participate.[36]

For people whose calling lies in the exercise of power related to fixed ideological positions, writers, readily assenting to Kafka's view that 'the negative is the task that awaits us, we already have the positive',[37] can easily appear contemptible, even treacherous, especially since their characteristic type of commitment is 'against abstraction, against ideology and its fronts of death'.[38] Commonly at home in the category of the 'homeless left', and incidentally with the danger of outsiderness deteriorating into a socially expected role,[39] the protest of the 'literary opposition' will be less directly political than subject to the rigours of literary form. For this new literary generation, one might say, 'politics is today the least revolutionary aspect of social protest',[40] language becomes a matter of major concern, its use a primary weapon. Eich describes the writer's task as 'to insert a word into the nothingness of directed speech',[41] and Enzensberger advises him to 'blow the fine deathly dust into the lungs of power'.[42] Significant is Walser's distinction between *wirklich* and *realistisch*, 'real' and 'realistic', the former denoting what is 'present' and 'exists', but 'not yet observed', the latter 'the relation of the observer to what is being observed'. *Wirklichkeit*, necessarily conservative, 'conceals or suppresses anything that does not help to preserve it', whereas a 'realistic' story is one that 'refuses to be dictated to by *Wirklichkeit*', but rather 'plays with it until it makes it confess "yes, I am like that",' and 'no exclusive attempt to explain the world can be allowed to disturb the dialogue'.[43]

The modern writer thus faces a twofold problem in a heightened degree, of identifying his own existence under conditions in which the notion of individuality has become more complex and elusive, and, complementary to this, of identifying the objective realities that constitute its environment. With the area of human activity of which the individual can have direct experience drastically reduced, and with consciousness deeply affected by scientific modes of thinking, the validity of symbols with transcendental orientation has been weakened. The stress is shifted from man's relationship to God (or to nature seen as God's creation) to man's relations in and to society.[44] Musil, who 'wrote novels in order to discover what he thought and felt about human life', and whose writing is to this extent 'experimental' and 'exploratory',[45] spoke with a very modern voice when, in 1918, he defined the task of literature as

B

'to discover ever new solutions, connections, variables, to find seductive examples of how one can be a person. It is the structure of the world and not of his own inner disposition that defines the task of the poet.'[46] This is a call to the writer to become analytical and experimental, 'so isolating natural phenomena that they become observable and measureable'.[47] With 'social structures' substituted for 'natural phenomena', this statement becomes relevant to the way nowadays the West German writer will often, on the lines adumbrated by Musil, tend to let his work assume something of the character of a 'model'. Examples are pre-eminently provided by the shorter prose forms, which in the last twenty years have acquired a quite new importance in Germany.

Even Gaiser's literary theory takes account of these aspects, although of the writers dealt with in this book he is the most conservative, and in his ideals closest to nature. Since for him reality is 'chaotic', and only few are successful in reading into it 'meaning and order', it is important to 'make a picture of things', as a 'way of arranging phenomena'. One does not thereby discover the deeper meaning, but 'one sees impulses, structures, connections'.[48] Helmut Heissenbüttel expresses the same idea more radically by contrasting the view of things surrounded by 'the fog of a pseudo-romanticism' with 'the model from which one can study one of the possibilities of human life and human community'.[49] This formulation is comparable to Siegfried Lenz's remark that 'I need stories in order to understand the world ... in the same way as other people perhaps need formulae',[50] and to the opening of a section in Max Bense's collection of 'attempts and models' in *Das präzise Vergnügen*:[51] 'as it was not possible to get a mould of the beautiful foot that had caught my attention, I transformed it wholly into words and transferred it to the sphere of language in order to study its connections'. Art of this kind, that is to say, only fulfils its task by relating itself to an idea of 'truth that presupposes a full measure of intellectual understanding (*Erkenntnis*)'.[52]

'The penetration of the experimental spirit', it has been stated, into art and scholarship[53] leads inevitably to the 'denaturisation of the object' and towards 'its decomposition and a redistribution of content'.[54] This is a principle now deeply assimilated into the way modern man analyses the complex and bewildering social reality around him, examines its 'impulses', uncovers its 'structures'. If for modern sociology the reality under investigation has to be 'denaturised' and 'distorted' by comparison with 'its "natural" appearance in the primary experience of the individual ... in order to become scientific fact',[55] similar trends are evident in many spheres of human activity, including those involving the creative imagination. Examples are provided by all those works of contemporary West German literature in which, in line with Zeitblom's impression in *Doktor Faustus* that the beautiful work of art had become a 'lie',[56] distortion becomes a necessary and accepted procedure.

Of the writers examined in this book only Gaiser, with whom we begin, and with one exception the oldest, still has any affinity with the ideal of a past when literature could live by other standards. He alone of the authors here represented can still express his faith in a society substantially deriving its standards from the cohesion of organic relationships, and in a style granting an important place to nature, myth and poetry. By contrast the work of the youngest, Uwe Johnson, with whom we conclude our inquiry, in its every feature, down to the seemingly tortured syntax of its sentences, declares its indifference to the ideal of the literary work as balance and beauty, its kinship with the principle that art 'has today to be dangerous in proportion as reality forbids it to proclaim harmony and peace'.[57] If nowadays we seek these qualities in the West German novel, together with roundedness of character,[58] narrative continuity, and a metaphysical sense of tragedy and fate, we find them pre-eminently in the make-believe world of the serial novels in popular illustrated papers.[59] Here at least the convention of the happy end provides a surrogate for faith in an intact order of human existence. Indeed, a criticism levelled against the contemporary West German novel by the publisher of a popular picture-magazine was that it did not 'want to reveal the world in all its fullness, beauty, tragedy, and joy, to help man regain the threatened harmony by showing him his place in the natural course of things'[60]—which is also to make the point that the gap between the literary and popular forms of the novel has never been greater than it is today.

Chapter 1

Gerd Gaiser

After an inconspicuous literary debut in the Nazi period Gaiser published his first post-war work at the age of forty-one in 1949, a collection of stories under the title *Zwischenland*. One of these (*Brand im Weinberg*) contains in bare essentials the theme of his first novel *Eine Stimme hebt an* (1950). The central figure in both is Oberstelehn, whose name, with the stress on the last syllable, indicates his descent from those who 'cultivated the uppermost fief', from a peasantry, that is to say, rooted in simple, integrated communities,[1] 'free from the seduction of arrogance'.

In a passage in *Brand im Weinberg*, suddenly 'all along the old vine terrace' he saw 'the old sunken temples conjured up out of the ground' and watched the 'spirits of the earth' bring in 'the sacrificial beast . . . and prepare the heathen feast'. Here a primitive, heroic and by implication nobler past is evoked, by the standard of which the modern urban community appears as corrupt and selfish, confused by petty aims, lacking in greatness and grandeur. Oberstelehn 'gazed at the cold, arrogant walls, and enmity overcame him; he suddenly hated the place', 'there seemed to be neither sympathy nor genuine suffering, no one seemed to be aware of having lost anything very much, even the whitewash had hardly been affected', and the people 'were all avaricious and callous'. Returning from the war, Oberstelehn feels himself a stranger in such a society. Like 'the lame officer' in *Das Schiff im Berg* (1955) and Soldner in *Schlußball* (1958), he belongs to a group of characters typical of Gaiser's work. Alienated by the rising affluence of contemporary society, they 'were tired of comfort before they had enjoyed it and had no time for accomplishments that had not been mastered the hard way'. They reflect Gaiser's sympathy with a more heroic view of man than is allowed for in modern society, with life in more direct touch with nature, more hierarchically

ordered, more firmly stratified. His idea is not, however, the
older status-order of peasantry, proletariat, bourgeoisie, and
aristocracy, but, in the Nietzschean mode, a hierarchy of merit,
with at the top men dedicated to an ideal not to be reckoned in
terms of security and gain, and at the lower extreme, for
example, nouveaux-riches and intellectuals.

The opposite ideal to the materialism that Oberstelehn rejects in *Eine Stimme hebt an* is described in the account in this
novel of the countryside that 'had lost its angel'. Devices like the
advancement of the separable prefix *(ihn abrief vom geschändeten
Boden, stand auf im graslosen Lande)* helps to contribute an
archaic tone, and alliteration *(lechzend im großen Glänzen, Geruch
der Geburt)* recalls the heroic style of the old German epic.
The names Gaiser uses also tend sometimes to have heroic
overtones, and they are important in other ways too. It was
suggested to him that 'one feels that no other writer loads
his names with so much weight and so many special characteristics'; he commented that 'the giving of names is obviously
an ancient way of achieving mastery', as in the second chapter
of *Genesis*, 'where man takes possession of the world by giving
names to things'. His further remark that 'through the names
the underlying strata become transparent'[2] links his attitude
to language with his view in *Eine Stimme hebt an* of nature as 'a
zone . . . stretching back to a time before organised religion,
a zone to which the modern city-dweller no longer has access'
and 'in which ancestor-worship and the veneration of the
dead play a major part, and ancient customs had authority
and magic'. So in *Das Schiff im Berg*, in an allusion to the
biblical account of Adam's part in the Creation, primeval
man is shown in the midst of nature giving everything its name:
'he saw all the life around him, immortal, because unconscious
of itself, mightier than himself, who had to die. Everything
turned towards him, as if called by him to receive its name . . . as
if coming at his command. And he spoke to it, caressed it with
names, called it bluegrass, hare's ear, sickle-wort'.[3]

The paratactic sentence-structure and the piling up of names,
reminiscent of the language of the Bible as also of magic chants,
constitute a typical feature of Gaiser's style. The tone of archaic
simplicity helps to immunise the world thus portrayed from
the rational and materialistic claims of modern life,[4] against

which Gaiser asserts all that nature represents to him. In imaginative, ecstatic language, sometimes mixed up with a sort of scientific shorthand, he describes in *Das Schiff im Berg* the ageless permanence of nature, its majestic cycles of creation, annihilation and re-creation, this 'terrible cycle, this continual change, creation and destruction'—in which 'terrible' implies not something to be deplored but, with its older associations, affirms awe-inspiring grandeur. The Mountain symbolises this aspect of nature: we 'meet nothing that has not already existed somewhere else before'. Epitomising a past more wonderfully mysterious, more elemental and more heroic than mere civilisation, it is an image of nature itself which, reaching back layer upon layer into the distant past, and destined with majestic indifference until the end of time to enact its blind processes of creation and annihilation, shames man's illusory faith in the progressive movement of history to rational and civilising goals. Man 'is no longer the measure of everything', runs a remark in *Eine Stimme hebt an*; 'all is subject to the lightning of the gods' is the Heraclitean motto of *Einmal und Oft*. Harsh, heroic struggle is the condition of moral and physical virility, the price of an easier life is spiritual unease (*Unbehagen*), disruption and decay: 'they were rid of the struggle for warmth and food, a struggle which once had taken up all their time. But security made them more sensitive to disease and doubt. There was an increase in illness caused by having too little and too much to eat, by poison, fear, and inner conflict.'

The quotation is from *Das Schiff im Berg*, one section of which shows what happens when man, who is 'merely transitory', tries to prove 'that he is superior to nature'. It describes how a lad, fascinated on his way home by a cavity on the mountain side, succumbs to the temptation to explore it, but its shape makes it impossible for him to get out. Nature triumphs over the human will 'presumptuously exploring and scheming'. The coldly indifferent tone of the conclusion ('of course he screamed a few more times, but there was not much noise left in him, and he became less and less conscious of himself') is Gaiser's comment on the 'transitory' fate of one arrogant enough to believe that he had nature in his power and for whom the price of education was fatal curiosity. This section of *Das Schiff im Berg* appears as a story in its own right in *Gib acht in Domokosch* (1959), where, as if

to point the moral, the next story (*Das Rad in Sghemboli*) opens
with the theme that the ultimately decisive forces lie beyond the
sphere of human will.

Contrasting with the precariousness of human ways, nature's
creatures are characterised for Gaiser by their instinctive
assurance, illustrated in the description of the narrator in *Am
Paß Nascondo* watching the fish crowding near the surface of the
lake: 'how could they manage to stick to the way they had
come, who indicated to them the direction?' This recalls the
parable of the ants in *Eine Stimme hebt an*. Their tactics, in
stripping the ground they cover, 'seem to be based on an
intelligent plan', but there is 'sheer lack of intellect behind its
execution': 'not a single insect performs either a leading or an
individual function. It exists within a context of action, of
which it is an unconscious, involuntary part. There is neither
intellect, nor goal, just sheer technical skill.' But they come to
lose their sense of direction, become a whirling mass stupidly
revolving, and soon 'one saw only columns of lesser species of
ants at work carrying the corpses away'. It is a parable of
humanity revolving 'like some senseless whirligig towards its
dissolution', and 'waiting for it are merely the undertakers of
some insignificant species, who will clear it away'.

Like the ants, the élite body of airmen in *Die sterbende Jagd*
(1953) form a unified community, without barriers of class or
calling, where 'even differences of rank had only a limited
significance'. Their existence has sense and purpose so long as it
is governed by collective ideals instinctively accepted. Betrayed
by men from outside, by the politicians, the airmen are doomed,
like the ants, to fight to the death in heroic but hopeless
struggle, their cherished ideals usurped by an 'insignificant
species'. Ennobled by constant confrontation with danger and
death, the airmen are contrasted with the representatives of
civilian life, preoccupied with security and prosperity. Begun
during the war, revised and completed when the domination of
civilian values was assured, *Die sterbende Jagd*[5] leaves no doubt
about the fate in store for this heroic community in a society
indifferent to its nobility.

'What will happen now?' asks Oberstelehn (in *Eine Stimme
hebt an*) about the situation after the war, and it is nostalgia for
the lost ideals of the Youth Movement that determines his

reply: 'the bourgeois installed in his own little world, idling away his break after a meal, with an indolent brain cheering himself up with poisons, because his intellect paralyses him . . . yet made envious by someone who has done better than he and who will go on improving himself'. It is the spirit of the Youth Movement too that is portrayed (in *Das Schiff im Berg*) in the unrest among young people who 'felt very clearly what was being lost', who believed that society should be renewed and, 'at once fleeing away and surging towards new horizons', pondered 'what they could take with them into this new and better world'. In *Die sterbende Jagd* Frenssen's virtues are attributed to his having come 'from the youth-groups (*Bünde*)', 'from the camp-fires'. Such people 'attracted followers not because they were appointed or wore bright-coloured badges of rank. They won obedience merely because they were as they were.' It is the cameraderie of his time in the Youth Movement that Oberstelehn recalls with his remark that 'the bleak open spaces (*Wüste*) make men brothers', the word having the Nietzschean association of standing for opposition to the enemies of 'life'.[6]

In *Schlußball* Soldner, too, belongs to this company. He also had 'slept in tents and kept watch at camp-fires', and his comments have the same contemptuous ring as Oberstelehn's: 'this world in which everyone all the time is preoccupied with being happy', a world 'full of gimmicks and articles to make one happy at the current market-price and of the best quality, happiness through manicure and radiograms, through bosoms, air-conditioning and vitamins, through dream-fulfilment, shaving lotion and easy spiritual relief'.

Those who in Gaiser's stories hold such markedly anti-bourgeois attitudes find themselves isolated in a society striving to re-establish bourgeois standards of behaviour when prosperity returns after the levelling effects of war and defeat. In this situation private dancing lessons assumed a new importance as a means of re-defining the mores of 'good society',[7] and of helping the children of better-off families distinguish themselves as a social group and lay the basis of privilege and influence in later life. In *Schlußball* Gaiser traces the growing self-awareness of a middle-class clique up to the point at which its members desire to arrange exclusive dancing lessons for themselves, even though this would socially differentiate people on familiar terms at school. Through Soldner's initiative this snobbish intention is frustrated and the 'last ball of the session' made open to all. When he asks some of the more affluent sixth-formers why they are so keen on forming a closed group, he is told that 'it's said to be an advantage. You get into certain circles and learn correct behaviour', 'in a couple of years or so it will be time to think of a job, and it's a help to be able to say that you were in the same dancing class as so-and-so'. The same tone of upstart affluence is also heard in the brash jargon of material success used by the ambitious entrepreneur Förckh: 'this was only the beginning, then came the establishment all in one go of a whole lot of different branches. I wanted to get out of that muck, out of it once and for all (*raus wollte ich ja aus dem Dreck, raus ein für alle Male*)'.

It is because Soldner despises such materialism that he intervenes. His protest however, is not a rejection in principle of class-distinction, but, as it seems to him, of distinctions of the wrong kind. As an outside observer at the ball puts it, the class-distinctions were continued, 'but on a false basis, determined merely by income', and a little later: 'those were the days when things that had been thrown into confusion seemed to be consolidating themselves in the old way again, but only on the surface, so that in reality nothing was quite as it was before, but also no new pattern emerged'. 'To be obliged to dance on particular occasions,' Soldner says, 'is part of social life. But what if there is no set society?' Seeing the dance-course merely as a degenerate form of old initiation rites, he sets it against the background of a society more primitive and more unified, less secular in its preoccupations and ambitions:

Such courses had taken on at the time, for the age-group involved, a singular and disproportionate significance. Only a total lack of other ways of proving oneself, of other preoccupations and ways of life with a different sort of content could explain this. . . . Since, therefore, ways of proving oneself did not exist, since initiation had been emptied of meaning and not even the mere forms for this were available, this introduction of young people into dancing seemed to be developing into a sort of baser initiation, with the difference that in these initiation-rites there was missing the suffering properly associated with such occasions. They compensated for this by a lavish output of money, which magically gave the people involved a sense of identity.

Gaiser's outsider-figures are not denied the consolation that so contemptible a society is foredoomed to perish. Soldner can look forward to the time when 'all this ghostly unreality will be swept away and swallowed up' and nature will see to it that of Neu-Spuhl there will remain 'just a stain on the ground'. Since, like nature, history creates only to destroy, the despised reality can be accepted as accidental and ephemeral: 'I will put up with prosperity till hard times come again.' Meanwhile he waits, as in some lonely garrison, for 'the dead times' of the present to pass.[8] Likewise, in a passage in praise of nature as 'the kingdom, the power and the glory', 'the lame girl' draws strength from a similar idea: 'nothing can happen to me that has not happened already and everything that has ever happened is mine'. The formulation recalls Nietzsche's doctrine of 'eternal recurrence' as the means of eliminating the degenerate, and fostering the survival of morally worthier people, capable of living with so tragic a concept.

Similarly Gaiser's reference (in *Die sterbende Jagd*) to the 'insignificant species' is close to Nietzsche's notion of the 'lower species',[9] and this, in turn, to Gaiser's question (in *Schlußball*) whether 'life really needs the vulgar mob'. The idea of the *Gesindel* as a baser, incompatible element in a naturally integrated community is among Gaiser's themes already in *Eine Stimme hebt an,* and in *Brand im Weinberg* there is talk of the 'gang of aliens' who 'had found their way into the place as a result of war and collapse, foreigners among them, people about whom one did not know what they lived on'. In *Schlußball* they are represented by the Rakitsch family, whose mother's shady business appears as an image of debasement through opportunities to make easy money by whatever means. Her son is a rather sinister figure, with a 'dark' accent and the 'social habits of a breed accustomed to doing obeisance in order to end up on top'—though the sentence was later modified presumably to avoid suspicions of anti-semitism. There is a certain ambiguity about Rakitsch's character. 'A crazy fellow', Ditta reflects, 'but there was something to him.' He offends Soldner's ideal of a community intact in composition and tradition, and so he

comes to see Rakitsch as a 'poisonous spider', a 'reptile', a
'cheeky fellow'. But his freedom from artificial social convention,
his readiness to act 'against the rules', and his cruder vigour, by
comparison with the snobbish habits of Neu-Spuhl, appeal to
him. When Rakitsch first appears at the grammar school in
Neu-Spuhl, he instinctively goes first to see Soldner, and at this
stage Soldner feels some affinity with him. Both come 'from far
away', both in their different ways are 'without a fixed abode',
'straying around like a dog'. Rakitsch is predisposed by nature
to distrust the 'official channels', so too is Soldner. When,
having been found to have lied about his qualification, Soldner
loses his job at the grammar school, this only implies criticism
of narrow-minded bureaucracy, since he had done his job
efficiently and won respect. It is not to his discredit that he finds
it hard to settle amid the greedy and snobbish materialism of
Neu-Spuhl, though it would be difficult to imagine him happily
at home in any modern democratic society. By democratic
standards he is conservative, but, in the context of Neu-Spuhl, a
conservative with revolutionary implications.

'Revolutionary conservatism', a familiar trend in German
thought, owes a number of its ideas to Nietzsche, like the
rejection of intellectual capacity as indicating superiority, of
metaphysical values as justifying human existence, and the idea
of cyclic time. Thus the allusion to Nietzsche in the sentence
from *Das Schiff im Berg*[10] about 'the days when God seemed to
them dead or to have abandoned them' is immediately followed
by the statement that 'nothing remained but this terrible course
and circle of events, these processes of digestion, these endless
acts of conception and destruction, fearful boredom, impotence,
joy, suffering, all indifferently distributed'. 'What's the aim of
anything coming into being? Fullness, Emptiness. Just a
terrible game', the clipped style reflecting the resignation of a
narrator who, like Nietzsche's Zarathustra, only with difficulty
confronts the tragic implications of such a view of nature and
history. Yet, still in the world of 'revolutionary conservative'
thinking, the chapter ends on a note of ecstatic acceptance of
'the glory of life (*herrliche Endlichkeit*)'.[11] The concept of 'eternal
recurrence' became a central theme of 'revolutionary conservative writers,[12] like Ernst Jünger. His views are sometimes
akin to Gaiser's remark 'that we never encounter any form that

could not already have been before', and to Soldner's observation that 'everything is different, but as it once has been'.

The idea of 'revolutionary conservatism' had owed a good deal in the first place to Hugo von Hofmannsthal, the title of whose *Die Briefe des Zurückgekehrten* (1901)[13] relates it to Gaiser's motif of the man returning to a drab, materialistic society that he cannot come to terms with. For when Hofmannsthal got back to Europe after some years in the Far East, he was repelled by the triviality of values, the addiction to money, the aridity of a 'civilisation' that was 'a breath not of death, but of the non-living, indescribable', and the apathy in face of the thought of death where 'no one is ready for the final act'. 'Here amid these cultured and property-owning Germans I can never feel comfortable.' The remark might have come from Gaiser, whose comment in *Das Schiff im Berg* about the two scientists who knew so little about themselves, because they had been 'poisoned through reason', matches Hofmannsthal's belief in the 'poisoning' of European life. Hofmannsthal brought back with him to Europe the impression of what has always obsessed Gaiser, of the sheer force of nature. 'Nature in them and the power of the human soul fashioned by nature', this was what struck him in the work of Van Gogh. For him union with nature was modern man's remedy for his desperate alienation: 'why should not nature, appealing without words to your loyalty and affection (*die stumm werbende Natur*)—nature which is nothing but life that has been lived and life impatient of your cold way of looking at it—why should it not in rare moments draw you into itself and show you that in her depths are contained sacred grottoes in which you, who are outside nature and are alienated from yourself, can be at one with yourself?'

Illustrating a paradox inherent in 'revolutionary conservatism' Soldner has 'ideas of reform on his mind', but not the will to radical change. An unrevolutionary figure for all his rejection of bourgeois values, he can say that 'basically I have never thought much of doing anything about it'. Like Herse Andernoth, his female counterpart, with her thought of 'sticking out the days to come', he looks to the inward consolation of some vague hope beyond the immediate prospect. In the context of some reflections in the language of nihilism, and embodying the Nietzschean terms *Ekel* and *Wünschbarkeit*, he has the idea that 'if you tell yourself that not much can come of it . . . then you will manage to put up with it all, but I'm waiting all the same'. Soldner's mixture of revolutionary awareness and lack of will to act is expressed metaphorically in the remark heard from a former fiancée of his, that 'he picked up stones and put them down again. The dragons he found were too puny to attack'. So he has not the possibility of standing apart from society in hostile disengagement, nor reserves of irony and sarcasm. His position can become inconsistent even on its own terms. 'I am still waiting', he says, but he had just remarked that 'I don't know what I am and what I am waiting for', thus irrationally falling back on a combination of faith and nihilism. 'The lame girl', too, when she asks why she should go on living, answers that only students at technical schools question the why and the wherefore—'with such questions you can become an engineer; that's something, but it's not very much. If you are speaking about life, don't start with asking about the reasons and the objectives.'

Gaiser does not disguise the slightly comic features of Soldner, letting him overplay his heroic posturing on occasions, and also his tone of rather self-conscious chivalry in his concern for Herse Andernoth. At the same time he endows him with a marked critical awareness. This Soldner directs both on himself and his generation, as when he now sees the idealistic enthusiasm of the Youth Movement in the 'twenties in relation to the terroristic tendencies of the time: 'what sort of people were we really? Well, the one lot had a golden band round the neck with a lute hanging from it. Very dangerous. The others knew where a case of hand grenades was buried or an aeroplane engine. Nearly as dangerous. Most dangerous of all, both together.' Against Soldner's tone here of critical, analytical awareness, has to be set his anti-intellectualist comment about a girl with whom he had once been in love; she 'could do nothing except what intellectuals can always do, even in situations in which words were least appropriate—talk'. She had nothing 'except what intellectuals have, a word for everything', 'a word and no instinctive, deeper feeling (*Ahnung*) for the reality'. There are echoes here of Nietzsche's idea of *Geist* as the great enemy of 'life', a barrier to its deeper understanding, poisoning the holy, chthonic springs of consciousness. The attempt to prepare young people in school for life in a technological world is ridiculed, and the sixth-formers of Neu-Spuhl, interested only in money and machines, are confronted with Diemut Andernoth, an unspoilt girl of whom significantly it is stated that 'you could tell just by looking at Diemut that she had grown up in the country'.

Though to a large extent *Schlußball* is thus a novel of social criticism on the theme of the affluent society, its setting is not any of the great urban centres where the social and economic pressures are present in their most up-to-date and massive form, but a provincial, small-town community. Among its characters the world of business is represented only by the industrialist Förckh, made to appear incidentally all the more contemptible for coming from plebeian stock. His wife, a woman of aristocratic origins, is driven to suicide, because her material comforts in Neu-Spuhl make existence too easy and, therefore, meaningless to her. In the town, naturally enough, this is not appreciated. Like Gaiser's general picture of contemporary society, Neu-Spuhl appears merely drab, and the language reflects this: 'well, it wasn't anything special, neither nice nor what you would call unpleasant'. 'Everything was petty', everyone 'just thought about money' and only talked about 'what this or that costs'. It remains a trivial, rather shadowy place, where little ever happens—'not much story, but a couple of deaths in the early hours'. Soldner describes it in an off-hand tone, mixing indifference and contempt, as a town without history, without distinguishing features except of a practical and utilitarian kind. Its very air is poisoned by the workings of local industry, and dust from the Pansalva works settles symbolically on it like a blight. 'I just get bored without being able to avoid it, it makes me sad in a sick, irrational way,' Soldner comments, and, as if to keep the hatred reality at a distance, Neu-Spuhl figures not at the height of the post-war affluence, but at the beginnings of prosperity soon after the currency reform, when 'prosperity had not yet broken out, but the new money had just appeared'.

The effect is to make the theme of *Schlußball* basically not so very dissimilar from that of *Eine Stimme hebt an*, with the important difference that nature figures hardly at all. It is absent from Neu-Spuhl itself, which 'had not even a moon'. When nature does come into its own at the end of the book, it

is in the description of the pools formed outside the town by
bomb-craters, and represents a 'place of transformation', the
reassuring symbol of Neu-Spuhl's ultimate disappearance from
the face of the earth, as history follows out its cyclic pattern, and
nature swallows up the trivial creations of calculating and
'transitory' man.

The image of the pool thus destined ultimately to play so
decisive a part appears first in the introductory section in
association with 'the lame girl': 'the world is a small place, but
in the pool the larvae were stirring. Larva, chrysalis, imago.
The time will come when only the husk remains. Imago: the
wings stir and become firmer. What will then be—but what has
been?' Associated with 'the lame girl' also is the motif of
'beautiful sound' ('Ball! A beautiful sound. I've never been to a
ball!'). *Larve* has two meanings, mask and larva, and they
interplay as—again linked up with 'beautiful sound' and
'Imago'—in the section in which 'the lame girl' recalls the
incident in the art-gallery. A group of schoolboys and school-
girls had been preoccupied with the market-value of the
pictures, and Soldner had objected to this mercenary attitude.
Why then, they wonder, should an artist paint at all, if it is not
for the money? Soldner, despising a society which sees everything as commodities, answers in a way true to his belief in the
ennobling challenge of risky and dangerous enterprises. The
conversation continues, with 'the lame girl' concealed behind a
partition in the gallery. She does not want to be recognised and
so, as the group approaches, she throws a silk cloth over herself:
'and I don't know what my class-mates thought, whether they
recognised me, or considered how to approach me. Amongst all
the pictures. *Imago*. A lovely sound'. The passage has far-reaching
implications, including the suggestion of her waiting for 'the
dead times' to pass, the theme being hinted at even in the way
she holds out until the episode of the materialistically minded
young visitors to the art-gallery is over. The Imago motif
completes its function towards the end of the novel, when 'the
lame girl' is wheeled by Herse Andernoth to the pools, the
description of these serving also as a sort of parable of nature as
the goal in man's return to the origins of a lost existence.

This major theme in Gaiser's works recall the way the
German Romantics, in reaction against the 'philistine' world

of emergent capitalism, endowed nature with its religious importance in pre-industrial societies, and it is in quasi-religious terms that in *Schlußball* nature is contrasted with the disruptive effects of a scientific, industrial society. Thus 'the lame girl' recalls an outing with Diemut and Herse Andernoth:

. . . Now and then I read in my magazines that nature is dead and has nothing further to say to us except by way of the test-tube or notes of an experiment . . . I remember the evening of the day they took me to Nonn . . . the sun had just gone down, and over the tall pale cornfields the sky was darkening, and higher up it was turning green, and the first star came out, and a smell, a warmth, rose from the fields. I sometimes think I can feel the warmth, the smell, still in my skin, on the skin of my hands that were lying in my lap. And I had to say to myself and ask myself, 'What is that?', and when I had thought it over I gave myself the answer, 'It's the glory of God.' And when it went away, I began to feel that I was nothing any more and that around me was everything; and because I was part of that everything and observed that I had now exchanged that nothingness for everything, I said to myself further, 'No, it's not enough. Not only the glory of God, it's also the power of God.' And finally I said to myself, 'It's everything together, it's what is said in the prayer, the kingdom, and the power and the glory.'

Variations on the theme are furnished by the travel-book *Sizilianische Notizen* (1959). Here matriarchal myths symbolise in their gods and goddesses the powers of mother-earth, whose creative and destructive forces are celebrated in the allusions of the motto-quotation from Pindar. The classical quotation, a favourite device of Gaiser's, here serves to lend mythical distinction to the landscape, the goal of a journey signifying return to nature, to myth, to the 'authentic existence' that Heidegger affirms and that the people of Neu-Spuhl have lost. For the various references throughout *Schlußball* to 'health' and 'healthy' life denote not physical qualities, but rather closeness to the primary experience of human existence, to 'authenticity', to nature. By the standard of Heidegger's philosophy, with which Gaiser's work has much in common and by which death should form part of man's everyday awareness, and facing up to death denote the measure of his 'authenticity', the world of *Schlußball* is casual and frivolous. To Neu-Spuhl, with its fast cars and

c

efficient streets, death is just a passing incident, a mere mishap. 'The lame girl' is able to accept the fact of blood on mother-earth ('the earth swallows it, that's not so bad, it's bearable'), but blood on a macadam road is only 'a smear, and the cars drive over it, it's never more than just dirt'.

So, if the descriptions of nature in *Schlußball* stand out by their richness of style from the deliberately insipid, chatty language of much of the rest of the novel, it is to contrast the rural and the urban, the simple and the unhealthily sophisti-cated, myth and intellect. They reveal a freshness of experience absent when the narrative is concerned with material things. On the one hand, for example: 'what had they to talk about, to get excited about, except the next fashion in trousers and the latest gramophone record? They had nothing to live for and in future would have nothing to die for except money', on the other, the ecstatic, expressionistic prose in which in a flashback Soldner's dead fiancée recalls a summer ride on horseback in the country. By contrast with this, cliché and jargon infect all the talk about Neu-Spuhl. The language of the introductory section imitates slogans of the kind familiar in advertisements and seeks to catch the spirit of the age in its arid truisms. Ditta's language, a mixture of the jargon of teenagers and nouveaux riches, and of trivial small-talk, expresses the emptiness of bourgeois values in Neu-Spuhl; 'in so small a world everything appears terribly important'. Typical is the way she speaks about her dress specially made for the ball:

... hinein in die weiße Wolke. Fünfunddreißig Meter Tüll, das wurde nicht zu viel. Es war ja gerade die Zeit, in der man wieder die Sachen haben konnte. Haben natürlich auch nur, wenn man was gehabt hat. Aber das walte Gott, wir brauchten nicht zu klemmen.

True, those who remain outsiders in this society—'the lame girl', Soldner, Diemut and Herse Andernoth—often also use such language, but only because they realise that the others cannot speak about even serious matters in terms other than what Soldner despises as *alte Platten*, the 'idle talk' that Heideg-ger refers to in his own characteristic language: 'and because this discoursing has lost its primary relationship-of-Being towards the entity talked about, or else has never achieved such a relationship, it does not communicate in such a way as to let this entity be appropriated in a primordial manner, but communicates rather by following the route of gossiping and passing the word along'.[14]

Some three generations earlier Paul de Lagarde[15] had commented about the decay of language into mere 'gossip', in conjunction with his antipathy to Germany's advancing industrialisation.[16] His desire to return to more integrated and patriarchal communities[17] was accompanied, like Gaiser's protest against the affluent society, by criticism of the 'drab materialism of middle-class life'[18] and the 'poisonous weed' of intellectualism.[19] Against the pressure of such a society Gaiser, like Lagarde, asserts the validity of older values, and this gives his language sometimes a traditional, even old-fashioned character.[20] But occasionally it can acquire a modernity inviting comparison even with the style of Uwe Johnson. This is the case, for example, when in *Schlußball* he writes about the educational bureaucracy. One sentence runs: 'die Behörden versuchten sie zu bilden auf die Weise, die auf die Herrn von Humboldt zurückging', and another: 'und ich guckte mir an, was ich arbeitete, machte die Sachen, in denen es die Noten gibt fürs Fortkommen und wo die Chefs drauf gucken, wenn eine sich meldet'. By advancing the verb in the first example, and, in the second, by using an unconventional circumlocution ('die Sachen, in denen es die Noten gibt fürs Fortkommen'), modern grammar-school education is made to seem remote and questionable. The element of intellectual insight and analysis here at work relativises the affirmation, in many aspects of Gaiser's work, of values hostile to the claims of modern awareness, as when in *Schlußball* the author summons an official—in the guise of one not without transcendental associations[21]—to take a cool intellectual look at what is involved. This is the function of the section *Aus dem Bericht eines Referenten*, a detached view of the situation couched essentially in the language of sociological analysis, despite, maybe, hints of irony or even of parody.

Already in the course of writing *Die sterbende Jagd* Gaiser had sometimes qualified directly emotional involvement by a more detached and generalising tone. In the earlier version published during the war,[22] when he could accept war in terms of the prevailing ideology, words like 'the English', 'the tommy', 'North American pilot', 'Americans', 'the Germans', 'the Führer', 'Organisation Todt', are allowed the full impact of their current emotional associations. When a captured English fighter-pilot is told by a German officer: 'whereas *we* struggle for food and life, *you* go to war just for the sake of money', the emotional force of the remark is as in any propaganda statement. In the later, completed version, however, England, for example, appears as 'the island', death as 'Master Death', and fame as 'that great deceiver', intruding 'harshly and strangely into the life of the fighter-pilots'. These tentative suggestions of allegory point forward to *Schlußball*, where the town is made to appear less an actual place than as representative of a general situation, of the affluent society. In the opening section occurs the remark: 'ought Neu-Spuhl to be rejected? The majority of people live in Neu-Spuhl'. The implication is of something like a parable of the affluent society. Also, the language of the novel avoids direct reference to actual dates and places, and in any case it is consistent with Gaiser's view of history as a blind cycle of recurrence that the particular ceases to have much importance.

Am Paß Nascondo (1960), too, goes some way to becoming a rather hazy parable, in this case of the political division of Germany, or Europe. Here the counterpart of Neu-Spuhl, the town without history, is Vioms, 'equipped with all the latest devices of hygiene', its opposite the older part of Sogno described in the last section of the book, with its great cathedral, its stately square, old palaces and artistic treasures, or Promischur, where life goes amid nature—'it's best in Promischur', the narrator comments. It is in Sogno that at the end we once again meet Hagmann, who first occurs in *Das Schiff im Berg*, now 'serene and rested', the leader of a travel-group which includes Herse Andernoth (from *Schlußball*). The 'dead times', it seems, are past or passing, and with the others she here awaits her resurrection, if that is the term, to a fuller and truer existence. The association of rebirth and renewal with the appearance from the wells of Sogno of water 'pure and unchlorinated' suggests the ultimate hope of a consummation beyond the corruptions of modern urban life, 'poisoned' and 'hygienic' at one and the same time, the attainment of a world beyond 'civilisation'—not to be identified with Sogno nor to be achieved by a mere return to the past.[23]

This conclusion of *Am Paß Nascondo* throws some light on the question as to where the 'voices' of the various narrators in *Schlußball* are located. Sometimes their existence seems to lie in the present ('in Neu-Spuhl people only think about money'), sometimes in the past ('that was a good time in Neu-Spuhl', 'in those days in Neu-Spuhl'). Soldner, it is clear, has left Neu-Spuhl at the time the story is narrated, but it is hard to know where he is, except that at some point he went away to take a job in business. 'The seamstress', now 'much older', speaks as though she is still there, and so does Förckh, who 'is getting on in years'. Ditta's contributions sustain a more or less straightforward narrative tone, but one at least of Herse Andernoth's monologues, which for a time is in rather the same style, ends disconnectedly, as in a state of dreamlike meditation. The same is sometimes true of the monologues of 'the lame girl'. Bearing in mind the 'resurrection' motif at the end of *Am Paß Nascondo*, and comparing it to the 'transfiguration' motif at the close of *Zwischenland*, the implication could be that at least Herse Andernoth is in some limbo—more or less identical, perhaps, with the 'world outside' from which come the 'four voices' of the departed in *Schlußball*—awaiting her release to authentic existence in some 'morning in Sogno'. The tone of the monologues of Soldner and 'the lame girl' sometimes suggests that with them, too, the process of 'transfiguration' and liberation has begun. As to what this means, the motto-quotation from Heraclitus at the beginning of *Zwischenland* may provide a clue: 'in waking consciousness we move in a world common to us all. In sleep, however, each person turns away into his own'.

Asked why he had chosen to tell the story of *Schlußball* by means of these different 'voices', Gaiser replied that he had originally intended to narrate it 'from a single point of view' but that 'the participants had hardly a single idea or basis of judgement in common, hardly a single word meant the same to them all. But since this was the heart of the matter, each of the voices had to have its own language. ... The perspectives had to change.' The words omitted from this quotation, and now quoted separately for emphasis, run: 'at the same time this seemed to the author the best way of withdrawing himself and of taking sides as little as possible'.[24] Whether the author of *Schlußball* really is impartial with regard to the various characters is a question about which, if the novel is taken in conjunction with Gaiser's work as a whole, there can be no doubt at all. Soldner, Herse Andernoth and 'the lame girl' command his sympathy, Ditta and Förckh obviously do not, If, departing from his previous practice, he is not present as narrator in *Schlußball*, this has deeper implications. *Eine Stimme hebt an, Die sterbende Jagd,* and *Das Schiff im Berg,* each contain a substantial sphere which clearly Gaiser is able and anxious to affirm, with which he can identify himself, and in which he can feel at home. Neu-Spuhl is a different matter. Absenting himself as narrator from *Schlußball,* Gaiser pronounces his estrangement from a society held to be trivial contemptible. He does so on the basis of assumptions about existence shared by writers like Friedrich Sieburg, Rudolf Krämer-Badoni, and Günter Blöcker, and their attitude to him helps further to define Gaiser's position in German cultural life.

'The art of keeping not merely one's fellow-men but also nature itself at a distance, in order that the loneliness of the creative individual shall not be disturbed, gives the book its grand authority.' This was Sieburg's verdict[25] on *Das Schiff im Berg,* the judgement of one whose relationship to contemporary society was from a position of a refined individual culture. Krämer-Badoni, whose sympathy for Gaiser is matched by his hostility to Gruppe 47, has praised Gaiser as a writer of the utmost significance,[26] and his own views on the nature of reality are very close to his. 'Our few deeds,' he says, 'the few so called successes and failures left by the wayside', are 'ridiculously unimportant'. Man's reality, 'hidden deep and invisible', is 'a sea of thoughts, yearnings, calculated striving, sacrifices, wasted efforts, *actes gratuits,* foolery, dreams, waking dreams and dreams at night, requests, desires, stammering, cries, rejoicing about nothing, animal-like roaming about, and the promise of dawn. In such a reality alone our existence is real and authentic.'[27] With his conservative scepticism about modern civilisation, technology and progress, and his affirmation of the irrational side of man, Krämer-Badoni occupies an intellectual position similar in a number of ways to that of Blöcker,[28] whose refined, élitist idea of discussion among writers as appropriate only in select, intimate circles, helps to explain his dislike of Gruppe 47.[29] His philosophy sounds the note of an heroic, exalted existentialism, [30] and, echoing the language of *Schlußball*, he praises Gaiser as one who 'is interested in a view of life, by the standards of which social forms are merely empty husks'.[31]

This requires qualification, for there is, indeed, a type of social organisation of positive significance for Gaiser. It embodies the principle of an essentially stratified society under the leadership of an élite, but without implying a simple return to the past. It is an ideal closer to nature than modern industrial society allows for, but not in the sense of a going back to any rural idyll. For this Gaiser's representative characters have not only too demanding and heroic a view of existence, but sometimes also, as in the case of Soldner, too keen and critical an awareness.[32] The intellectual, however, as such, radical in his critique of society as a whole, always earns his contempt. His characters may feel estranged from their particular society, but alienation in the larger sense is not part of their experience, if only because, in however utopian a guise, the vision is always present in their minds of integrated social existence remote from the disruptive pressures of modern industrial society. For them the problem of identity never for a moment arises, and, opposing the notion of firm and forceful 'character' to their image of social decay, they are not troubled—or enriched—by that sense of the diversification of personality with which, in its negative and positive aspects, the contemporary West German novel is, as will be seen, often so profoundly concerned.

Chapter 2

Wolfgang Koeppen

Towards the end of the Weimar Republic it was said of the cultural situation in Germany that there were on the one hand those who saw 'the perfection of human existence exclusively in "the momentum of the unconscious", in "the unconscious process of life" ', who 'know how questionable is a type of culture holding to intellectual values'. Striving 'to establish firm roots amid reality', they look to 'the maternal forces of blood, of nation, and of landscape', and their 'soul derives its sustenance from the original and the unspoilt (*das Ursprüngliche*), from the organic, from the old and the genuine'. The others were those to whom 'the world only becomes interesting in the mind of intellectual man' and for whom man 'is only important as a being divided between mind and nature, head and body, a problematical figure with spiritual obligations'. They saw 'a society rationally organised throughout' as alone worthy of intellectual man, and aimed at 'advancing step by step under the leadership of reason, in constant protest against the vestiges of stupidity, confusion, instinct and barbarism in whatever shape and form'.[1]

The description of the first group fits Gaiser more or less, whereas the other writers dealt with in this book correspond rather to the second category.[2] All the same, adherence to the idea of a 'society rationally organised throughout' has implications that, in contrast to representative left-wing writers of the 'twenties, these writers would find distasteful. The reasons have been stated by Walter Jens. Writers of his generation—whose literary career, that is to say, started after the war—regard concepts like 'class', 'worker', 'bourgeois' and 'party-political ideology' as merely 'shorthand references suitable for a textbook', and, in so far as notions of class indicate ideological unity and solidarity, they find them meaningless. 'Acting not on behalf of any class, without any fatherland to protect him, not in alliance with any form of power', the writer is well advised 'not to be over-hasty in looking around for new kinds of affiliation'.[3] If class and ideology have played a more positive part than this with Gaiser and Koeppen (born in 1906), this is connected with their belonging to an earlier generation than the one Jens is referring to.

Koeppen's spiritual beginnings lay, at the opposite pole from Gaiser's, amid the left-wing debates of the 'twenties. As a schoolboy he made no secret of his enthusiasm for the new Republic as a devotee of Kurt Wolff's radical literary series *Der jüngste Tag*, of the *Weltbühne*, the *Berliner Tageblatt*, *Vorwärts*, and the *Rote Fahne*. The rationalistic element in his political thinking was, however, qualified by romantic yearnings, and he was later to describe his youth in these terms: 'I cut school, I hid behind the hedges. I embraced the earth, which was to me like a sphere bearing me at a hectic speed through a mysterious universe. I wanted, as it were, to run away with a circus. I admired the graceful amazon and loved the horse she rode. She disappointed me when I offered her my heart and life.'[4] He 'loved the anarchists . . . and those whose dream was of eternal peace, and those who enthused about freedom, equality, and human brotherhood'.[5] This tension between cooler rationality and emotional affirmation, was to leave its mark on much of Koeppen's work, and the mood of romantic revolt evident in this retrospective account of his youth is exemplified in his first novel *Eine Unglückliche Liebe*. This was published in 1934 by the firm of Bruno Cassirer, shortly to be put out of business by the Nazis because of its Jewish connections.

This novel concerns the infatuation of a young man by Sibylle, an actress in a variety company, a 'wild group' of people constantly on the move from place to place, outside the sphere of bourgeois order and convention. It comprises people without home or roots, 'refugees', 'nihilists', singing of 'distress and revolt'. Sibylle's very name has for Friedrich associations of a seductive romanticism not provided for amid the restraints governing his own social background. In pursuit of her he is lured away to the south, to forms of existence far removed from his bourgeois world. Having reached the town where for the moment the company has pitched its tents, his one desire is 'to be accepted here and to be able to remain'. His love for

Sibylle is impulsive and commanding: 'he was chosen by fate—demonic, devilish fate which always destroys people in one way or another—to love this one girl among all others on earth'. The bourgeois in him offers resistance to the spell to which the romantic appeal of Sibylle exposes him, which is why he speaks of his resolve to raise her out of her sphere into his: 'to lift her up is my destiny, and I must take it upon myself'. Moods of love and hate alternate between Sibylle and himself, between her way of life and his. There is a barrier that can never be broken down: 'the invisible wall rose up; you on the left of the wall, I on the right, thus we can proceed, but the wall remains between us'. They can be 'one heart and one soul' only 'if they respect the frontier, and contemplate each other as objects in a shop-window'. Fulfilment is possible only within the limits of discovering a common way of accepting the barrier: 'they both laughed and knew that nothing had changed and that the wall, of the thinnest glass, transparent as air and perhaps even sharper, and revealing the appearance of the other, remained between them. It was a frontier that they now respected; Sibylle remained destined for him, and Friedrich belonged to her. Nothing had changed.'

Also separated by many years from the books with which Koeppen made his name after the war, but no less significant in the longer context is *Die Mauer schwankt* (1935), with its theme of adventurous vagrancy in a pre-1914 setting between the settled conventions of the bourgeois world and the riskier spheres of less civilised society, and confirming the mood later indicated by Koeppen in a remark about his past: 'I lacked the ability to adapt myself to normal, bourgeois, commercial life. I swam against the tide and had difficulty in preventing myself from going under.' [6]

The central figure is Johannes von Süde, whose family is rooted in the firm traditions of the Prussian middle class and whose forbears had faithfully served the state as administrators and officials. He had wanted to become an artist, but, as his father had resisted this departure from the family tradition, he had compromised by becoming an architect. The story springs from the tension in von Süde between the two worlds, of art and imagination on the one hand, of discipline and order on the other. Like Friedrich in the earlier novel, von Süde's escape from the commitments of duty and of service to the state takes the form of a journey to the south, to Italy: 'it was here that the adventure started', here 'his longing was fulfilled'. It may have been a similar restlessness amid bourgeois values that had led his sister to marry a man from the theatre. He had later disappeared, and the immediate reason for von Süde's journey to Italy was to try to find out what had really happened to him. His efforts bring him into contact with people whose existence is far removed from the world in which he had grown up, 'with conspirators, with murderers', with people 'who disturb the peace and undermine order'. These people come to exercise a powerful fascination over him, particularly Orloga. Like Sibylle, she is a romantic, gypsy-like creature, and his falling in love with her symptomises his revolt against his inherited social world. Her father, Orloga explains to him, was a 'hero, always fighting, and always on the side of people threatened and oppressed, of nations anxious to assert themselves against those who represent the corrupt world of business and want to make the world a uniform and boring place. The trader is our enemy.' 'What can I do for freedom?' von Süde is led to ask with impatient enthusiasm, and under her influence, he learns to look forward to a revolutionary break with the past. But his position remains uncertain and even contradictory. In formulating it he echoes the frontier-motif of *Eine unglückliche Liebe*: 'he knew that, while he could vaguely feel what it would be like to have crossed over to the fresh, new age, he himself was bound to remain on this side of the dividing river'. Recognising this, he comes to see his duty as carrying out his day-to-day tasks in the small town in the eastern part of Germany where meanwhile, after his return, he settles down as municipal architect.

Von Süde's belief in a radical transformation of society derives from the conviction 'that the age referred to by . . . historians as a bourgeois age was drawing to its close at the approach of an era of a different kind'. His language in this connection is ambiguous in its possible implications. Phrases like *die junge Zeit, der grosse Umbruch, die grosse Weltwende,* can be linked with the utopian expectations of Expressionism or with the vocabulary of certain kinds of radical right-wing thinking of the 'twenties, or with an imagery familiar in National-

Socialism. Orloga remarks about her father that 'there are always a few people in the world who are to be found where destiny is at work and the fate of the nation is in the process of being accomplished', and she tells von Süde that he is standing 'on hollow ground, in a disintegrating country yearning to divest itself of its present form and to discover a new life'. There are suggestive overtones too, for example, in a passage about the dangers threatening the coming of the new age, the 'attacks of the hordes of barbarism', the 'way the forces of chaos seduce people', and about how in earlier times 'knights and priests' had stood united 'in a common front' in defence of order. Now, however, 'orderly, human, positive and moral values (*die Kräfte der Ordnung, des Menschlichem des Aufbauenden und der Gesittung*) have become fragmented . . . and the forces of chaos, secretly and unchecked, are winning back the ground they had lost'. If language such as this can be thought of as having associations with National-Socialism, it is largely because it is characteristic of the phraseology of certain writers familiar in the German tradition especially since Nietzsche, whose thinking is too permeated with apparently socialist notions to be properly described as conservative, too conservative to be classified as socialist, writers whose thinking is exemplified in Moeller van den Bruck's theory of socialism as a corporate conception of the state, on a revolutionary foundation, but aiming at conservative stability.[7]

Thus, at this stage of his development, Koeppen, like Gaiser, is seen to have associations with 'revolutionary conservatism'. In his case one might think, too, of the kind of thinking known as National Bolshevism,[8] in so far as what emerges from *Die Mauer schwankt* is a picture of a romantic anti-capitalism, nurtured by anarchistic impulses and not immune to the fascination of terror. In 1962, taking stock of his earlier position, Koeppen said that he had tended to see the writer as 'among the outsiders of society', as one 'who suffers, pities, and revolts', as 'the spokesman of the poor, the advocate of the oppressed, the champion of the rights of man against his tormentors'. He now dismissed this attitude as 'romantic', but his account in the same context of his current views might in a sense still be so described: 'the writer is committed against power, against violence, against the pressure of the majority, of the masses . . . against unmasked convention, he belongs to those who are pursued and hunted'.[9]

In the first of his post-war novels, *Tauben im Gras* (1951), he says, with the sarcastic irony now becoming characteristic of his work, that it dates from the time 'when the German economic miracle was rising in the West, when the first new cinemas, the first new insurance palaces, were rising above the ruins and the improvised shops', when 'the nouveaux-riches still felt unsure of themselves . . . the profiteers of the black-market were wondering where to invest their gains, and those who had saved money were paying for the war', and when, with war raging in Korea, 'there was a hectic search for sensual satisfaction before the Third World War broke out'. The point of the quotation in the title from Gertrude Stein emerges in the account of the lecture by Edwin, an American poet of distinc-tion, a conservative and Christian writer, whose theme is the dependence of mankind on the preservation of values associated with 'Western civilisation'. He attacks those writers who seem to him to regard human life as a mere haphazard accumulation of fortuitous circumstances and whose view of life is one of men living a free but pointless existence, 'like pigeons on the grass'. The setting is Munich, and the story takes place within a space of twenty-four hours: 'midnight strikes. The day is coming to its close'. Several threads of interrupted action are followed out, and the elements of each section are so distributed as to allow ironic juxtaposition, as if adapting for narrative purposes the resources of the film. When there is any commentary, it is within the inner monologue, or by means of interpolating a newspaper heading or some current slogan.

The style of narrative, combining the ironic detachment of reportage with insistent elements of caricature, communicates an attitude of seemingly bored indifference to the society in question. Wide aspects of significant experience are necessarily excluded. In language and in every other respect, the overall effect is bleak and arid, in contrast with the richly evocative qualities in much of Gaiser's work. *Tauben im Gras*—its setting the modern city, its characters fully at home amid the pressures, opportunities, and temptations of city life, and its language to a considerable extent that of advertising and the newspaper—has in common with *Schlußball* the rejection of modern urban civilisation, though Gaiser has at his disposal the vision of alternative possibilities, archaic and utopian though they may be. To the total character of Koeppen's rejection corresponds a style of language, constantly engaged in labelling things and situations simply to debunk them, a style with which in Gaiser's work only *Schlußball* offers any comparison. Koeppen's picture of Edwin, with his views on the futility of modern capitalist society, is rather a mocking one, and this is partly at least because Edwin has positive criteria of his own to apply to the problem of social morality presented by this kind of society.

Koeppen's social criticism is so wild and indiscriminate as to suggest motives of some deep resentment, the underlying reasons for which emerge from an examination of *Das Treibhaus* (1953). Its central character, Keetenheuve, is of the greatest interest for an understanding of Koeppen's work. He is a disillusioned parliamentarian of the Social Democratic Party, whose frustration and disappointment form part of a contemptuous picture of government and society in West Germany. This stresses the return to power of former Nazis, the petty intrigues and opportunism behind the political scenes, the undemocratic workings of the party organisations, and so forth. As in *Tauben im Gras*, the background is flashy prosperity and greedy materialism, the recurring image likening it all to 'the atmosphere of the hot-house'.

When we are told about Keetenheuve that he was a bachelor, a person who liked to follow an independent and individual path, 'perhaps a libertine, perhaps an anchorite, he did not know quite which he was, he hovered between different possible forms of existence', this reminds us of the tension in von Süde between the claims of bourgeois order and the attraction of romantic revolt in the political underworld of the Balkans. Friedrich's relation to Sibylle, and von Süde's to Orloga, provide a comparison with Keetenheuve's to Elke. She is the child of a former Nazi Gauleiter, young enough to be his own daughter, a girl whose background associates her with values other than those that he himself publicly adheres to. His marriage to this sensuous and passionate girl is in the nature of a romantic adventure, and what attracts her to him is indicated by her statement, referring in the first place to his wanderings as an emigré in Nazi times, that his life was 'full of movement and colour . . . almost the biography of an adventurer'.

Yet Keetenheuve has allowed himself to become a respectable parliamentarian, 'the loyal colleague of his chancellor', 'a man of the opposition, dutiful and submissive', the man counted among the moderates. He cannot forgive himself for having thus 'failed', for having betrayed himself, so that he is now trapped in the cage of parliamentary conformism and convention. His public image, too, is affected; people 'sensed his doubts, and this they could not forgive him'. Nevertheless, he remains a revolutionary at heart, and one of his political rivals can describe him as 'a man with romantic notions of human rights, seeking the pursued and the enslaved in order to remove their chains, seeking people who had suffered an injustice'. But, 'always on the side of the poor and of people with some special problem of their own', his sympathy was with those 'outside any form of organisation, but never with the churches and the cartels', and his loyalty to his party, to politics altogether, is qualified and reserved, producing a destructive inner tension.

To the question as to whether Keetenheuve really wanted revolution, the answer is that he 'did not, because he could no longer want it—such a thing no longer existed'. Revolution, he had come to feel, was 'a child of romanticism, a crisis of puberty', and now the idea of revolution 'had had its day', it was a 'corpse', a 'dry leaf in the herbarium of ideas', an 'antiquated word from the dictionary, but without existence in everyday speech', an 'idea as from a dream, a sweet smelling flower', 'the blue flower of romanticism preserved in a herbarium'. The time 'of the tender and delicate belief in freedom, equality, and brotherhood, was over, this idea had vanished once and for all'. Keetenheuve's 'zealous and sincere championing of human rights' had all the time been 'only one last wilful and playful remains of a romantic delight in revolt', of 'the joy of being in opposition', and his sense of frustration, with himself and with society, leads him—now 'without faith, and full of doubt, desperate, sceptical'—to the belief, typical of the romantic idealist, that politics in general is contemptible: 'politics was dirty, like a gangster fight, and its means were filthy and destructive. Even someone who wanted to achieve good easily became just another Mephistopheles, always creating evil. For what was good and what was evil in this sphere, stretching out far into the future as into some dark kingdom?'

Whereas von Süde has accomplished without bitterness or despair his compromise between his ideals and the reality imposed upon him in the bourgeois sphere, had carried with him into his small-town environment a sense of liberation gained by knowledge of other values and more heroic objectives, and could philosophically accept that their realisation lay in the future, Keetenheuve has the bitter awareness that he has lived out his instinct for revolt. His frustration, and the sense of damage to his own integrity, turn into a cynicism affecting his whole view of society and politics, which he now rejects as inherently evil and absurd: 'the devil had seized upon every social community and held it fast in his clutches'.

Keetenheuve is a man, who, while serving a political party, questions its ideology, and cannot really give allegiance to any institutionalised values. Hence he 'provokes rejection and hostility everywhere', as he senses in a moment of interior monologue when he has the image of himself as a 'stumbling block'. His loss of faith in his earlier values makes him uncertain of himself as a social being and weakens his sense of identity—a problem to which Gaiser's characters are significantly immune. What is Keetenheuve really, 'a monk who has lost his way', a 'vagrant who has got caught in a cage', 'even perhaps a martyr who has missed the cross', a 'crazy knight fighting against power'? These are a few of the possibilities suggested in the novel. It could be said about him, as Koeppen says about a number of authors, that he embodies 'the attitude of a secular monasticism, an asceticism relishing the joys of asceticism, a celibate way of life that does not always avoid marriage, concubines and the brothel, an attitude combining love of life with . . . cool and analytical detachment'.[10]

Disorientated and subject to inward contradictions, in flashes of interior monologue (printed in italics) Keetenheuve tries to imagine himself as actor in a variety of social and political roles. Some of them are incompatible with his present existence as a deputy and a person to whom all along marriage had really been 'a perverse way of life'. They are experimental roles, never in practice adopted, suggesting themselves for brief moments in a chain of associations, as in this example: 'how he longed for bourgeois family-life, for a wife who was also a mother. For a pretty wife naturally, for a charming child. *He lifted a little girl on to a swing, he stood in the garden, a beautiful wife and a beautiful mother called him to lunch, Keetenheuve father, Keetenheuve lover of children, Keetenheuve cutting a hedge'.* While the imagined role can borrow features from membership of a consumer-society (*Keetenheuve purchaser and consumer, useful*), often it will reveal him possessed by 'the age-old dream of renunciation of desire', and wishing to dissociate himself from such a society (*Keetenheuve the ascetic, Keetenheuve disciple of Zen, Keetenheuve Buddhist, Keetenheuve the great liberator from self*), or exploring various functions within a single role, or in a number of different and even incompatible roles: 'he had his portfolio with him, the important looking portfolio used by deputies. Poems of Cummings, Verlaine, Baudelaire, Rimbaud, Apollinaire— he had them all in his head. *Keetenheuve manager, Keetenheuve Excellency, Keetenheuve Sir, Keetenheuve traitor, Keetenheuve the man who wants to do good.'* At one point, in the cinema, and thinking about the crowds at a football match, another imaginary role suggests itself to him: 'what accident of fortune was responsible *Keetenheuve Pharisee* that he too was not squashed to pieces in this seething mass of twenty thousand people'. This is soon followed by: 'Keetenheuve saw the masses in a negative light. He was alone. That was the position of a leader. *Keetenheuve Führer.'*

The italicised features within such interior monologues serve to bring to full awareness possibilities of Keetenheuve's character and mirror his own uncertainty about his identity. He may appear to the outside observer as a person of clear-cut character, holding firm to certain views and rejecting others, but his intellectual complexity and his inward isolation in organised society make him in reality a person torn by scruples and doubts. Unable, Hamlet-like, to make clear decisions ('thousands of pros and cons attached to every decision, liana-like, lianas of the virgin forest, practical politics was like a jungle'), he is a 'dreamer sicklied o'er by the pale cast of thought'. His problem is an intellectuality very modern in character, complex, searching, disillusioned, classless, laying him open to a wide range of conflicting possibilities and temptations, positive and negative, and conditioning his mode

D

of existence as a plurality of roles. Plagued by his 'awful, oppressive, fluid, jumping, elusive intellectuality', confronted in the end with nihilism, and unable to see himself other than as an allegory of emptiness, he commits suicide: 'only the sorrow remained. For here there was nothing to uplift, no guilt, no love, here yawned a grave. It was the grave within himself', 'the deputy was quite useless, he was a burden to himself, and a leap from the bridge gave him freedom'.

There are close connections between *Das Treibhaus* and Koeppen's next story *Der Tod in Rom*. In the theme of a man who, morally rotten, dies in Italy, in references to the artist as 'fop', 'liar', and 'conceited fellow', the association of music with death and adventuring, of art and homosexuality, there are connections, too, with Thomas Mann's *Der Tod in Venedig*, which in occasional features it obviously parodies. Just as in *Das Treibhaus* the satire is spiced with references to Nazi elements in West German democracy, *Der Tod in Rom* focuses on a former Nazi boss, by the name of Pfaffrath, now enjoying power and prestige as mayor in prosperous West Germany, and on the one-time SS general Jüdejahn, whose wife still 'mourned for Greater Germany' and for the Führer. Pfaffrath, related by marriage to Jüdejahn, wants to get him back to Germany, where his influence could help him to establish a respectable existence again, but the plan is frustrated by Jüdejahn's sudden death after shooting a Jewish woman in a frenzy of hatred and sex. His son who, having broken with his family, is now an avant-garde composer, protégé of an eminent conductor (whose wife it is who meets a sudden death at Jüdejahn's hands), happens to be in Rome for the first performance of a symphony of his at a congress of modern music. Its music, passionate and demonic, is 'an approximation to the truth of things, a truth that can only be inhuman', but to Siegfried's dismay it becomes under Kürenberg's baton 'humane and bright', 'music for cultured listeners'. Siegfried, an artist and also an intellectual, a man of inwardness and not of action, who at heart lives his life aside from the prosperous world of moral futility and corruption described in *Tauben im Gras*, reveals in a modified and sometimes intensified form some of Keetenheuve's characteristics. These are the very qualities that Kürenberg's interpretation of his music concealed, where what he had set out to express was the 'suppressed, romantic and flawed feelings' of a 'secret resistance'.

Thus one might apply to Koeppen's work the remark about the poetry of contemporary experience that it manifests 'the newly sharpened break between individual and society, between the desire to change things and an equally radical scepticism'.[11] It is also true that in *Tauben im Gras* and *Das Treibhaus* 'the characters remain strangers to one another, they do not exist with one another, but side by side with one another', that, for all its realistic detail, the world of Bonn emerges in *Das Treibhaus* as an Angst-ridden world, the expression 'of a ghostly unreality, of a nightmare world', in which reality is attenuated 'to a sequence of experiential fragments',[12] of life as 'encounters rather than relationships', 'ephemeral, non-repetitive, and optional'.[13]

Consequently, in *Tauben im Gras* and *Das Treibhaus*, straightforward narrative, interior monologue, journalese, newspaper headlines, and concealed and overt breaks in the flow of narrative, combine to form a restless kind of prose. Enumeration, the piling up of sentences, and the off-hand interpolation of telegraphese words and phrases, help to create a syntactical structure which strives to convey the author's experience of the confused haste of life. Curt, staccato sentences alternate with cascades of words as in this example from *Tauben im Gras*:

Das Frühjahr war kalt. Das Neueste wärmte nicht. SPANNUNG, KONFLIKT, man lebte im Spannungsfeld, östliche Welt, westliche Welt, man lebte an der Nahtstelle, vielleicht an der Bruchstelle, die Zeit war kostbar, sie war eine Atempause auf dem Schlachtfeld, und man hatte noch nicht richtig Atem geholt, wieder wurde gerüstet, die Rüstung verteuerte das Leben, die Rüstung schränkte die Freude ein, hier und dort horteten sie Pulver, den Erdball in die Luft zu sprengen. ATOMVERSUCHE IN MEXIKO, ATOMFABRIKEN IM URAL, sie bohrten Sprengkammern in das notdürftig geflickte Gemäuer der Brücken, sie redeten von Aufbau und bereiteten den Abbruch vor, sie ließen weiter zerbrechen, was schon angebrochen war: Deutschland in zwei Teile gebrochen.

This montage-technique, with origins in Expressionism, is used far less in *Das Treibhaus*. The author's attention is here for the most part focused on the protagonist, on Keetenheuve, and so there is little room for passages which, narrated as it were from a detached point of view in the future, serve to conjure up the atmosphere of a time without reference to a particular character. The problem of embodying them in the text, without their appearing as mere background material, would not in any case arise in *Das Treibhaus*. With the narrative dominated by what the central character of the novel feels, hears and sees, the author, limiting himself to this single perspective, can use interior monologue in order to achieve a corresponding effect— as when the Rhine near Bonn is described through Keetenheuve's eyes:

> Villen standen am Wasser. Rosen wurden gezüchtet, die Wohlhabenheit schritt mit der Heckenschere durch den Park, knirschenden Kies unter dem leichten Altersschuh, Keetenheuve würde nie dazugehören, nie hier ein Haus haben, nie Rosen schneiden, nie die Edelrosen, die Nobiles . . . Gesundbeter waren am Werk. Deutschland war ein großes öffentliches Treibhaus. Keetenheuve sah seltsame Floren, gierig, fleischfressende Pflanzen . . . aber es war alles morsch, es war alles alt, die Glieder strotzten, aber es war eine Elephantiasis arabum.

In this passage the enumerative sentence-structure gives it a resemblance to the previous one. Here, too, the aim is to achieve detachment from the present by the use of a seemingly past tense. If in *Tauben im Gras* the familiar, in the form, for instance, of newspaper extracts, is given remoteness by using the past tense, in *Das Treibhaus* this achieves added effect through being incorporated into the interior monologue. Adopting the perspective of the protagonist, the author is able to alienate the familiar by metaphorical utterance that justifies the claim in the introductory note that 'the dimension of all statements in the book lies beyond the actual context of people, organisations, and events in the practical world of the present. The novel has its own poetic truth.' The writer remains in the detached position of the observer who, like Philipp in *Tauben im Gras*, is at once outside and inside contemporary time: 'but he, Philipp, stood also outside this flow of time, not actually pushed outside it by the stream of time, but called to this position—an honourable one perhaps, because he wanted to observe everything'.

Koeppen's work, we can agree, 'proves that the great school of melancholy, of which Chateaubriand is regarded as the originator, is not yet closed. Each century has its own sorrow, and no switch can turn off Hamlet's name. On the contrary, we are perhaps the first who in their thousands experience the mournful fate of Cassandra, of being endowed with knowledge and awareness and yet being lost.[14] Indeed, the range of values that can be called into question by Koeppen's hurried, enumerative style, with its undercurrent of pessimism and the resulting elegiac tone, is unlimited. Emilia in *Tauben im Gras*—an aristocrat who, if the war had been won, would have inherited a family fortune—illustrates this. Ill-adjusted in a society where everyone has to fight for survival, and feeling isolated, she is driven to sexual perversion and the sense that all traditional values have lost their meaning. This is narrated as the interior monologue of a woman whose perverted sexual behaviour, presenting a thoroughly debased image of man, stresses the profound pessimism that the author is concerned to communicate, as when she falls into a nihilistic frenzy inspired by titles of modern books in her lover's library:

. . . les fleurs du mal, Blumen aus dem Nichts, der Trost in Dachkammern, wie-hasse-ich-die-Poeten, die-Pumper, die-alten-Freitischschlucker, Geist Trost in verfallenen Villen, ja-wir-waren-reich, une saison en enfer: il semblait que se fut un sinistre lavoir, toujours accablé de la pluie et noir, Benn Gottfried Frühe Gedichte, La Morgue ist—dunkele-süße—Onanie, les paradis artificiels auf den Holzwegen, Philipp auf den Holzwegen, ratlos im Gestrüpp in den Fußangeln Heideggers . . . Schrödinger What is life? . . . die Seele, Deus factus sum, die Upanischaden . . . die Seelenwanderung, die Vielheitshypothese . . . das Geworfensein, Kierkegaard Angst tagebuchschreibender Verführer . . . Sartre der Ekel ich-ekele-mich-nicht, ich treibe dunkele süße Onanie, das Selbst, die Existenz . . . Millionärin, war-mal . . .

Extending over more than a page, her enumeration is built, in a way reminiscent of Joyce (whose use of interior monologue fascinated Koeppen from the beginning[15]) on a pattern of associations. 'I am convinced', Koeppen has said, 'that nowadays one has to go in Joyce's direction even if one does not actually use him as a signpost. His style corresponds to our feeling, our consciousness, our bitter experience.'[16] By describing a situation in which the most eminent contemporary philosophers—Heidegger, for instance—and what are regarded as the highest ideas of mankind are brought into association with a perverse sexual act, the author creates the image of man as a lonely, degenerate being, capable of attaining individual heights, but hampered always by primitive and ugly impulses. There follows from this the frequent references to the animal functions of man, and many images of man's need to cleanse himself of the filth that is of his essence.

Thus in *Tauben im Gras*: 'drunks staggered out of the Hofbräuhaus. They pissed against the houses. . . . The hotel was the devil's beehive. . . . Behind the draughty walls people were bawling, belching, clearing away the mess. . . . He (Philipp) stopped a moment in front of the Hofbräuhaus . . . from which came the smell of vomit. . . . Two women were cleaning up the night's filth from the road.' In *Das Treibhaus* there is a description of the temporary wooden huts erected in Bonn after the war to house deputies and the staff of the various political parties: 'they resembled the headquarters of some huge circus, or the booths in an exhibition; they were built to be pulled down. A secretary was having a bath. You could hear the water in the pipes through the wall. The secretary was having a good wash, with plenty of soap, and rinsing the soap away, the dirt of officialdom was being removed. . . . Lavatory chains were being pulled, water was taking the mess away. People were divesting themselves of muck.'

Here the effect of a quick series of short sentences is to poke mockery at the sophisticated world of Bonn, and of modern society in general, by reducing it to its most trivial and ephemeral elements. Nothing assumes an outstanding importance, everything is reduced to its meanest denominator, man and the world are portrayed as base and transitory. In the passage just mentioned this is embodied in an image linking up with the disillusioned Keetenheuve's view of parliament as a circus, and the participants as buffoons: 'in the committees, in the plenary sessions, he saw his worthy colleagues as clowns performing in the ring'. Again this background of transitoriness, life in general appears an absurd game: 'even when his life was endangered, he had never failed to see the grotesqueness of the situation'. The sense of transitoriness is unrelieved by any compensating hope of salvation. It only leads to an awareness of unfulfilment, as in a passage, built around the word *Öde* ('waste'), stressing Keetenheuve's nihilism, and in which all experience is interpreted as 'nothingness', providing also a good example of repetition and the stringing together of short sentences as the stylistic equivalents of the drab meaninglessness of existence that Koeppen is clearly anxious to convey:

> Die Arbeit genügte ihm nicht. Die Politik genügte ihm nicht. Sie schützten ihn nicht vor dem ungeheueren Nichts. Sie griff nicht nach dem Abgeordneten mit langen Gespensterarmen. Sie würgte ihn nicht. Sie war nur da. Sie blieb nur. Die Öde hatte sich ihm gezeigt, sie hatte sich mit ihm bekannt gemacht, und nun waren ihm die Augen geöffnet, nun sah er sie überall, und nie wieder würde die Öde verschwinden, nie wieder würde sie seinen Augen unsichtbar werden. Wer war sie? Wie sah sie aus? Sie war das Nichts und sie hatte kein Aussehen. Sie sah wie alle Dinge aus. Sie sah wie der Ausschuß aus, wie das Parlament, wie die Stadt, wie der Rhein, wie das Land, alles war die Öde, war das Nichts in einer schrecklichen Unendlichkeit, die unzerstörbar war.

This recalls a comparable experience in Gaiser's *Schlußball*, where in an interior monologue Soldner voices a similar feeling of nausea: 'but after a while you are no longer aware of anything and, full of nausea (*Ekel*), you would prefer just to lie flat on the ground'. Yet while nature plays an important part in Gaiser's work as a whole, it figures only incidentally in Koeppen's, where the only aspect ever commented on directly is that it reveals the eternal flux of time: 'time which kept standing still and was the here and now, that moment of infinite extension fled past'. As 'the sum of all days, the sequence of light and dark given to us on earth', time 'was like the wind, it was something and nothing, to be measured by cunning devices, but no one could say what he was actually measuring', time 'flowed round one's skin, formed people, and vanished incomprehensibly, beyond control: whence? whither?'. A suggestion of the language of the Bible ('given to us on earth') does not conceal the fact that transitoriness without a meaningful goal is here the theme. It is as if nature has no further significance for man in the urban civilisation that leaves its stamp on the vocabulary of Koeppen's novels. Characteristic of his language are words like *Krankenkasse*, *Wohnungsbedarf*, *soziale Eingliederung*, *Psychiater*, *Komplexe*, *Volksvertreter*, *Organe der Exekutive*, side by side with English words mirroring American influence on post-war Germany (*Highlife*, *Publicity*, *Manager*). At the same time there is an element of ironic detachment in the use for satirical purposes of certain compound words constructed of officialese, like *Verfahrenshasen* and *Geschäftsordnungshengste*. If we add the montage of newspaper headlines, and a persistent habit of enumeration to convey the impression of man's hectic and ephemeral activities, we have most of the essential features of Koeppen's style, illustrated in the following passage from *Tauben im Gras*:

STADT BRENNPUNKT DES WOHNUNGSBEDARFS. Sie waren wieder zu Hause, reihten sich ein, rieben sich aneinander, übervorteilten einander, handelten, schufen, bauten, gründeten, zeugten, saßen in der alten Kneipe, atmeten den vertrauten Brodem, beobachteten das Revier, den Paarungsplatz, den Nachwuchs der Asphaltgassen, Gelächter und Zank und das Radio der Nachbarn, sie starben im städtischen Krankenhaus, wurden vom Bestattungsamt hinaus-gefahren, von Straßenbahnen umbimmelt, benzindunst-umschwellt, glücklich in der Heimat. SUPER-BOMBER IN EUROPA STATIONIERT.

These features of Koeppen's style in *Tauben im Gras* marked a new development as compared with his pre-war novels, and in *Das Treibhaus* they firmly established themselves as char-acteristic of this later stage of his work.

His more recent travel-books, *Nach Rußland und anderswohin* (1958), *Amerikafahrt* (1959) and *Reisen nach Frankreich* (1961), also utilise a style of enumeration rather than sustained con-tinuity of narrative flow—appropriately so since what they describe is a succession of casual experiences. Between the appearance of the last two, Koeppen was awarded an important literary prize by the city of Munich, and the following year the Büchner Prize. Whether or not this recognition was influenced by the seemingly more accommodating character of the travel books as compared with the novels it is impossible to say. More important here is the close connection between Koeppen as tourist and Keetenheuve. For if, as Alfred Andersch has said, the tourist is a 'key figure of this century', it is partly because, like the modern picaro who will occupy our attention later, he is a 'man on the move'.[17] A common denominator between Keetenheuve and Koeppen on his travels is what Andersch refers to as 'consuming unrest', and it is this that can make the tourist in a rather special way 'a man chasing the impression of the moment.'[18] So, while the general tone of the travel books is in some ways different from that of Koeppen's post-war novels, it is an oversimplification to say that they 'discover a system of relationship between things and experiences necessarily lacking in the novels'.[19]

Yet, when in *Amerikafahrt* Koeppen notices the way the word dollar 'was always uttered with reverence' and how the dollar 'links you up with other people, makes you equal', or when he calls America the 'egalitarian race of purchasers', the New York Stock Exchange the 'dancing house of the dollar', and the attendant girls the 'vestal virgins of high finance' and 'beautiful sirens singing money's Song of Songs', these are rather the playful observations of a kindly visitor without bitterness or malice. Phrases in *Reisen nach Frankreich* like 'the cunning business man, the privileged child of his time', his 'every thought concerned with profits', have only the friendliest tone of satire or caricature as compared with the attitude in the post-war novels to capitalist society, and now they are unostentatiously embedded in a context of affectionate description. Whereas in *Tauben im Gras* and *Das Treibhaus* the material reality in which the characters live out their anxious and troubled existence appears bleak and contemptible, in the travel books Koeppen is always on the search for things of significant interest.

The mood, however, of *Die Mauer schwankt* will occasionally reassert itself, as in the account in *Reisen nach Frankreich* of French writers in their rooms filled with books and home-made furniture, without any of the trappings of 'the European economic miracle', 'eloquent and poor in a world of fear and greed, with its petty concern for security, and enormously sloppy', 'guarding the heritage of Voltaire' and alert 'to fight for the freedom of everybody, against every system of power, and against all oppression of thought'. There is rather the same mood in the description in *Amerikafahrt* of the crowds at a Paris station, a place, Koeppen remarks, where 'people loved the revolution, the never-ending attack on all the fortified citadels', where 'for ages past the spirits of uprising were invited to the feast' and where 'people liked unrest'.

In *Reisen nach Frankreich* Koeppen describes the modern Marseilles created by Le Corbusier, from the roofs of which the 'part of Marseilles looking out on the sea appeared like some age-old den of pirates', but the old 'harbour quarters of the drinking sailors, of the deserters' was now replaced by cold 'cement castles' for 'affluent tourists'. Yet it is 'good to sit on these terraces' and, 'lulled by all this kitsch', to enjoy 'this strange French Biedermeier'—an odd confession, this, from Koeppen's pen, but less surprising if we recall the stage in *Das Treibhaus* when, after Keetenheuve has rejected the idea of revolution as an outdated, romantic illusion, his resignation is thus described: 'he did not want to lower his gaze at the sight of horror. But he wanted to live in comfort and steal a march on the devil. He was for happiness amid despair, for happiness and solitude, for the idea that each person should enjoy comfortable and despairing happiness in the technical world that we all have to accept.' The ensuing passage in the novel, prefiguring the account in *Reisen nach Frankreich* of Le Corbusier's buildings, interprets the hidden implications of this in advance, and brings it into relationship with the theme of isolation and alienation, central in Koeppen's post-war novels:

And so Keetenheuve wanted to build new houses for the workers, Corbusier-like dwelling-machines, domestic fortresses for the technical age, a whole town in one single giant house, with artificial roof gardens and artificial climate. . . . Keetenheuve wanted to house ten thousand people under one roof in order to isolate them from one another, just as the large cities lift the individual out of his links with his neighbours, leave him quite alone, a lonely beast of prey, a lonely hunter, a lonely victim. Thus each space in Keetenheuve's huge building was to be sound-proofed against every other, and each person was to create in his own particular space the climate that suited him, he could be alone with his books, alone with his thoughts, alone with his work, alone with his idleness, alone with his love, alone with his despair and alone in his sweating human flesh.

The bitterness of these lines should be taken in conjunction with the part of *Reisen nach Frankreich* where Koeppen speaks admiringly and enviously of the vigour of political and ideological discussion among French intellectuals in a certain bookshop catering for political interests, and also of the old parts of Paris 'heavy with the sweat of the centuries and all their ecstasies and excesses', the haunts of beggars 'with the moving face of the old Verlaine or of God himself', of women 'stamped with all the marks of a disordered existence . . . in the style of Hieronymous Bosch'. Then follows a crucial comment, mingling relief at the thought of his own happier existence with a guilty sense of loss:

I have had an evening meal, I shall sleep in a bed. I shall be warm, but I think I could be like these people, the outcast, the negator, and perhaps it is a vestige of Christianity that makes me feel for a moment that I should like to be like them, not a monk in a beautiful monastery, but an anchorite of the streets, someone who has left the fateful sphere of action and of guilt, and it is fear and greedy bourgeois cowardice that saves or stifles me.

It would be misleading, therefore, to attribute the seemingly more carefree tone of *Reisen nach Frankreich* to Koeppen's having left behind the problems which preoccupied him as a novelist. Renunciation is only lightly concealed beneath the surface of contentment, bourgeois satisfaction is not something he can talk about with an easy conscience, and the question is left open whether it will prove to have been his salvation or his ruin.

The intellectual, that is to say,—as Koeppen said a little while ago in memory of a friend of his own generation, and, we may think, as a comment on himself—'has suffered an irrevocable loss', has 'developed a limp'. His explanation was that the intellectual 'had come to suffer from the fact . . . that enlightened people are no longer revolutionaries', 'perhaps the idea of revolution has been stolen from them or they have overhastily given it away'.[20] Here lies the source of Koeppen's, and Keetenheuve's, melancholy resignation, and the reason why, in the figure of Keetenheuve, the intellectual is portrayed as a flawed existence. Younger writers, however, of a generation without the experience of having been actively involved in this renunciation of revolution are, as the following chapters will show, now inclined to give the intellectual's existence a more aggressive purpose, uninhibited by the frustrations of disillusioned revolutionary ideology.

Chapter 3

Heinrich Böll

Born in 1917 and the only other writer represented in this book who lived through the whole of the Weimar Republic,[1] Böll was sixteen when Hitler came to power. The thought that he was born a subject of Wilhelm II 'seems to be about as fantastic as if my father were in all seriousness to tell me that he had taken part in the Third Punic War—it seems to me quite unreal'.[2] Older than Grass and Walser, who could at the most only have childhood memories of the Republic, and of quite a different generation from Johnson, born a year after its collapse, his literary career, like theirs, belongs wholly to the period after World War II. But he alone made the war, in *Der Zug war pünktlich* (1949) and *Wo warst du, Adam* (1951), and its aftermath in *Und sagte kein einziges Wort* (1953) and *Haus ohne Hüter* (1954), a central concern of his novels. This makes him a middle figure between the two older writers who have preceded him in this book, and the younger ones who follow him, like whom, in contrast to Gaiser and Koeppen, he has been closely associated with Gruppe 47.

As compared with these younger writers, Böll's earlier novels are closer to the realistic tradition and more concerned with straightforward moral issues. His principal theme originally was the 'little man' in the war and the difficult years just afterwards. As to his attitude to the social change meanwhile taking place in West Germany, there is an element of self-confession in Johanna's remark, in Böll's first longer work set in the world of the upper middle class (*Billard um halbzehn*, 1959), about the situation in the later 'fifties: 'not even in 1935 or even in 1942 have I ever felt such a stranger among people', and with the growth of prosperity an increasingly satirical tone is heard in his work. This can be seen by comparing the stories published in 1950 under the title *Wanderer kommst du nach Spa* with the selection of stories, half of them dated between 1953 and 1958, in the volume *Erzählungen, Hörspiele, Aufsätze* (1961). In 1958, moreover, in *Doktor Murkes gesammeltes Schweigen*, Böll published a collection of stories specifically labelled satires, and dealing with the world of business, of institutionalised culture, of officers and politicians.

In one of these, *Hauptstädtisches Journal*, a former colonel goes to an unnamed town for the ceremonial opening of an Academy for Military Memoirs that he has been instrumental in establishing. Here 'every former soldier from major upwards is to have the opportunity, in conversation with his comrades and in conjunction with the Department of War History in the Ministry, of writing his memoirs', and where he himself is to give the opening paper on 'Memory as a Historical Task'. The Chancellor honours the colonel with a telegram of congratulation, and when the latter remarks how delighted he is 'that one of my youthful dreams has become reality—and moreover in a democracy', one of his friends replies that 'a democracy in which we have the majority in parliament on our side is far better than a dictatorship', and the new academy receives the ceremonial blessing of the church. This, then, is a story firmly in the main tradition of satire, exposing long familiar targets of the satirist—the military, the politicians and the church— to ridicule by exaggerating selected characteristics and making them look silly in the light of changing conditions.

The problems, however, are more complex in the case of another of these stories, *Der Wegwerfer*, about a man, well-educated, well-dressed and thoroughly respectable, who is employed by a firm to throw things away, circulars, wrappers, and other kinds of packaging—an existence by ordinary standards so absurd that, as he says, he would not think ill of anyone who thought him eccentric. Social respectability under the guise of a fatuous job might suggest itself as the object of the satire, but obviously other things, too, are satirised—people, for example, who review books without having read them. Or if we take the story as satirising adventurous and successful opportunism, there is the difficulty that we might want to rate him higher for his ingenuity than less resourceful people content with more humdrum ways of earning a living, and laugh as much at a kind of society that could justify such an existence as much as at the man who exploits it.

Ambiguities of this kind also confront us very delicately in *Unberechenbare Gäste*, published in 1955,[3] told by a husband whose wife, unable in the kindness of her heart to say no to anyone who calls with something to sell or to dispose of, starts by buying handy things like soap and razor blades, proceeds to small and harmless animals, and ends up with an elephant and a lion. 'It is very unusual', the husband says reproachfully, 'you must admit that', to which his wife replies with a simple question, crucial to the point of the story: 'what is not unusual?'. Her behaviour may not be exemplary by practical domestic standards, and she is not entirely outside the range of the satire, but neither is the husband, with his smugly conventional ideas about reality[4] that leave him without an answer to his wife's question.

There is a link here with the story *Hier ist Tibten* (1953) about an intelligent and cultured young man who makes his living by announcing at a station over the loudspeaker the arrival of trains, the name of the place and appropriate items of information about it. As to what exactly is being satirised, one obvious possibility, apart from references to the commercialisation of culture and the persuasive powers of propaganda, would be a wasted education. But in that case it would not be clear whether the young man is being satirised for wasting it, or society for causing him to do so. Not to be overlooked in any case is that the story is as much about the passengers as about the announcer:

. . . then I go to work, hang my cap on the hook, take off my coat, put my sandwiches in the drawer, arrange my cigarette papers, tobacco, and the newspaper, and, when a train arrives, say the sentence that it is my duty to utter: 'This is Tibten! You have arrived in Tibten! Passengers wanting to see Tiburtius' grave should alight here . . . ' I say it very softly, so that those who are asleep do not wake up and those who are awake do not fail to hear me, and I put just enough feeling into the pronouncement that those who are dozing reflect a moment and ask themselves whether after all Tibten was not their destination. And I don't understand how anyone can consider my occupation unworthy of me.

Reality, that is to say, is not as self-evident as one might assume and, since the announcer's job helps people towards this discovery, his work is not so silly after all, bearing in mind the remark that it is only 'people without feeling' who easily take for granted that things are as simple as they seem. The passengers wake up to discover that what in their prosy, practical way they had assumed—that Tibten was not their destination—was false, and the story moves in the direction of parable, with the suggestion of likening the concept of man with that of the traveller to form a general statement on the condition of man in the modern world. This equation was completed in an essay of the same year:

Modern man is like a traveller who gets into a train at the place where he lives and sets off through the night to a destination without knowing how far away it lies. In the darkness the traveller will be startled from his light sleep by the voice from a loud-speaker on some unknown station, telling him where he is for the moment. He will hear names that he does not know and which seem to him unreal, names from some strange world that does not seem really to exist. A fantastic event, but absolutely real. For the real is fantastic, but one has to know that our human fantasy operates always within the limits of the real.[5]

This questioning of conventional attitudes to reality by exposing them to the force of an outsider position, itself not necessarily without absurdity, provides the context in which to consider *Das Brot der frühen Jahre* (1955). This story, in which 'bread' is the symbol in the first place of hungry greed, in the second of a just wage, concerns a mechanic whose job had been mending washing machines and who, having suffered hunger at school and after the war, had taken to stealing food. Money becomes an obsession with him, partly because of his privations in the past, partly because he can now earn so much. A letter from his father reminds him that the daughter of an acquaintance is coming to the town where he works and that he is to find lodgings for her. He fetches her from the station, and the meeting transforms his existence, setting in motion a process of remembering the past and reinterpreting his life. Imagery and symbol enforce the idea of rebirth and purification. The decision to break completely with the past, to be for ever one with Hedwig from one moment to the next, so drastically negates any calculating materialism as to flout standards of common sense, and to put both Hedwig and Fendrich at such a distance from ordinary social criteria as to make these appear questionable and irrelevant. This is not a didactic piece on the theme of conversion from materialism to God, as if Böll were recommending the actions of Hedwig and Fendrich as a pattern to be followed—they are too absolute and in their way too ridiculous.

In this story, with the past re-lived under the impact of a transforming experience, past and present come to coexist within a pattern of simultaneity, as in the later radio play *Bilanz* (1958) and *Klopfzeichen*, (1960)[6] ('and you do not know whether the past is the present or the present the future. It is all one'), and in *Billard um halbzehn* ('the present appeared to me as the completed past'). In this novel Böll again exploits the use of symbols, also with near-religious associations, but the social setting is now transferred to the world of the upper bourgeoisie.

Billard um halbzehn concerns three generations of a family of architects, and their association with a monastery which Heinrich Fähmel, as a young man in 1908 in the time of Wilhelm II had won the commission to build, and which his son, Robert, blew up towards the end of World War II, because of its support for the Nazis, whereafter Robert's son, Joseph, was in charge of its reconstruction. There is a sharpening of Böll's political attitude, and more concern than in any previous work of his with Germany's historical development, with the tradition in this case of militarism from the time before World War I until the recent period. For the first time in Böll's work the resistance to the Nazis occupies an important place in the story; Heinrich Fähmel comes to realise that 'secret mockery' is not enough, and his wife, Johanna, insists on the need for 'powder and lead'. However, Schrella, once in the resistance against the Nazis, and whose sister Robert Fähmel had married, in a mood of cynical despair considers returning to emigration, recognising the Germany he had once known 'rather as one recognises a woman whom one had once loved as a girl and sees again twenty years later', more portly, more prosperous, married now to a rich and industrious husband—'under such circumstances love inevitably turns into irony'. He sees the realities of the present situation clearly enough, but, lonely and resigned, turns his back on politics. Again, a central symbol of the novel, the 'sacrament of the lamb', embodies the idea of

withdrawal from the world of power. Those who participate
in brutality are represented by the 'sacrament of the buffalo',
which interplays with the symbols of 'boar' and 'blood of the
boar'. People associated with it—Hindenburg, for instance,
Otto Fähmel, the Nazi brother of Robert killed on the Russian
front, Nettlinger, an active Nazi and now a high official of the
Federal Republic—stand for the principle of harsh power, of
rigid subordination to authority. The suggestion[7] that Böll breaks
the Biblical pattern—requiring, as the opposite of the lamb,
not the buffalo, but the wolf—in order to stress not just strength,
but also primitiveness and stupidity in the militaristic tradition,
finds support in the metaphor of an earlier story *Mein trauriges
Gesicht*: 'he was as serious as a buffalo that for decades had fed
on nothing but duty'.

From early days Heinrich Fähmel's behaviour had been
characterised by a rather superior delight in play-acting, reflected in his account of his way of life as a young man: 'from
the moment I entered the town I had prescribed for myself all
my actions, my movements, a precise daily programme, I had
sketched for myself a complicated dance-routine in which I was
solo dancer and ballet-master in one; supporting actors and
stage-setting were at my disposal free of charge'. His account
of his behaviour as a young man during his visits to the Café
Kröner is similar to Sartre's portrayal in *L'Etre et le Néant* of
human life as a theatrical 'dance', symbolised for him in the
actor-like demeanour of waiters and relying on images of the
'rope dancer' and 'ceremonies'.[8] Heinrich's description leans
heavily on the language of the theatre:

No other guest was in sight, inside the café everything was clean
as in a hospital before the doctor's round, the ballet of the waiters,
through which I passed with light steps: supporting actors and
stage-setting were ready for me; this was a rehearsal, it was excellent,
and I was delighted with the way the three waiters went from table
to table with revolving movements: putting the salt cellar in place,
the vase too, slightly adjusting the position of the menu which
obviously had to be at a certain angle to the salt cellar; ashtray,
snow-white porcelain with a golden edge; fine; I liked that; I was
pleasantly surprised; that was as things were done in a town, I had
never seen anything like this in any of the out-of-the-way places
where I had had to exist hitherto.

E

It is his new experience of urban life that tempts him to think of human existence as a setting in which each individual can choose his role, and his interior monologue abounds in theatrical terms presenting human life as scenes on a stage— 'ballet of the waiters', 'soloist', 'supporting actors', 'stage-setting'. By contrast to the village, derogatively referred to in the above passage, town life appears to him in a positive light, as enabling man to free himself from the bonds fettering his personality in a narrower society, showing him that he can act his life as deliberately as waiters going about their work. The role Heinrich Fähmel chooses—and is free to choose, since as the heir of rich parents he does not need professional security— is that of free-lance architect. As such he feels a strong relationship to the bohemian artist, as in his account of what is, in effect, the first scene of his 'performance':

Ich sah sie alle an und hörte ihnen zu, meinen Komparsen; zeichnete Stuhlreihen, Tischreihen mit Kellnerballett, verlangte zwanzig vor elf die Rechnung: sie war niedriger als ich erwartet hatte; ich hatte mich entschlossen, 'großzügig aber nicht verschwenderisch' auf-zutreten; das hatte ich irgendwo gelesen und für eine gute Formel befunden. Ich war müde, als ich, vom Kellner mit Dienern verab-schiedet, das Café verließ, den mythosbildenden Mund des Kellners mit einem Extratrinkgeld von fünfzig Pfennigen honorierte; und sie musterten mich eingehend als ich das Café verließ, ahnten nicht, daß ich der Solist war; aufrechten Ganges, elastisch, schritt ich durchs Spalier, gab ihnen zu sehen, was sie sehen sollten: einen Künstler, mit großem schwarzem Hut, klein, zart, wie fünfund-zwanzig aussehend, mit dem unbestimmten Air ausländischer Herkunft, doch sicher in seinem Auftreten. Noch einen Groschen dem Jungen, der die Tür aufhielt.

If any feature of Heinrich's behaviour does not fall in the category of an 'act' (*Spiel*) or a 'performance' (*Auftritt*), this calls for comment: 'the fact that I went into the church was not part of any performance'. Other people are just his puppets: 'my supporting actors had well oiled joints, they were moved by invisible threads, their mouths were opened to allow them to utter the phrases I attributed to them'. As to why Heinrich Fähmel plays his existence as a role, Sartre provides an answer in his analysis of the café waiter acting his position to prove to himself that he is what he acts. Heinrich Fähmel acts the role of architect in order to become in reality what he had wanted to imagine himself to be.

Character and personality appear as deliberate self-manipulation. At first the actor, as we may call him, may be non-committedly involved, but in due course he is no longer free to call the game off. Heinrich Fähmel's taking part in the competition was just *ein Spielchen*, ('a little game') and anyhow he expected to lose, but it soon becomes *das große Spiel*, 'always with him', because, being now expected of him, he has to play it. The initially tentative role of architect becomes willy-nilly his role in society, and, realising that he is no longer a 'soloist' in sovereign command, he becomes 'afraid of the great acting game'. A provisional role has become a determining force. He has to commit himself to it entirely, and it subjects him to outside influences beyond his control once his role is taken seriously by society. Thus, awaiting the decision of the jury on the choice of architect for the new monastery, Heinrich realises that he was 'no longer master of the performance', and he is seized by a sudden longing for the 'strict liturgy of my daily routine, when I alone still held all the threads of the act'.

Earlier his monologue had suggested the dictatorial tones of one organising his fellow men as pawns in the background of his own freedom: 'abbots and archbishops, generals and waiters, they were my supporting actors; I alone was the soloist'. He had been able so to manipulate time that time itself became unreal: 'I still swam about on time . . . crossed the oceans of past and present and, protected by my own loneliness from the danger of sinking, penetrated into the icy cold of the future'. But at a very early stage of his play-acting, when he submits his plans for the competition, there is the first suggestion that everything is not happening in accordance with calculation; he falls in love with his solicitor's secretary, and her words wishing him luck for the competition ('all the best, Herr Fähmel!') were 'the first for some weeks that wounded time, the first that reminded me that there were traces of reality in this play-acting of mine,' that made him aware that 'time was not controlled in the chambers of dreams'. The prisoner of a society which accepts his play-acting as commitment to a profession, he has to recognise that 'time had suddenly become a force'. Later he no longer merely acts the role of architect, but, fully identified with it, is enslaved by it. The pattern of life devised for himself in youth becomes a meaningless ritual in old age, and he the prisoner of its senseless mechanism; 'he began to run along after his own legend, he was incarcerated by the liturgy of his existence'. In understanding life as play-acting, and adopting a role, he has found a way of withdrawal from the depressing development of politics—which means that he had some responsibility for the fact that two of his children Heinrich and Otto, were infected by the political ideologies of the day, although he did not directly contribute to their indoctrination. So not only in his role as architect, but also as husband and father, he loses control of the situation. When he deplores this, his wife points out: 'it's no use weeping about it, my old dear, you chose to play the game'.

However, though the actor has become enslaved to this extent by his milieu, Heinrich retains a measure of ironic detachment both from his position in society and from the life of that society. He is not an outsider, nor does he feel estranged from his profession as an architect, but viewing life as *Spiel*, remains psychologically at a distance from his job and from politics. At the dedication ceremony of the new abbey Johanna realises 'that it was all a game', played by one whom she liked to think of as her 'little David with the sling, with the sad eyes hiding mocking laughter'. This is Heinrich Fähmel's way of distancing himself from the corrupt world of power of imperial Germany, glorified by those he heard singing *Die Wacht am Rhein* shouting the praises of Wilhelm II, and calling out enthusiastic-ally 'the name of the fool'—whereas he can say of himself: 'I waited in vain for any feelings that I could share with all those people. I felt empty and lonely, incapable of any kind of en-thusiasm'. A spectator isolated from the society he is observing, he acquires a position of elevated detachment from everyday life, even where he wants to share it, as when he is watching the women workers returning home: 'I liked the sensuous look of their faces . . . and would have dearly loved to go dancing with one of them'.[9] But his is a way of life enforcing aloofness, and so Johanna can say that 'it's the others who make history'. His compensation is irony, but he comes to realise that, since ironic detachment is escapism and a shunning of responsibility, this does not entitle him to feel superior, 'that irony was never

enough and never would be', that it was only a 'narcotic for
the privileged few', that, having been merely ironical, he had
morally failed vis-à-vis those who had suffered. Yet the aesthete
in him still finds satisfaction in imposing on his way of life
patterns of behaviour, like the ritual of breakfasting every
day at the same time in the Café Kröner, and his delight in
billiards.

Johanna will sometimes tease Heinrich about his type of
life, but really she is in agreement with it. She had begun her
adult life in the same spirit of revolt against the bureaucracy,
the military, and the ideals of the Wilhelminian bourgeoisie.
Like her husband she looked for the liberating experience of
irresponsible play-acting, deploring that this was taboo in a
society obsessed with ideals of duty: 'only one thing was for-
bidden, to want to live and treat life as a game. Do you get me,
Heinrich? Playing and play-acting was regarded as a mortal sin.'
Though *Spiel* for her has rather a more domestic application,
it is for her, too, a way of gaining freedom in relation to one's
milieu. Unwilling, however, to remain content with irony and
passivity, she alone makes an unequivocal protest against Wilhelm II by openly calling him 'the imperial fool' during a party
of high-ranking officers and their wives. Under Hitler she is
courageous enough to tell a prominent Nazi official, an old
acquaintance of hers, that all Nazis should hang themselves,
and there is a strong suggestion later that she shoots a min-
ister of the Federal Republic who, to gain votes, cultivates
relations with a group of right-wing extremists. 'Woe to those',
she even declares, 'who have not eaten of the sacrament of the
buffalo'.

From 1942 she had been living in a mental home, suffering
from an illness that it is possible to interpret as a camouflage
to enable her one day to take revenge on behalf of her two sons,
estranged from the family by their adherence to Wilhelm II
and Hitler respectively: 'the Lord says: "vengeance is mine",
but why shouldn't I be the instrument of the Lord?' She warns
Robert: 'don't imagine that I am mad, I know exactly where I
stand'. If she seems to live entirely in her memories of the past,
this is only the psychological mechanism of revenge, her reluctance to forget the things she wants to avenge: 'I will do it.
Robert, I shall be the instrument of the Lord; I have patience,

and time does not enter the sphere of my existence'. The exact circumstances in which she went to live in a mental home are not made clear; there is only the reference in one of her husband's monologues about 'the taxi in 1942 that took her to the home in Denklingen'. At one point there is a suggestion that she agreed to be taken there in order to escape persecution by the Nazis: 'and I knew of one possible way of escaping from the murderers—being declared insane', and a little later she says: 'I lived in inner emigration', which would be in line with the idea of her madness as an assumed guise for her later to be able to take revenge. In the mental home she play-acts successfully enough to be considered 'harmless' by the doctors, and when she comes out in 1958 with the intention of taking revenge, she acts another part, this time of the old granny who has been ill for a long period, but is now recovered. So she says to her husband: 'I shall be your dear old wife, a good mother, and a charming grandmother, whom one can describe to one's friends as a jolly nice sort of person.'

To the function of role-playing as a means of social and ideological detachment (in the case of Heinrich Fähmel) and, with Johanna, as a way of more active protest against the inhumanity of certain forms of political organisation, must now be added the function it has with Robert Fähmel.

If one applied to Robert's fastidiously superior response to the world around him, as one could apply it to his father, the idea of the snob, it would be in the spirit in which Böll himself has said that, 'in every snob there is an element of the aesthete'.[10] Outwardly this reveals itself, as Robert's secretary notices, in the 'meticulous orderliness' that he insists on in the office, his distaste for the vulgar realities, his reluctance to be seen 'in any intimate activity'.[11] Emphasis is laid on Robert's sense of intellectual superiority as a youth, particularly in his attitude to games. In handball 'it was all a matter of calculation', he realised, all you needed to succeed was 'a bit of physics', 'a little mathematics and practice', and the others were 'fools' not to grasp this. The father's delight in translating the movement of waiters into terms of ballet is matched by a corresponding feature in his son: 'my memories of people and events had always been linked with memories of movements, and these had always stuck in my memory as dance-figures', 'memories of movements translated themselves into lines, assuming the form of figures, green, black, red figures were cardiograms representing the rhythms of a particular person'. Hence his delight in billiards: 'red on green, white on green, new figures emerge like signs; quickly fading, nothing remained; music without melody, painting without image; just rectangles, rhombuses in varying numbers', 'the balls rolled about, white upon green, red upon green', 'a new geometrical figure arising out of green nothingness'.

'Just formulae,' he sums up, and this would also not be a bad way of describing the narrative technique of *Billard um halbzehn*, whereby three main first-person narrators and a number of minor ones are so ordered as to present basically the same material in ever changing patterns. The language too, has something of the brevity and conciseness of the formula, as can be seen in a quotation from Robert's interior monologue. Apprehending at one point that he will not be able to avoid a serious talk with his father, he imagines the following scenes, seeing it all through his father's eyes:

... diese Begegnung, auf die der Vater vielleicht seit zwanzig oder dreißig Jahren gehofft hatte; Gespräch mit dem gereiften Sohn, der nicht mehr Kind war, nicht mehr an der Hand zu nehmen, mit auf die Reise ins Seebad, zu Kuchen und Eis einzuladen; Gutenachtkuß, Morgenkuß, Frage nach den Schularbeiten, ein paar Lebensweisheiten: Ehrlich währt am längsten; Gott trügt nicht ... Robert ging nach den Mahlzeiten mit Vater ins Atelier hinüber, saß nur da, zeichnete, spielte mit Formeln in dem leeren großen Raum, wo noch die Zeichentische von fünf Architekten standen; leer; während der Alte müde seinen Kittel überzog, dann zwischen Zeichenrollen kramte, immer wieder vor dem Plan von Sankt Anton stehenblieb, später wegging, spazieren, Kaffee trinken, alte Kollegen, alte Feinde besuchen. ...

The way in which childhood memories are condensed here into single nouns (*Gutenachtkuß, Morgenkuß*), the use of terse and rather arid phrases (*Frage nach den Schularbeiten, ein paar Lebensweisheiten*), postscripts added to main clauses (*leer, spazieren, Kaffee trinken*), and the length of the sentence in its entirety (more than twice as long as the excerpt quoted)— all this is reminiscent of the enumerative style in Koeppen's novels. Present throughout *Billard um halbzehn*, it is the stylistic equivalent of a type of imagination which here reduces experience to mathematical formulae and transforms impressions into geometrical figures.

Robert Fähmel's decision to abandon his career as architect and to set up a Bureau of Statics is inspired in part by his wish to satisfy his abstract interest in mathematical formulae, and thereby to withdraw from the world of corrupt power known to him above all through his experiences in Nazi times, when he was tortured and persecuted, and some of his friends were killed. His father remarks that he 'was always shrewd and cool', but 'never ironical', and it is this lack of irony that distinguishes him from Heinrich Fähmel. Despite occasional traces of irony, Robert is too serious to rely on it, and his daughter Ruth notes how solemn he has become. It is not an act of personal irony against his father that makes him blow up the monastery, but of political protest against a régime with which the abbot had temporarily sympathised with an act by which he destroys where his father had built. His wartime occupation is closely related to what he is doing now. Demolishing, he says, 'is only the inversion of statics, so to speak its reciprocal'. The reason why he is not capable of his father's degree of irony may be seen from the list of hardships he had experienced as a man 'hard hit by fate through the death of his wife', a man who 'had emigrated and returned', had been 'betrayed and tortured'. His life after 1945 has been a retreat from all involvement with people outside his family circle and his secretary 'had never seen him talking with anyone—except with his father, his son, his daughter'. His new profession is only a facade, and he hardly ever works in his office, which is closed in the afternoons anyhow. It gives him the opportunity both to contract out of participation in society and to satisfy that 'abstract interest' which had always made mathematics for him 'sheer delight', and which now provides his point of withdrawal from the world of power. Thus, when asked by his émigré friend Schrella whether he bore in mind the suffering and atrocities inflicted on his family and friends by the Nazis, Robert replies: 'I do think about it, and perhaps it is one of the reasons why I collect formulae'. In billiards he can apply his 'abstract interest' to the behaviour of the balls and relish their ever-changing patterns, and playing billiards becomes part of his ritual of withdrawal into formulae and remembrances of the past. He always plays with Hugo, a lad who, having no parents, has no past, and so serves him as a symbol of Christ-like innocence. 'I am going to my father,' Hugo characteristically remarks, and again someone says to him: 'they are waiting for you, you are our lamb'. Robert's adoption of Hugo is a gesture symbolically expressing his wish to be one with timelessness and innocence. Playing billiards with Hugo, he can enjoy to the full 'a feeling of eternity' 'on this rectangle of green blotting paper' time is 'wiped out' for him, 'nothing of reality entered in . . . reality lost its dimensions'. Likewise in the structure of the novel past and present fuse into one.

There is thus a sense in which Robert's way of life can be likened to a role, but, since his aim is retreat from society, it is the negation of a social role. In contrast, Otto Fähmel plays a fully articulated ideological role. The same 'abstract interest' that motivates Robert's withdrawal into formulae and figures gives Otto an unsentimental approach to power, divesting him of all lovable human traits: 'there was nothing to touch the heart about Otto . . . in his mind power had become a formula, stripped of all considerations of utility, freed from instinct'. From a lively and gay child he turns into an instrument of brutish force: 'he betrayed us to the police, suddenly he was no more than the outward form of our son'. Unable to comprehend the change, his mother asks: 'how did he come into our family? I have not the consolation of the foolish hope that perhaps he got mixed up with another baby; he was after all born in this house.'

So in *Billard um halbzehn* the individual is seen above all as someone who may choose, or be conditioned by circumstances to assume, a role, and this may even imprison him. This applies also to the minor figures: Nettlinger, a former Nazi, now chief of police in a big town, is analysed by Schrella, who had known him at school, and who emphasises both the 'genuineness of your motives and feelings' and also 'the role that you were playing then and are playing today'. As if realising the problem of moral responsibility involved, Schrella adds resignedly: 'you won't be able to understand, don't try, because you did not play your roles consciously—otherwise you would be a cynic or a criminal, and you are neither.' The question of guilt in such a case is clearly other than with men like Heinrich and Robert Fähmel who, because they choose their roles knowingly, are ultimately responsible for what they have done or left undone. Heinrich, for instance, committed nothing that according to the law could be called a crime, but, since he 'played his role consciously', he could be held the more guilty for not having revolted openly against Nettlinger. This, the reader may feel, would not be an adequate ethic, and, bearing in mind the scope of irony in the novel, it need not follow that Böll does either.

In this novel irony is least involved when the narrator is present in the traditional sense, as a person telling the story with at least as much knowledge of the circumstances as the individual characters. He will also abdicate his authority and let an event be talked about from the subjective angle of individual characters through interior monologue. He is, however, always implicitly present as the agent by whom the pattern of the novel is arranged, and, applying a remark by Robert Fähmel, the nature of the pattern can be defined as 'imagined simultaneity'. Robert's phrase is reminiscent of Thomas Mann's *Joseph* novels or of *Lotte in Weimar*. With Mann the notion of time—'the "once" in its double meaning of "as once it will be" '[12] —is closely bound up with his view of the 'mythical', and this in turn with irony: 'this is the way the mythically orientated narrator sees things, and, you observe, it combines irony and a sense of superiority'.[13] If, in a way foreshadowed in *Das Brot der frühen Jahre*, in his handling of time in *Billard um halbzehn* Böll operates by analogous 'mythic' devices, an important and related fact is that here for the first time in a major work the setting is in the world of the well-to-do bourgeoisie, to which on this evidence Böll's attitude could be described as 'ironic' and 'superior'.

As in Proust the narrative has two levels, with the difference that in Böll the present carries the main weight, while Proust's concern is with the recovery of the past. Memory, we read, 'was not feeling, it remained a formula', and 'it is not wise to release formulae from their rigid form, to express secrets in words'. We hear a good deal about Robert's youth and about the anti-Nazi activities of the pacifist circle he had belonged to, but exactly what went on is somewhat obscure. In the account of the scene in which Johanna shoots, where much of what happens is known to us only through Johanna's inner monologue, the picture is far from clear. Often in this novel it is rather like looking out over a landscape, anxious to pick out its details and contours, when haze keeps drifting over and confusing the view, creating interesting patterns all the same. History tends to become allegory, and the novel does rather seem to strain after those 'far-reaching allegorical constructions' that Günter Blöcker has condemned,[14] but which are only an extension of those aesthetic patterns which the characters delight in and through which they shape the memory of their individual experiences. In fact, one reason why on the whole *Billard um halbzehn* was so well received in West Germany was that it satisfied for this reason those who had criticised Böll for having been too long involved with sordid and petty material. Also he had at last written a novel with a very sophisticated literary technique, very much at home, in Mann's terms, in the 'interesting' sphere of art, and, in Nietzsche's, undeniably an 'aesthetic phenomenon'.[15] A writer whose fame had rested largely on his treatment of the problems of the 'little man' and on his handling of the smaller forms, had switched to a less episodic treatment of a more exalted milieu. But, in the process his characters had become in some respects so passive that Johanna's active intervention towards the end would, if less obscured, verge on melodrama. Also, by the standards of his earlier novels and stories, in *Billard um halbzehn* reality tends to be somewhat out of focus. His next novel was to show that the passivity of the characters and the loss of focus had been related aspects.

The central figure, and narrator, in *Ansichten eines Clowns* (1963) is Hans Schnier, son of a wealthy business man. He was ten at the end of World War II, twenty-one when, after having been educated at a Catholic school, he left his family to follow the career of clown, to which by the end of the book he has devoted himself for five years. He is 'a poor, recalcitrant outsider', the opposite of his brother Leo who, as a candidate for the priesthood, had entered a world demanding conformity to a rigid system of beliefs. Schnier's position is as far removed as could be from ideological commitment and from the 'unscrupulous demagogues', 'pure tacticians', and 'opportunists' whom Böll mentions in one of his essays as endangering society by the ideological violence they do to language. Schnier therefore refuses 'to join in with those who beat the air with high-sounding words' and to bind himself to any set of ideological principles. He is always deeply distrustful of the jargon of ideology in any shape or form, and the very phrase 'principles of order' re- minds him of the 'torture chamber', in the same way as the hero of *Entfernung von der Truppe* (1964) can say that the word 'service' always fills him with fear. Hence Schnier's love of children, creatures uncorrupted by opportunism and ideology: 'I love children, I can get on very well with them, especially with babies'. Hence, too, his respect for people who, in secret defiance of their chosen or accepted role, succumb to some personal and hidden fancy. He delights in being privy to a scene in which, unaware of being watched, his conventional mother steps outside her role of social respectability and quietly and crudely tucks into some delicacies in the cellar, and he despises the preacher who talks all the time about 'laws' instead of about 'a woman's hands', about abstractions instead of individuals. He scorns those who see their own and other people's actions merely as means to an end and judge them only for their effect. When on one occasion a speaker, unable to see himself except as an actor playing a role, asks him: 'how was I? Did I make a good impression?', Schnier contemptuously likens the query to 'the sort of questions prostitutes ask'. People, he comments, 'accustom themselves to a prostitute's vocabulary'. Marie means all and everything to him because on the one hand he finds her a person content to be true to her own nature, and on the other because his relationship to her is absolutely personal, neither having to play a role vis-à-vis the other. She alone takes him for what he is, does not seek to use him for any ulterior purposes, ideological, political, or of any other kind, whereas others 'believe in nothing but man, God, or abstract money'. Marie's desertion is correspondingly catastrophic, all the more so since it is accompanied by her being won back to organised Catholicism, by her allowing herself to be 'used'. His art immediately declines. His father then offers to pay for him to be trained by a professional mimic, but he refuses, for the cause of the trouble is not just faulty technique, and in any case he will not be forced into a role or a pattern by somebody else, treated as a commodity that only needs to be better processed in order to succeed.

The function of a clown is by nature of his trade to appear at once lovable and absurd. His method is parody and carica-ture, but he is not out to convert his audience any more than *Ansichten eines Clowns* aims to persuade us all to play the fool. This novel is a true successor to those earlier short stories in which with ironic effect Böll alienates the familiar and con-ventional by exposing it to the light of absurdity, and signifi-cantly this is something that Schnier himself is particularly good at: 'I am most successful at portraying everyday absurdity'. 'What the others call non-fiction', he says, 'always seems to me to be fiction'. A fool, Böll wrote on one occasion, 'who every now and again is beaten up by his moody master for his im-pertinence and always displays the outward signs of his trade, a clown's cap and rattle, leads a dignified existence compared with the person who performs on the stage of public opinion like a marionette always ready to turn somersaults'.[16] In *Ansichten eines Clowns* Böll enjoys the liberties of the fool as a weapon of social criticism. He is not, as some have assumed,[17] treating Schnier as his *alter ego*, and so it is inept to criticise him for too trivial a kind of commitment[18]—as if, as one writer wisely observed, he ought to let his clown, 'draped in the "great questions of our day", wander through the streets of Bonn like a sandwich man'.[19] Schnier pokes fun again and again at Catholicism, but at much else as well, and he is as good at parodying tycoons as cardinals. It is ridiculous to imagine that because Schnier is anti-clerical, Böll is too, and to say that because Böll loves humanity, he ought not to caricature it—an odd criticism, incidentally, to come from the editor of *Der Spiegel*.[20]

Rather, in *Ansichten eines Clowns* Böll adopts a position from which he can react to the 'great questions of our day' other than in the drab and banal form of merely ideological comment, however worthy its intentions may be.[21] 'Between the impos-sible values of ideological systems, possibilities',[22] 'between the songs of the barbarians (*Ungesänge*), counter-songs, parodies'— this formulation can be applied to *Ansichten eines Clowns*, whose author operates with a double process of alienation, between himself and the clown, and between the clown and society. Hardly any type of figure can be imagined better fitted to enforce the principle of non-identification of author and protagonist, and the author never for a moment intrudes as narrator, Schnier lives fully and actively, becomes familiar with the world around him, but remains unintegrated. As the virtue of his outsiderness, he is endowed with a highly critical sensitivity, grotesquely epitomised in his ability to smell what is happening at the other end of the telephone, and with a gift of formulation such as Martin Walser takes as a characteristic quality of the intelligent outsider.[23] Schnier, however, is by no means a passive observer, for a clown is necessarily actively engaged in working for his public, and it is not by any act of withdrawal that he keeps society at a distance, but in simply being a clown. Adopting a variety of roles within the framework of his professional role as clown, he can be in the social world, but not of it, and pass judgement on all manner of situations, 'but one does not have to believe him'.[24] There are those, the novel tells us, who expect of him that he should become 'grown up, mature, no longer merely subjective, and this, like the infant-like gnome in Grass's *Die Blechtrommel*, he refuses to do. This is also more or less what at least one critic[25] demanded of the youthful rebel against the 'phoney guys' in Salinger's *Catcher in the Rye*, the hero of which is certainly a kindred spirit of Schnier. Böll translated Salinger[26] into German, a fact that should be seen in connection with his remark in the *Frankfurter Vorlesungen* about why 'I often preferred to translate more than to write': 'to take over something from a foreign language into the area of one's own language is one way of getting firm ground under one's feet'. This comment links up with his stress throughout these lectures on the extent to which post-war West German writers have had to operate without any reassuring sense of being rooted in familiar territory, of having *Orte und Nachbarschaft*.[27]

Existentially committed to the role of clown and unable to be anything but a clown, Schnier is constantly tempted into clownish acts, sometimes most obviously when his finances are involved. When he has just received a small sum of money from a friend, he goes and spends it on a taxi ride instead of taking the bus, and when he has run out of money, he tosses his one remaining coin out of the window. When his father offers to have him trained as a mimic instead of a clown, he evades the issue by suddenly acting a blind man, and he does it so well that his father really believes for a moment that his son has lost his sight. He can thus show both his disgust at the thought of changing his proper métier, and also prove what an excellent mimic he already is, though his father does not grasp the point. As a clown he can imitate and assume many roles from every-day life, but, different from Robert Fähmel in *Billard um halb-zehn*, he does not act his profession as a role, although as a clown he is a professional role-player. His nature is to make a sharp division between lying and acting, and so on one occasion, catching himself lying about some trivial matter, he reproves himself with the thought that 'that was false because it was a lie, and everyone will immediately recognise when I am lying'. Since his concern to preserve his innocence leads him, like Robert Fähmel, to refuse complicity with the corrupting pres-sures of power and convention, he has the makings of what might perhaps be described as a secular saint. The inversion of his situation is that of the little community portrayed in Böll's radio play *Die Spurlosen* (1957), seeking to live an innocent existence in retreat from society only to discover that, in order to survive, they have to plunder. In the interests of innocence they have to become criminals.

The structure of *Ansichten eines Clowns*, based on a series of events presented by the clown as first-person narrator, is made up of episodes with minute descriptions of people's milieu and behaviour, 'an almost uninterrupted chain of miniatures',[28] leading Böll away from the large symbolic constructions of *Billard um halbzehn*. The dialogues are embedded in narrative focused on a number of loosely connected events in Schnier's life. The language of these passages, comprising more than merely an objective record of impressions, has a highly sub-jective and also a very intellectual quality, the world being pre-sented in the grotesque light in which the clown himself sees it. Things may thereby reveal greater complexity than they are normally thought to have, or equally may become grotesquely simplified. An instance is the way Schnier deals with the problem of commuting. Since every large station is packed daily with people arriving to work in the town, and also with people leaving it to work elsewhere, why, he wonders, don't these people simply swop their jobs? The episodic structure of the book, corresponding to the way the clown behaves and

reacts, with his astonishing memory for details and his sensitivity to impressions, results largely from the principle by which
Schnier calls reality to account by subjecting its most ephemeral
incidents to critical and detailed scrutiny. The arena of any
clown's performance, it has been said, is 'a distorting mirror
reflecting the truth embodied in a moment of time'.[29] So in
answer to a question about what he does, Schnier replies that
'I collect moments', and it is exercise of this predilection that
gives the novel the vividness of detail that most differentiates it
from *Billard um halbzehn*.

The reference to the intellectual element in Schnier can be
clarified by comparing him to the young poet in Böll's radio
play *Zum Tee bei Dr. Borsig* (1955).

Here, Robert has been commissioned by a large concern to
write a monograph on the founder, but his picture has turned
out to be that of a 'sceptic on the grand scale'. It is, therefore,
rejected for publicity purposes, and modified without his con-
sent. The vigour with which he defended his version impresses
the firm, and he is envisaged as a suitable person to help
advertise a product claimed to cure colour blindness. Dr.
Borsig, an executive, invites him to meet the President at tea
to discuss the matter. Robert's wife is fearful of the prospects:
'I have heard the voices of these people, and I am sure that
they want something from you that you should not give'. He
is privately warned by Dr. Borsig's wife, whose father, also a
poet, had once in rather similar circumstances allowed himself
to be persuaded to run the firm's advertisement department.
The President, she tells Robert, belongs to the 'world of smooth-
shaven swindlers'. Robert rejects the role demanded of him; his
wife says in the same spirit that she does 'not want to fall into
such a mould and find that it fits me like a glove'. Meanwhile
the discussions betweeen Robert, the President, and Dr. Borsig
are in progress. Dr. Borsig tells him that the public need to be
shown, and this would be Robert's job, that behind the abstract
looking trade-name are the interests of living men and women.
The considerations motivating Robert's resistance make it easy
to understand how he could present the hero of his rejected
pamphlet in the way he did, for it is essentially scepticism that
Robert opposes to the blandly confident assumptions of his
would-be employers. If the product in question stands or falls

as a cure for colour-blindness, his 'scruples begin at the point when I can't be sure that colour-blindness is a real danger', and in any case, if he accepted the plan and wrote the required advertisements, he would be merely increasing people's fears. So Robert refuses to participate, to the joy of his wife, who is relieved to find that 'you have returned to me as the person I thought you were'.

Dr. Borsig had told Robert that 'you look too far and too deep', but Robert comments to his wife that 'one can't look far and deep enough'. Schnier would have a lot of sympathy with this attitude and as a clown he is armed against the conformist pressures of a world of organised success and power, and against the clichés built into its language and its values. He is essentially an intellectual clown.

The fool, Ralf Dahrendorf has said, 'has the special character-istic that he does not want to fit any role. His role is to play no role'. Ideas 'of "what is becoming" and "how one behaves" mark the opposite of what the clown does'. He 'is not at the top, because he cannot dictate to people the laws of behaviour'. equally he is not at the bottom of the social system, 'for he is present among the ruling people as their critical conscience, and he allows himself liberties that would not be forgiven any-one at the bottom'. His power 'lies in his freedom from the social hierarchy, in the fact that he speaks both from outside and within, that he belongs and yet does not belong, that he can express the unpleasant truth'. Modern democratic societies, Dahrendorf argues, also need their fools, and the corresponding figure nowadays is the intellectual. As the 'court fools of modern society', intellectuals 'have the duty to cast doubt on whatever seems obvious, to relativise all authority, to ask all those questions that otherwise no one dares to ask'. For 'every position the opposite of which cannot at least be discussed is a weak position', and it is the function of intellectuals 'to strengthen accepted positions—political, moral, educational, religious, or whatever—by calling them into question and therefore compel-ling people to justify them'.[30]

Schnier would agree with a good deal of this, but hardly with the last part of the argument. He would be in sympathy with the idea of 'turning every thought around' that conceals its reverse side',[31] and with the notion of the 'opened' society,

one, that is to say, ready to 'admit its own negation'.[32] He
would be fully in accord, too, with the related argument of the
contemporary Polish philosopher Leszek Kolakowski in a book
translated into German in 1960 and ending on the theme of
the 'antagonism of priests and fools':

> The priest is the guardian of the absolute, he is the servant of the
> final truth and everything regarded as self-evident in tradition. The
> fool is sceptical about everything that claims to be self-evident. He
> moves in good society, but he does not belong to it and he is cheeky
> to it. He would not be able to do this if he belonged to good society.
> Then he would be no more than a priest causing a scandal in the
> drawing-room. The fool must stand outside good society, look at it
> from the side, in order to see how little self-evident things can be
> that it regards as such, how little final are the things it treats as final.
> But he must move in good society in order to know what is sacred
> to it . . . The philosophy of the fool in any epoch unmasks as dubious
> precisely what is most firmly accepted, discovers contradictions in
> what appears obvious and incontrovertible, makes all the so-called
> obvious truths of commonsense look ridiculous and lays bare what
> is reasonable in what seems to be absurd. The attitude of the fool
> consists in constant reflection about whether perhaps the opposite
> may not be right . . . but it is not governed merely by the desire to
> contradict, but by distrust in relation to all stabilised values.[33]

Kolakowski's conclusion that 'we stand for the philosophy
of the fool, for an attitude of negative watchfulness against
all absolute claims' raises the problem of commitment, and
there arises the question whether so apparently negative a type
of commitment can correspond to any conventional category.
'Left' might seem a possible label, and the definition of this
term in the contemporary context is a question to which both
Dahrendorf and Böll have offered answers.

The important thing, Dahrendorf wrote[34] in this connection,
is 'that the politicians should listen to the intellectuals and that
the intellectuals should speak to the politicians', for 'the intellectuals are so to speak the permanent element of constructive
distrust in society—or they ought to be, in order to be aware of
their task at the head of the "left" '. But the term 'left', he
remarks, must today be seen in rather a new light. It is con-
ceivable, runs the argument, that 'today a new form of liberal
thinking can claim the position of the left, a form characterised

above all by a 'constructive distrust . . . of the constant extension of the power of private and public interests', and by an
attitude 'whose critical hope accompanies the forces of power as
a goad and thus replaces the utopian left'. In Germany, he
comments, the notion predominates 'that unity is strength, so
that all criticism is considered malicious and total', but 'only
when . . . the view establishes itself that the security of the whole
is better served by opposition than assent, can "left" in the
sense here intended have a practical basis'.

Clearly, commitment in this context cannot correspond to
the sense in which it is used, for example, by Wolfdietrich
Schnurre when he defines the committed writer as one 'who . . .
tends not so much to distance and objectivity as to adherence
and involvement'.[35] The paradox is involved of commitment
to what (by political or ideological standards) should perhaps
be referred to as non-commitment, but with more than merely
negative features, and comparable to the idea of commitment
implicit in some remarks of Hannah Arendt. Adopting a
position typical of the modern intellectual, she argued that
those who failed in their personal responsibility under Hitler
were those who, disposing of 'a set of learned or innate rules',
apply them in such a way 'that every new experience or situation is already pre-judged, and we need only to act out whatever
we learned or possessed beforehand'. Those who are reliable
under such circumstances, and Schnier would add under any
circumstances, 'are not those who cherish values and hold fast
to moral norms and standards', but 'the doubters and sceptics
not because scepticism is good or doubting wholesome, but
because they are used to examine things and to make up their
own minds'.[36] We might here fall back on Silone's phrase about
'commitment as personal vocation', in conjunction with his
remark, fully in accord with Schnier's view of things, that those
who accept it 'must never identify their ideal with institutions
or with powers'.[37]

Böll's answer to the question about the left[38] has points of
contact with Dahrendorf's in its doubt about the usefulness of
any too firmly defined ideological position. The 'official left',
he says, 'has its right wing, the right its left wing', in addition to
which there are 'many centres'—'the centre of the right', 'the
centre of the left', 'the centre of the right wing', 'the centre of

the left wing', not to mention 'the centre of the right wing of the left'. Thus, taking so familiar and seemingly obvious a concept as that of the political left, and assuming a tone of intellectual clowning (like Schnier's on the question of commuters), Böll analyses it in such a way as to make it appear less self-evident than might be assumed, and also to set it in a rather grotesque light. This corresponds to Schnier's procedure, based on the notion (as Böll puts it in this essay) that 'all I see around me are mechanical stereotypes'.

In a world where these predominate, as Schnier well realises, the identity of the individual person is constantly under threat. Professionally he adopts the role of clown, but, since he *is* a clown, this is not just a role. He thus has the freedom that Heinrich Fähmel gains within certain limits for himself through mere role-playing, but without his irony, the moral uprightness aspired to by Robert Fähmel, but without his passivity, and, all in all, qualities of resilience that differentiate him from his fictional contemporary, the less articulate and more naive clown-hero—or rather clown-victim—of Eckhart Kroneberg's *Keine Scherbe für Hiob* (1964).

Hans Schnier is outside the confines of respectable society, but by no means without dignity. In *Ende einer Dienstfahrt* (1966) the two accused place themselves in a similar situation by their defiance of the law, and in their case too moral dignity is not lacking. The Gruhls, father and son, are jointly involved in setting fire to a jeep belonging to the army, at the point when the younger Gruhl is finishing his army service. The army here represents the world of administrative authority and control, which in the story includes also a relentless and merciless taxation system ruining the small-scale family enterprise. A 'giant organisation' whose purpose is described by a witness as consisting 'in the production of absurd kinds of nothingness, almost total nothingness, of utter senselessness', confronts an absurdity of a different kind. For the Gruhls stage their act of sabotage and destruction as a Happening, with appropriately absurd ritual, singing the litany and tapping their pipes rhythmically together. They are by temperament clowns, and as witnesses too they give clowning answers, about 'always being cold when it is hot' and being 'absent minded and mentally wide awake at the same time'. The prosecutor calls this 'latent frivolity', which in a way it is. Commonsense, it is true, must brand this kind of thing ridiculous, but the standard of so absurd a logic exposes the absurd practical logic of the army administration, which requires for reasons of administrative convenience that, if a jeep will not reach the mileage required by the scheduled servicing, it should be aimlessly driven around till it does. It is as if to add to their own absurdity that the Gruhls stage the destruction of the jeep as more than a mere act of sabotage but as an absurd Happening, and comparably, this particular practice of the army is interpreted by a defence witness Heimüller, as itself only part of a larger absurdity. His testimony on behalf of the army authorities amounts to a philosophy of nihilism, so that he can compare the 'arrangement of operations' with his own philosophy of art, namely that art 'consists in arranging nothingness into its different forms of nothingness'. By the same standard the attitude of the Gruhls, too, has features of nihilism. Their 'indifference' is often stressed, and Heimüller mentions this in the context of praising the younger Gruhl as having been a meritorious soldier. Needless to say, his evidence is not particularly effective for the purpose of the prosecution.

If in *Ansichten eines Clowns* there was, as the public reaction showed, often the danger of the author being identified with his first-person narrator, in *Ende einer Dienstfahrt* a third-person narrator serves mainly the function of merely reporting on the confrontation in the court-room, and on a few marginal activities connected with the case. For further detachment the story is placed in the trivial and slightly comical setting of a quite unimportant small town—a setting in which incidentally representatives of order and bureaucracy can appear in less anonymous guise as personally, at heart, essentially 'human'—and the effect is increased by the ironic humour brought to play on every aspect of the case, on prosecution and defence alike, and by the quaintly idyllic character of the whole affair. The effect of the story depends to a great extent on the effect made by the discrepancy—and on the irony by which this is brought about —created between seeming triviality and deeper and more serious import. For in its guise as Happening the sabotage of the jeep can be called by one witnesss an act of 'de-formation' (*Entstaltung*), and 'disarrangement' (*Entstellung*). These are terms

that can be taken into service to describe social criticism of the
kind whereby—as increasingly in recent German literature and
art—an institution of authority is 'deformed', stripped down,
to reveal the components of absurdity out of which it is constructed, which the general image will obscure, and which
generalising ideology will be at pains entirely to obliterate.

This, it must be added, is the critical procedure of intellectuals
as critics of society—and their retort to ideology is as anti-
ideological as the Happening staged by the Gruhls, and sometimes in the guise of equivalent absurdity. A Happening, says
the same witness (in language reminiscent at this point and
elsewhere of the in-group terminology[39]), is an 'attempt to
create salutary disorder', and he goes on to speak of the creation
'out of de-formation of new form'. The remark needs to be
taken in conjunction with what we come to know about the
Gruhls as men marked by particular sensitivity and intelligence,
as essentially 'artistic natures', endowed with an 'astonishing
ability to recognise . . . and reproduce different styles'. If
in his way Hans Schnier could be compared, behind his
mask of clowning, with an intellectual, the same is true of the
Gruhls.

There is another comparison to be made with Schnier, as a
destructive critic, but representing also a certain type of innocence. The older Gruhl is commended by the parish priest for
his 'almost innocent piety', for being, though he was not a true
believer, and even occasionally was caught smoking in church,
'one of the few Christians in his parish'. Returning now to the
earlier quotation, 'salutary disorder' is revealed as not a wholly
satisfactory translation, and *heilbringend* as applied to 'disorder'
comes to demand also the notion of salvation. The relationship
between innocence and clowning is indicated in the evidence of
the prosecution witness, who, testifying about the elder Gruhl's
financial affairs, says that, while there was 'nothing whatever
ethically . . wrong about Gruhl's behaviour' the financial
bureaucracy could not tolerate "anachronistic court fools"'.

The idea, in the phrase we used earlier, of secular sainthood,
becomes relevant again in the case of the Gruhls, and this
brings us back to Böll's *Frankfurter Vorlesungen*. Humane humour,
he says there, will set out to 'define what is sublime in what
society contemptuously casts aside'. Only the 'asocial is sublime'

but 'to recognise it as sublime demands a sense of humour'[40]—
which helps to explain why, for all its depth of theme and
content, *Ende einer Dienstfahrt* is to date Böll's most delicately
humorous book.

Chapter 4

Günter Grass

Up to the time when at the age of thirty-one Grass won the prize of Gruppe 47 in 1958 he had a limited reputation as a graphic artist, as the author of a volume of poetry (*Die Vorzüge der Windhühner*, 1956), and of a few short plays in the manner of the theatre of the absurd. His fame has come to rest largely on two novels (*Die Blechtrommel*, 1959, and *Hundejahre*, 1963), in the interval between which appeared a further volume of poetry (*Gleisdreieck*, 1960) and the story *Katz und Maus* (1961).

Reporting the 1958 meeting of Gruppe 47, one critic wrote: 'Grass writes an unconventional, powerful, even rather wild prose, with its own individual rhythm. He can observe and describe, his dialogues are excellent, his humour is angry and original and he has much to say. His prose carries one away and sometimes provokes resistance. But one can never be indifferent to it.' [1] The last part of this statement was illustrated in 1960 when Grass was proposed for the award of the literary prize of the city of Bremen. The city fathers, shocked by the improprieties of *Die Blechtrommel*, rejected the committee's recommendation, and the prize went instead to Siegfried Lenz. Grass then addressed an Open Letter to Lenz [2] in which he referred to Lenz's remark, in his speech of acceptance, about the way such an award honoured the freedom of the writer. He concluded by giving Lenz the number of his bank account with the request to hand over the prize money. The incident, like Grass's public offer once to Anna Seghers that, if she would make a public declaration in East Germany on the issue of freedom he would make it his business to spit in a church in the Federal Republic, [3] exemplifies his delight in self-dramatisation, which is something he shares with Oskar Matzerath, the clowning hero of *Die Blechtrommel*, and Joachim Mahlke in *Katz und Maus*. 'People like us,' Oskar is told, 'have no place in the audience. We must go on the stage, into the arena.' When in the 1965 West German election, for instance, Grass himself went 'into the arena', with a series of much publicised political addresses on behalf of the Social Democratic Party in various towns of West Germany, the tone of his speeches could, however, lead Max Frisch, in a tribute to the intellectual nature of Grass's contribution, to say that 'the decisive thing about what Grass did . . . was to indicate by his personal example that one can choose rationally how to use one's vote without being blindly carried away'.[4]

Oskar, too, has features associated with the intellectual, and familiarity with the phenomenon of the intellectual in France[5] may well help to explain the enthusiasm with which *Die Blechtrommel* was acclaimed there. In England its reception was mixed, often cool and reserved, sometimes downright negative. 'Every kind of social criticism', one commentator wrote, 'meets with understanding in England. What is not understood is the total withdrawal from and disavowment of social and therefore moral values.'[6]

True, the hero of *Die Blechtrommel* is a rootless wanderer from place to place, irresponsibly unwilling, it might seem, to settle down to the obligations of a fixed occupation. Even when in the end he withdraws to a mental home, the indications are that before so very long he will move on again to new adventures and fresh forms of existence. So Oskar Matzerath is a modern picaro, a 'man on the move',[7] a rebel. If he is not prepared to surrender his privacy in order to make his revolutionary enthusiasm a means of social change, this, too, is typical of the picaro who, while he may cherish utopian hopes for the world, holds back from the exercise of organised power. Thus, refusing to be regarded as a 'resistance fighter', he begs to be seen merely 'as a rather eccentric person who . . . registered some sort of protest on nothing more than a toy'. A pragmatist dealing with each problem as it comes, Oskar, like any picaro, has no interest in ideological commitment, is too disposed to want to go it alone to have the desire or the will to instigate any kind of political organisation. He is too much governed by motives of private interest, self-preservation, and the satisfaction of his own pleasure. Important too is that the typical modern picaro, Oskar included, tends to belong to a petty-bourgeois setting, and this provides both a colourful background, and a basis of discontent and frustration from which social criticism can be launched. For 'in this new, mobile society a thinking person born in the middle or lower classes had more grounds to question his inferior position because so many of those above him on the social ladder were there not because they "belonged" but simply because they had amassed more capital than he. The new industrialised, bourgeois society, moreover, promulgated a standard of mediocrity and crass materialism that was likely to embitter or estrange the sensitive individual.' [8]

Significantly, a number of recent West German novels link up with the picaresque tradition. They include in addition to *Die Blechtrommel*, Paul Pörtner's *Tobias Immergrün* (1962), Heinz Küpper's *Simplicius 45* (1963), Martin Beheim-Schwarzbach's *Die diebischen Freuden des Herrn von Bißwange* (1964), Gerhard Ludwig's *Tausendjahrfeier* (1965), Helmut Putz's *Die Abenteuer des braven Kommunisten Schweyk* (1965), and Gerhard Zwerenz's *Casanova oder der kleine Herr im Krieg und Frieden* (1966). *Die Blechtrommel* may be assumed to have provided the immediate stimulus. [9]

In all these works a life of adventure serves as a way of protest and detachment of the kind indicated in Walter Mehring's lines:

> Abenteuernd, abenteuernd
> Trotte ich durchs Land,
> Bin nicht Euren Seelen, Euren
> Herzen nicht verwandt.
> Jegliche Verkleidung paßt mir,
> Der ich bin in Ewigkeit,
> Bald Trappist und bald voll Freßgier!
> Meinen Namen fraß die Zeit!
> Meiner alten Mutter Erde
> Riss die Nabelschnur entzwei;
> Die Chimäre, die mich nährte,
> War des Alltags Einerlei!

The hedonistic cynicism usually in some degree characteristic of the picaresque adventurer, grasping at opportunities for personal advantage, is of the sort expressed in the final verse of this poem:

> Abenteuernd, abenteuernd
> Trotte ich durchs Land,
> Und der Tod, den Bund erneuernd,

Frißt mir aus der Hand!
Jegliche Vermummung paßt mir,
Henkerkleid und Ordensstern,
Wird der Körper einst zur Last mir,
Diene fromm ich meinem Herrn!
Oft schon schlief ich unter Leichen,
Selig wie ein müdes Kind—
Oft auch mäste ich die Reichen,
Die lebendig Tote sind![10]

A social outsider, an adventurer, even an hedonist, the picaro has always, nevertheless, been able to represent in some measure the interests of humanity. This is by virtue largely of his protest against the intrusions of authority and power, and in his dream of happiness and freedom—in short, of those features that make him in certain respects a childlike figure. The yearning for the cosy security of babyhood and childhood, a central motif in *Die Blechtrommel*, figures also in *Tobias Immergrün* and *Simplicius 45*. In the former, Tobias in hospital cherishes his need for attention as a way of being watched over like a child, in the latter Simplicius actually is a child. The motif of innocence may, as in the continuation of Mehring's poem, be linked with the picaro as saviour of mankind:

Meine Träume sind das Eiland
Der enterbten Kreatur—
Bald ein Vieh und bald ein Heiland
Ringe ich mit der Natur![11]

Oskar can be viewed by himself and others sometimes in the image of Messiah, but his actions are not always saintly, and Rasputin is one of his models. In *Die diebischen Freuden des Herrn von Bißwange* the New Testament is among the hero's favourite books. But the title was originally to have been *Der Unheilige* ('the unsaintly man')[12]—not to indicate that he was a figure of evil, but that his virtues were other than those provided for in the orthodox canons of holiness.

The picaro has traditionally also been something of a clown. This obviously applies to Oskar, and also to Joachim Mahlke in *Katz und Maus*. Clearly here Grass has devised a story lending itself to treatment in the traditional manner of the *Novelle*, which it purports to be. It has substance and extension, and

something analogous to the dramatic 'turning point' demanded
by orthodox theory. Yet the conventions of the form are somewhat at odds with the way Grass handles his theme. He 'has
taken on the task of writing an extended story', but sets out 'to
relativise it, to interrupt it, to make it appear questionable',
and this he does by building into it 'motifs that do not firmly
follow in their chronological order', and above all by the way
it 'digresses into episodes and incidents serving to characterise
the hero and define the area and the milieu, but which are not
integrated into the story'.[13] To this extent Grass narrates
against the features that give the *Novelle* its intrinsic character,
and a note of parody is clearly caught towards the close in the
question as to 'who will supply me with a good ending?'.

Traditionally the *Novelle* operates with the development of
character, but Mahlke remains little, if at all, changed by the
end of the story. The point of the *Bildungsroman*, to which *Die
Blechtrommel* is related, had been to show a personality developing to wholeness in the light of experience. However, the
irrelevance of the notion of growth is a central theme of *Die
Blechtrommel*, and here too there is an element of parody. It is
a novel about someone 'who was to be so superior to the grown-
ups, who did not want to measure his shadow against theirs,
who inwardly and outwardly was ready and finished, while all
those people right into old age had to keep waffling about
development'. It concerns someone 'for whom it was not necessary each year to have larger shoes and trousers merely to show
that something was growing'. Yet, if *Die Blechtrommel* negates
the principle of growth, its style of narrative has much in common with that of earlier periods when, as with the realistic
writers of the nineteenth century, development of character
was taken for granted. Here, too, Grass indulges his delight in
parody, combining drawn-out and detailed narrative with
ironical comments about the realistic novel and the omniscient
narrator. 'I shall begin', Oskar declares, 'far away, for no one
ought to tell the story of his life who hasn't the patience to say
a word or two at least about half of his grandparents before
plunging into his own existence. And so to you personally, dear
reader, . . . to you my friends and weekly visitors who suspect
nothing of my paper supply, I introduce Oskar's maternal
grandmother.' Oskar then quickly reveals himself as one who

has, or appears to have, at his command a store of relevant information.

The flow of narrative, however, is often checked by the way episode after episode assumes an importance exceeding that of an incident in a developing sequence of events, which is one reason why *Die Blechtrommel* frequently gives the impression of throwing up 'symbolical overtones of its own accord', creating 'seductive invitations to allegory', and requiring on the part of the reader 'a quick response to symbolical gestures, however lightly sketched'.[14] Such a moment is the account, early on, of the baby Oskar observing a moth beating against the electric light bulbs. Allegorical possibilities inevitably suggest themselves, on the lines maybe of the 'desire of the moth for the star' or of Goethe's poem *Selige Sehnsucht,* familiar to the German reader, and Oskar himself gives it an allegorical touch by speaking of 'the moth's last confession', and of its beating against the light as 'a kind of absolution'. Again, in the final chapter of Book One ('Faith, Love, Hope'), household gas grotesquely acquires an allegorical relationship to the Holy Spirit, with Christ as the 'holy gas man' lighting the stars. Oskar's existence teases us all the time with possibilities of allegory. We may sense the allegory of a successfully absurd existence evidencing the general absurdity of life, or, in conjunction with the suggestion (referred to by Grass) of 'denaturisation as a parable', 'mutilation as the opposite of an original totality',[15] or, as Oskar appears to one of the characters in the novel, of 'the destroyed image of man', the 'madness of the century', or of the rebel fashioning for himself an autonomous position free from the restraints of moral and social responsibility, of the degeneration of bourgeois freedom into anarchism. In much the same way in *Katz und Maus* references to the 'eternal cat' and the 'eternal mouse' are bound to stimulate curiosity about possible allegorical equivalents, but the answers that suggest themselves are likely to prove just as partial and inconclusive.

The clowning side of Mahlke's nature is constantly stressed in *Katz und Maus.* Early on, the narrator recalls the moment at school when Mahlke remarked that he was 'going to be a clown and make people laugh'. He returns to this aspect again and again: 'You were not afraid of the blackout, and yet you

fastened five or six plaques, a luminous school of fish, a flock of
gliding gulls, several bouquets of phosphorescent flowers, first
on the lapels of your coat, then on your muffler; you had your
aunt sew half-a-dozen luminous buttons from top to bottom of
your coat; you turned yourself into a clown.' He 'was planning
to go into the circus later or maybe on the stage', and already
he 'was almost a clown when he did his knee swings on the
horizontal bar'. His natural clowning manifests a style of life
which finds satisfaction in play-acting. 'At the height of his act'
he 'practised his turn'—these are characteristic ways of describing him. Applause 'did him good', and he has a 'dangerous
attachment to outward forms'. He does not necessarily play
the same role all the time, but he is always role-playing—in
the company of school friends, at communion in church,
in his relationship to the Virgin Mary, as a soldier (in this
case consciously modelling his role on the airman who had
lectured at the school about his exploits), and not least, as
Redeemer.

In a sense Mahlke, like Koeppen's Keetenheuve[16] in this
particular respect, 'fluctuates between different forms of existence'. Clever and full of ingenuity, he is given nevertheless to
pursuits comparable to primitive magic. The equivalent extremes in the case of Oskar are represented by Goethe and
Rasputin: 'I fluctuate between Rasputin and Goethe, between
the faith-healer and the man of highly informed intelligence,
between the dark spirit who cast a spell on women and the
luminous poet-prince who was so fond of letting women cast a
spell on him.' These provide patterns of alternative roles. So
Oskar can say: 'Rasputin with the help of Gretchen Scheffler
taught me the big and little alphabets, taught me to be attentive
to women, and comforted me when Goethe hurt my feelings.'
The language of role-playing stamps his account of a variety of
activities: 'it was by no means so easy to learn to read and at the
same time play the role of someone who knew nothing. That
was to prove harder than year after year pretending to wet my
bed like a child.' Like Mahlke, too, he loves an audience: 'how
I would like to remove the glass from the peep-hole towards the
top of the door, so that Bruno, my keeper, could watch me more
directly', and early on he 'plays the role of the tempter.' When
his mother takes him to see a play, he interprets it to mean that

she had noticed 'my direct relationship to the theatre'. Though when Bebra wants to engage him as a clown, his answer at first is rather coyly to say that he regards himself as belonging 'to the spectators', and that he would prefer his 'little art to flourish in seclusion, far removed from all applause', Bebra has little difficulty in gaining his objective, and he has a correct insight into Oskar's nature when he tells him that people like them belong 'on the stage': 'we must perform and run the show. If we don't, others will run us.' Bebra becomes for Oskar his 'teacher and master', and it is he who, in a scene paralleled in the earliest of the Spanish picaresque romances (*Lazarillo de Tormes*), initiates him with a kiss into his calling as rogue. It was Bebra's task 'to open up the world to Oskar and to make him what he is today, a person whom for want of a better term I inadequately label a cosmopolitan'. It is Bebra who tells Oskar about the court fools in the Middle Ages and, as if to lure him into a corresponding role, shows him pictures of 'powdered clowns got up in frilly, grotesquely pointed dress, whose appearance was like Bebra's or even Oskar's'—pictures that Oskar found extremely attractive. That Oskar actually goes on to the stage is less significant than that he is so often talking about his activities in theatrical terms: 'ashamed, unsure, not trusting such stirring in my body, I left the hospital after these tender curtain raisers (*nach solch zärtlichen Vorspielen*), as if to avoid the main performance (*einer Hauptaktion ausweichend*), went to get some air, walked in the garden . . .'

Oskar's decision to remain a three-year old is the adoption of a role, and there comes a point in his existence at which his role-playing, with its tricks and impostures, and its nearness to the dimension of the circus, assumes varied dimensions. This is reached when he is living in a large modern city, in Düsseldorf, soon after the currency reform, when West Germany was in the process of becoming a model of an affluently pluralistic society. In this context the question of Oskar's marriage to Maria presents itself, and *Hamlet* and the theatre provide the framework within which he now contemplates the problem: 'he looked down on the slate roofs of the village of Oberaussem. The village cemetery became for me the centre of the world, while the factory of Fortuna North stood there as the redoubtable demigod, my antagonist. The fields were the fields of

Denmark; the Erft was my Belt, whatever rot lay about was rotten in the state of Denmark—and I was Yorick. Charged with high tension, crackling, the high-tension angels, in lines of three, sang as they made their way to the horizon, to Cologne . . . But for me, Oskar, Matzerath Bronski Yorick, a new era was dawning, and scarcely aware of it, I took another quick look at Hamlet's worn-out fingers on the blade of my shovel.' Then, 'turning to Korneff or more to the pylons of the power-line, I said—my decision was made, but before coming out with it I felt the need of a theatrical question that would cast doubt on Hamlet but legitimise me, Yorick, as a citizen—turning then to Korneff . . . I, stirred by the desire to become an honest citizen, said, slightly imitating Gründgens, although he could scarcely have played Yorick, said across the shovel blade: "To marry or not to marry, that is the question".' Very soon follows the scene in which Oskar dresses up to take part in Carnival: 'my first idea had been something in the style of Velasquez. I should also have liked to appear as Narses or as Prince Eugene', but finally 'I said to myself softly and none too happily: Now, Oskar, you are Yorick the fool. But where is the king for you to play the fool to?' It is not long before Oskar is identifying himself, as 'Oskar the fool', with 'Parsifal the fool'. Of this period he says that the currency reform 'compelled me to reform Oskar's currency. I was obliged to capitalise, or at least make a living from my hump.' Thus begins the chapter in which we see Oskar as model, in partnership with Ulla, in Professor Kuchen's studio. Here he collaborates in yielding a whole variety of theatrical motifs—'faun and nymph', 'Beauty and the beast', 'the lady with the unicorn', 'Christ and Madonna'. He is by now so at home amid an existence of role-playing that 'neither the sixteen students, gifted as they may have been, nor Professor Kuchen with his supposedly unique charcoal stroke, succeeded in turning out a valid portrait of Oskar for posterity'. In the final chapter he remarks about the way people 'want to pin me down', but, 'so many possibilities are open to a man of thirty'. The paragraph continues with a proliferating list of alternative choices: 'I might, for example, should they really throw me out of the hospital, propose to Maria a second time . . . Or I could stay single and marry one of my professions . . . Or I could revive my partnership with the Muse Ulla . . . Or, should I grow weary of Europe, I could emigrate . . . Or I could give in . . .'

Life is thus seen not as a process of growth towards unified personality, but as the discovery, under the impact of modern life, of a variety of different and maybe simultaneous possibilities of existence. Oskar does not gain the wholeness idealised in the *Bildungsroman*; if he 'develops', it is not in the traditional sense of the term, and when he 'grows', it is, negating nature's expectation, grotesquely to produce a hump. Professor Kuchen's difficulty in catching Oskar's personality in a clearly delineated picture reflects the extent to which Oskar has profited from experience. The professor's problem is of an equivalent order to that of the reader of *Die Blechtrommel*, confronting what he discovers to be a variety of shifting possibilities of meaning. They can co-exist rather in the same way as Oskar is not at any moment either wholly one person or another. He is a 'face with a thousand masks' such as Jens recommends[17] in *Herr Meister* (1962) as a fitting protagonist for the contemporary novel.

In Oskar's case one of these 'faces' is that of Oskar as narrator. Having stage-acted the part of a person guilty of a crime and successfully thereby got himself confined in a mental home, he uses the peace and seclusion to write the account of his life. In doing so he further extends, as narrator, the scope of his role-playing.

Oskar describes his bed in the mental home as 'a goal attained at last, my consolation', and would like to have the bars at the side raised 'to prevent anyone coming too close to me'. So he can call himself an 'incorrigible aesthete', which he is, too, in the sense that, having acted his life, he then narrates it as an artist, a comedian, with words. He does not just record the past, and, however detailed the record of the past may be, it stands at the opposite extreme from Naturalism, because 'the sum of all the detail yields an entirely imaginary result',[18] as when the account of one particular experience is staged as a set of variations rhythmically so ordered around a single substantive (*Kreuz*) as to suggest a parody of litany, also thereby relativising with mocking effect essential symbols of faith and ideology, or when in the chapter entitled 'Should I or Shouldn't I?', beginning with the history of Danzig, nouns and historical detail accumulate so as virtually to obliterate the historical reality.

What we remember is above all the dance of words around the motif 'he is growing', which gives this particular episode an appropriately theatrical setting. So *Die Blechtrommel* is not a sort of disguised autobiography, despite the fact that Grass and Oskar were both born in Danzig and stayed there till 1945, found their way to Düsseldorf, where they attended art classes— Oskar as model, Grass as a student—and both played the drum in a jazz group. Grass renders his experience artistically fruitful by turning it into fiction, and in a sense this is what Oskar does, with the difference that, while the author is free in his imagination, Oskar is manipulated by him.

As narrator Oskar talks about himself sometimes in the first person, sometimes in the third, varying his practice even within a single sentence: 'however, and here Oskar must confess to development of a sort, something did grow—and not always to my best advantage'. True, a baby will in real life often refer to itself both as 'I' and by name, but Oskar goes far beyond parody of baby-talk in confronting himself as first-person narrator with earlier experiences referred to in the third person. Engaged in an act of creative fantasy, he treats the Oskar who had the experiences as raw material for Oskar as narrator, and as such, role-playing now in his art as in his life, he adopts amongst other things the role of omniscient narrator, rather as in *Katz und Maus* the narrator, in the process of self-dramatisation, borrows the role of one composing a *Novelle*. (The parodistic query as to 'who will supply me with a good ending?' is seen as, indeed, a 'theatrical question'.) Adding, as he writes the account of his life, to all his previous roles that of living himself into the roles that Oskar adopted, or is imagined as having adopted, Oskar is one stage beyond Beheim-Schwarzbach's *Die diebischen Freuden des Herrn von Bißwange* in which, while the narrator distances himself from the rogue by telling his story in the third-person, as the 'source of the facts' he identifies himself by implication to some extent with him. The opposite extreme is embodied in Pörtner's *Tobias Immergrün*, where the picaro is more or less a puppet, a feed for the narrator's verbal virtuosity.

By the time Oskar embarks on his narrative his role-playing has, as we have seen, become complex and varied. This is associated with what is referred to as his 'demonic intellectuality', the beginnings of which take us back to his infancy. He

was 'one of those highly aware infants whose mental development is completed at birth', with so critical an awareness that
'the moment I was born I took a very critical interest towards
the first utterances of my parents beneath the light bulbs'. He
has an ability to remember things exactly and, as is frequently
evident, is a man of considerable and varied learning. If his
work, as he says, is 'destructive' ('and what I did not defeat
with my drum, I killed with my voice'), it is basically because
he holds to the view that 'there are things in this world which,
however sacred they may be, cannot be left unchallenged'. His
is a many-sided protest: 'for it was not only demonstrations of a
brown hue that I attacked with my drumming. Oskar huddled
under the rostrum for Reds and Blacks, for Boy Scouts and
Spinach Shirts, for Jehovah's Witnesses, the Kyffhäuser Bund,
the Vegetarians and the Young Polish Fresh Air Movement.
Whatever they might have to sing, my drum knew better.'
Alienation is with him both fact and ideal. He 'achieved distance by means of his drum', and he plays roles so that reality
will not 'play him', following Bebra's advice to him that the
alternative to going on the stage and 'running the show' is that
'people will run us'. An opposite type is represented by John
Belitz in Heinz von Cramer's *Die Kunstfigur* (1958), 'a very
model of adaptability', whose role-playing, very different from
Oskar's calculating iconoclasm, is governed by the instinct to
trim his personality to prevailing fashion and convention. The
drum, traditionally associated with summons to order and
obedience, is Oskar's ally in establishing with society a relationship combining participation and detachment, in the further-
ance of which he utilises the resources of the child, the clown
and the intellectual. Grass, that is to say, operates with Oskar
in a different way from Hubert Fichte with Detlev in *Das
Waisenhaus* (1965), where response to the barbarous forces of
reality is through the consciousness of a child whose naivety is
never infringed, and who is therefore denied any adult powers
of analysis and critical manœuvre.

As characteristically an intellectual figure as Grass, Enzensberger has also declared his interest in the sphere of children,[19]
in the 'anarchic humour' of their verse 'against which all
ideology breaks down'. This 'immunity' stems for him from the
fact that such verse is 'the servant of no one . . . and acts on

nobody's behalf', is 'entirely lacking in respect and pokes fun
at God and the world. Authority makes it laugh.' It 'helps the
child to find its place in the world, to master it'. Oskar himself
sometimes slips very consciously into the tone of the simple fairy
tale, into the mood of 'there was once upon a time a tin-
drummer, his name was Oskar' (to which corresponds in
Hundejahre 'there was once upon a time a girl, her name was
Ulla'). But what emerges is an alienating style of fairy-tale
narrative, and Oskar's pranks always have adult sophistication.
This makes him a close literary relation of the hero of G. B.
Fuchs's *Krümelnehmer*, who in his battle against the 'crazy logic'
of society and the clichés of its 'textbook of applied realities'
becomes preoccupied with 'beautiful irrational things'.[20] Characteristic of Oskar is his capacity to make, or imagine himself
making, things behave in a fashion perversely inconsistent with
the self-evident logic of the everyday, and to describe the effect
with equal virtuosity. One example is the scene where he tries
to make the figure of Jesus play his drum. A cough ceases to be
a simple physical fact and acquires an independent, bizarre
existence of its own, thereby also providing a setting in which
in retrospect Oskar, in characteristic style, can the better
dramatise one of his experiences:

I coughed. My cough hopped over the checkerboard pattern of the
flags, down the transept, up the nave, hoisted itself into the choir.
Multiplied by sixty, it organized a Bach society that did not sing but
specialised in coughing, and just as I was beginning to think that
Oskar's cough had crawled away into the organ pipes and wouldn't
be heard again until the Sunday chorale, a cough rang out in the
sacristy and another from the pulpit, until at length the cough died
down, coughed out its soul behind the high altar, not far from the
Athlete on the Cross. It is accomplished, said my cough; but nothing
was accomplished. The boy Jesus sat there stiff and proud, holding
my drum-sticks, but drum he would not . . .

It would, therefore, be more correct to speak of Grass's
'sensitivity to the magic qualities of things'[21] than merely of a
matter-of-fact preoccupation with objects, of an *Objektsperspek-
tive*.[22] To say merely that Oskar observes everything, from a
figure of Christ to acts of copulation, with the same detached
matter-of-factness, too easily suggests a comparison, for example,
with Robbe-Grillet's notion that the aim of the novel is to

'insert the object in a dialectic of space',[23] and with the way in which in the *nouveau roman* 'objects are neither associations nor symbols, but things in themselves, virtually fetishes'.[24] The difference between Grass and the practitioners of the *nouveau roman* becomes obvious if we think of Marcel Butor's remark about 'the image of your life which is about to be realized without your will being involved',[25] and his statement that in the *nouveau roman* 'we are taught to look at the world with the eyes . . . of a man who walks about town with no other horizon but what he sees before him, and with no power other than the vision before his own gaze'.[26] The principle that 'henceforward we refuse all complicity with things' will not fit Oskar, who continually manipulates them, is in active relation to them, and mobilises them in relation to himself. If he observes things so closely and exactly, it is not least in order to mobilise them as a setting to meet the demands of his constant self-dramatisation. His account of the cough becomes theatre, or he will so describe an episode of his physical growth as to stage it, in Enzensberger's phrase about some of Grass's prose, as a 'syntactical ballet'.[27] Not to be forgotten, too, is the Nietzschean principle that existence as role-playing calls for a high degree of attentiveness and concentration[28]—and, as far as exactness of observation goes, there is little, as we shall see, to choose between Oskar and Anselm Kristlein in Walser's *Halbzeit*.

This embodiment in Oskar of 'the principle of unlimited freedom vis-à-vis objects in time and space'[29] is symptomatic of the high degree of alienation, that makes this kind of freedom possible. The history of Oskar's alienation begins with his relation to his father, from whose world it is early on his desire to escape, and Oskar is never more blasphemous than in his mockery of God the Father, and of Him whose mission it was, as Son of God, to establish His Father's kingdom. Important in this context are the figures he mentions in connection with what he characteristically thinks of as 'playing the game of guilt and innocence', for in the following paragraph he describes himself as performing, as a model with Ulla, 'as Vulcan, as Pluto with Proserpina and . . . as a humpbacked Ulysses'. Now, what Pluto received from his father's empire was the kingdom of the infernal regions, Proserpina owed her sojourn in hell to her father, and Vulcan was cast out of Olympus by

Zeus for siding with his mother in a conjugal quarrel. As to
Ulysses, he has in this connection all-important associations of
the outcast who sets out on adventure, suffers and returns home.

The theme of return is, in fact, central to *Die Blechtrommel*,
as when, with wide experience now of life as a diversity of roles,
Oskar comes to feel the need to raise the question as to who
basically he is, if he can have existed under so many masks.
'Just wait a minute,' he says, 'let's see now who you are and
where you're from.' Thereupon he conjures up the memory of
an opposite situation to that created by the exercise of his
'demonic intellectuality'. One who has meanwhile lived out his
existence in adopted roles, evokes, but in a tone of far from
baby-like consciousness, the situation of union with his mother,
of 'the childhood that means so much to me': 'and there they
glowed, the two sixty-watt bulbs of the hour of my birth . . .
Mama promised me a toy; at the age of three I would be given
a drum . . . I ate, drank, evacuated, put on weight, let them
weigh me, swaddle, bathe, brush, powder, vaccinate and
admire me. I let them call me by name, smiled when expected
to, laughed when necessary, went to sleep at the proper time.'
Remembrance, alienated and nostalgic, of the past, of Poland,
of childhood, marks the yearning of one on whom the problem
of identity presses with the question as to who, if he can fill so
many roles, he really is.

What his mother, and all she represents, means to Oskar
corresponds, in the case of Mahlke, to his preoccupation with
the Virgin, with strongly sexual motivation. That his pro-
tuberating Adam's apple, and the screwdriver worn around his
neck to conceal it, have a phallic significance, is clear in the
account of him, characteristically with an audience and not
least for effect, letting water: 'thus he stood, showing his profile
from the toes extending just over the edge to the watershed in
the middle of his hair: strangely enough, the length of his
sexual part made up for the otherwise shocking protuberance
of his Adam's apple, lending his body an odd, but in its way
perfect harmony'. At communion he is presented to us with his
'agitated mouse so exposed and defenceless that I might have
caught it in my hand'—'perhaps he intentionally accentuated
its frenzy with exaggerated swallowing, in order to attract the
glass eyes on the Virgin standing to one side of him; for I cannot

and will not believe that you ever did anything whatsoever without an audience'. One of the most important episodes is that in which, in a way carefully contrived to suggest an act of sexual intercourse, Mahlke is described as boring a hole in the ice to get access in the wreck to the shrine constructed there for the adoration of the Virgin: 'he always had an audience. When I say that, even while cutting his circular groove over the ice-bound barge, he had the Virgin Mary behind or before him, that she looked with enthusiasm upon his little axe, the Church shouldn't object; but even if the Church refuses to put up with the idea of a Virgin Mary forever engaged in admiring Mahlke's exploits, the fact remains that she always watched him attentively'.

The sexual imagery of *Katz und Maus*, giving this withdrawal to peace and happiness in the bowels of the wreck nuances of return to the womb, adds point to Mahlke's remark that he 'just couldn't manage without the Virgin'. As he played it in the inner recesses of the wreck, given over to the cult of the Virgin, a record that moved Mahlke to tears was one in which the singer 'sang something from an opera with which we had been familiarised by a film called Homeland—"AlasIhavelost-her," she moaned. "Thewindsangmeasong," she sighed. "One-dayamiraclewillhappen," she prophesied.' When Mahlke finds the entrance to his hideout in the wreck, he says: 'I've camou-flaged it. Nobody'll ever find it. But it was lots of work. It's my private property now, in case you have any doubts. Cosy little spot. Good place to hide if things get hot.' In the same spirit Oskar describes his bed in the mental home as his 'goal' and 'consolation', and in the description of it some features are significantly suggestive of a cot.

If the father-image is allowed a Jungian association with the burden of consciousness, the mother-image with the uncon-scious, and water association 'with a number of numinous or magical qualities peculiar to the mother' as the unconscious and the place of rebirth,[30] an important connection suggests itself. Mahlke's yearning to disappear in the dark waters around and within his point of retreat (whence in the end he is never seen to emerge), and Oskar's desire, initially in revolt against his father, 'to return to his position as a baby in the womb (*in meine embryonale Kopflage*)' belong together. So also, perhaps, does this aspect and Grass's affection for Mother Church—it is, he said, not least the 'heathen elements' in catholicism that attract him.[31] Not to be overlooked also is Oskar's predilection for nurses' care, and his desire to be buried with his mother.

When at the end of *Die Blechtrommel* Oskar contemplates possibilities available to him, he does so characteristically with critical and intellectual detachment, but also with the knowledge that, whatever kind of existence he chooses, it will be 'in the shadow of a buggaboo . . . getting blacker and blacker', of the 'black wicked Witch'. Of this sinister presence, evident earlier in the book, and hinting at the dark and even seductively elemental forces of life, he becomes fully aware only when he has reached the farthermost extremes of an alienating intellectualism. 'First she was behind me,' Oskar says right at the end, 'now, now and forever, she is in front of me, coming closer and closer,' this too pointing to the conclusion that in Grass a high degree of intellectuality cries out for reassuring compensations at an opposite pole, whether in the *nostalgie de la boue* evident in a celebrated revolting description in *Die Blechtrommel* of crude physical matter, or in the impulse of Oskar Matzerath and Joachim Mahlke towards the union and integration denied them as the bearers of so critical and intellectual an awareness.

Thus it is that in *Katz und Maus* and in the drawn-out evocations of *Die Blechtrommel* and *Hundejahre*, Grass returns so often and so persistently to Danzig and Poland, to the world in which he enjoyed the unreflecting innocence of childhood. Lying in his bed in the mental home, Oskar searches in memory for the details of his childhood 'at the same time he has to search for the land of the Poles': 'und ich suche das Land der Polen, das verloren ist, das noch nicht verloren ist. Andere sagen: bald verloren, schon verloren, wieder verloren'. There are ironic references to the Germans 'searching for Poland with credits, Leicas, and compasses, with radar, divining rods, delegations, and moth-eaten provincial students' associations in costume', and the paragraph concludes (in the English translation); 'I, meanwhile, conjure up Poland on my drum. And this is what I drum: Poland's lost, but not forever. Poland's not lost forever.' Important in the original, however, is the weight that reiteration gives the motif of 'lost' (*verloren*), in a context in which the 'not lost forever' appears rather as the heart's resistance to the knowledge that the loss is irrevocable: '. . . suche ich Polen auf meiner Trommel und trommle: Verloren, noch nicht verloren, schon wieder verloren, an wen verloren, bald verloren, bereits verloren, alles verloren, Polen nicht verloren.' [32] So when, remarking that in Grass's work Danzig enters German literature just when it ceased to be Germany's, Enzensberger says that this 'Danzig saga' signifies a 'search for a lost dimension',[33] we have to give this more than a political sense. Not every search, however, is in the rational hope of finding, and for all Oskar's—and Grass's—nostalgia for 'the protective folds of his origins',[34] he is in touch with them only grotesquely as an adult in the role of a child, and ironically through the mediation of a little toy drum.

Chapter 5

Martin Walser

Two years after the publication of a volume of stories entitled *Ein Flugzeug über dem Haus*, Walser's first novel *Ehen in Philippsburg* appeared in 1957. Set in a provincial town, it is a partial picture with little interest in proletarian or lower middle-class aspects. These we experience only incidentally, mainly through the eyes of Hans Beumann, who finds them sordid and repulsive —the squalid world of howling children, the prostitute, the teacher with her married lover. At the focus of interest is the upper middle-class life of Philippsburg, which the Sebastian Club epitomises in its most arrogant, snobbish and exclusive form: 'only people of social standing could have a key', 'to be a member meant that one was above financial worries'. This is a world where only affluence and social prestige count, a community without deeper human relations, and where friendship is little more than the gesture of ambitious men seeking to further their private intrigues.

Ehen in Philippsburg is in large part a novel of social criticism, directed against a society seen as morally bankrupt and in which all higher ideals are crushed or perverted. The newspaper office, the broadcasting organisation, the television chairman, the local prize-winning poet, the writer down on his luck, and suchlike, provide pictures of social interest, characteristic of which is that they show ways in which under pressure human values can become corrupted and distorted. Volkmann, a radio manufacturer in close contact with influential people in radio and television, is a man of few words and with little understanding of anything outside his narrow world of practical and profitable efficiency, a calculating opportunist, whose conception of freedom is the jungle warfare 'of all against all'. His preoccupation with the exigencies of profit and loss cuts him off from warm human relationships and makes his wife's existence rather bleak. So she adopts the role of a connoisseur of culture, inviting poets and painters to her house as a means of asserting a sphere of personal freedom against the world to which her husband condemns her, self-consciously cultivating freer forms of social relationship, tilting at bourgeois convention by being ostentatiously informal with her daughter. Anne, too, is bored by her father's business values, and also by her mother's pseudo-teenage behaviour. Her escape expresses itself in a risky defiance of convention, and paradoxically also in the adoption of maiden-auntish habits (her constant knitting, for example) as a protest against the falsely modern airs of her mother. Among the other characters is Dr. Alwin, whose petty-bourgeois father had regarded himself as a staunch democrat, which had not prevented him from rejoicing in the advantages accruing from his son's marriage into an aristocratic family. His mother as garderobière in a theatre had taken pride in the opportunities this afforded of contact with upper-class people, if only by handling their coats. He himself is interested only in power and prestige, which he pursues without qualms. The history of his family shows the decay of democratic, even revolutionary values, and his own development leads him to a confused and compromising political opportunism, typified in his chairmanship of a 'socialist-liberal-conservative' party: 'he did not want to take over any of the undemocratic aspects of an aristocratic family. But why should one simply deny the real values taken for granted in families that have developed through the centuries? Why be an iconoclast like some colour-blind fanatic?'

It is into this community, ruled by the 'cat-and-mouse game of powerful groups', that Hans Beumann comes, 'a wanderer . . . who can build with words a bridge from one kind of loneliness to another'. The illegitimate child of a humble mother who had earned her living working in a public house, his student friends had been mainly 'petty-bourgeois and working-class people like himself'. A recommendation to a newspaper editor gives him the sudden chance of a break, but he is cold-shouldered. When Volkmann offers him a job on the publicity side of his firm, he is delighted, for 'someone now actually wanted him for the first time in his life'. He was no longer a person 'who hesitated, breathless with excitement, in front of a door shut to keep him out, hardly daring to knock. For the first time a door opened amid this sea of hostile houses to let him in, and a man stepped out and said: I am expecting you. He could have embraced Herr Volkmann.' He 'who . . . had always been a spectator . . . who envied everyone so sure of his own usefulness that you see it at a glance', delighted now in the prospect of justifying his existence by practical and useful activity. Eager to conquer his sense of 'superfluity', he is driven to give his existence meaning by integrating himself in this society, whose values he nevertheless continues to query. He had always been 'against the manufacturers, against rich people who have a fine life', and he wonders by what right their particular ability to handle money is regarded as a general law of life, the condition of a really worthy existence. But Volkmann was after all 'a kind man', and in any case it is 'not his job to raze the villas of the rich to the ground'. The successful men of affairs, the economic experts, would tell him, he knows, that his misgivings have ceased to be relevant, that 'that was all nineteenth-century stuff'. In the past, they would say, and he virtually concedes the point, 'it was perhaps enough to have a hot head and a strong heart, but today one must be intelligent, be a specialist, to prevent unemployment and inflation'. Beumann realises that he could not even read the financial page of a newspaper and that the cause of human welfare had to be left to people 'who could speak with authority at an international conference on wheat, who were informed about the convertibility of currency, who could calculate the social product, who distributed pleasure and suffering at their discretion'. All the same he has 'a bad conscience', the sense of having been guilty of 'betrayal', of having been 'seduced'. Walser is at pains to let this aspect of Beumann appear as of general, typical significance, and so, in the context of Beumann's pondering on the 'betrayal' of which he feels guilty, Walser has him reflect that such a 'biography was commonplace in Central Europe', that the course of his life was a 'stereotype'. Beumann retains, however, a fundamentally critical, though vague, attitude to society; he 'was a grumbler (*Nörgler*), although he knew that people like himself could not keep a tram-line running, not to mention some larger social body, although he knew how useless he was, how superfluous in this well organised world, and that his ideas of an alternative kind of social organisation amounted to no more than the principle that "everyone should have the same standard of living" '.

The party given by Frau Volkmann marks his entrance to the higher society of Philippsburg, his engagement to Anne Volkmann, his official introduction, his admission to full membership of the Sebastian Club a first stage in his initiation proper, and his action in throwing the proletarian intruder out of the club the final rite, his demonstrative act of loyalty to his new class. He is instinctively anti-capitalist, he hates the rich and all ideals of practical success and efficiency, and is contemptuous of a society 'where efficient people grow like weeds', though he despises himself for being useless and superfluous. His inferiority complex finds compensation in the 'intoxication' of his aggressive action in the Sebastian Club, which gives him 'the feeling of having accomplished something'. Although he feels an outsider in Volkmann's world, he recognises its validity, and is contemptuous, in the case of the writer Klaff, of his egoistic and artistic ideals, his 'coldness' and 'arrogance'. But he lacks a positive conception of an alternative way of life, and all that remains is an empty idealism, vaguely coloured by socialistic ideals. Committed in the end by the force of circumstances to marry Anne, but drawn by instinct to the humbler Marge, he would like, if only it were possible, to combine both worlds. 'Torn into two halves' by conflicting desires and also by a sense of guilt, and with his social identity virtually destroyed, he is reduced in the end to renunciation and resignation: 'the world can jolly well go on without me'.

Walser himself has chosen to live at a distance from the centres of economic power and the high spots of affluence—near Germany's geographical limits in the small town of Friedrichshafen on the Lake of Constance, not far from Wasserburg where he was born. A comment on Walser's choice of abode might be provided by the remark in one of his stories in *Ein Flugzeug über dem Haus*: 'the more isolated Herr Templone became, the more keenly he observed'. In *Ehen in Philippsburg* Hans Beumann, 'who was always a spectator', has uncommonly sharp powers of observation, illustrated in the scene when, sitting in the café, he was the 'motionless onlooker' as two girls approached:

Rasch wischte sich Hans die Hände noch einmal ins Taschentuch, am Eingang erschienen die Mädchen. Sie kamen auf hohen Absätzen durch den hellen Gartenkies, daß es weithin und ohrenbetäubend knirschte. Sie kamen auch kaum vorwärts. Mit jedem Schritt, den sie taten, wobei sie Sohle und Absatz gleichzeitig aufsetzten, schienen sie wieder stehenzubleiben, eine halbe Stunde nur drehten und mahlten ihre Schuhe im Kies, hin und her, und gingen weiter, nein, es war kein Stehenbleiben, es war der ruhigste Punkt in diesem Schreiten, der Punkt, wo sich das Gewicht des Körpers den vorgesetzten Beinen nachschiebt, über die Beine gelangt und wieder zurückfällt, weil die Beine inzwischen schon wieder weitergegangen sind. Er hatte noch nie Mädchen so gehen sehen. Die Schenkel führten den Gang an, vor allem bei Marge; die Füße und der übrige Körper wollten immer wieder zurückbleiben. Schwanken und ganz gebändigte Stärke in einem, das war ihr Gang.

Walser, in fact, made reference once to the remark that 'God exists in the little details'.[1] If, for example, he explained,[2] one narrates an incident by saying simply about somebody that 'he then went home', the result is so sparse as to make one feel that one might just as well have said nothing at all, and so 'I only get pleasure from writing when I list everything that happens when someone goes home'—whereupon without more ado he elaborated the imaginary incident thus:

Let us suppose then that someone is going home, meets the schoolgirl who lives in the same road, who does not see him, he is now on the path to his house, then he treads on a snail, its shell crunches, let us suppose that it is six o'clock in the evening now, so at this moment the bells are beginning to sound, just as the snail's shell is heard to crunch, and rather powerfully, because he does not expect it; and because of the noise of the bells the two young swallows lose their direction in a flight of swallows practising in the afternoon flying round the houses, the two swallows hit against the gable of the house that the man wants to enter, while the bells naturally are still sounding, fall at his feet, they are dead or as good as dead, and only when he has this experience of the dead swallows behind him is he at home, but things are different from what they would have been if this had never happened.

These, Walser admits, 'are all very incidental details', but 'without such detail I would not want to tell a story about someone going home'. This aspect of Walser's work is more significantly and extensively in evidence in his second novel, *Halbzeit* (1960).

The central figure is a commercial traveller, Anselm Krist-lein, who at the beginning of the novel has recently returned home from hospital, his health having been undermined by his efforts to earn a living in a harshly competitive world. We meet him first of all with his family, in bed with his three children playfully enjoying their father's company, a setting that illu-sorily suggests domestic bliss. Anselm departs after breakfast, ostensibly on business, but it will be his intention to stay away from his family as much as possible and, when he returns from time to time, it will be because he cannot very well avoid it. He loses his job with a firm selling heating equipment, but gets another in the advertising department of the large Frantzke concern. In business, as with women, Anselm shows himself as a weak person, without guiding principles, self-indulgent amid the temptations of sex and commerce. Though not without subtle powers of self-assertion, he remains attached to his wife, but her possessiveness and the monotony of married life make their relationship degenerate into a series of trivial and obscurely motivated quarrels. Aware of the inroads made on his integrity by a job requiring him to be all things to all men, in his heart of hearts he yearns for the chance to be able to assert himself.

The scope of the satire in *Halbzeit* embraces the consumer society and the newly rich. At one point the ideology of anti-communism is singled out as a target. When one character, a writer who acts as consultant to the advertising agency, argues that those who serve affluence are 'playing into the hands of the Communists', the narrator expresses ironic surprise at the cun-ning thus attributed to the Communists. Particularly the 'very old among us, the wise', he says, seem to be aware of this pervasive Communist infiltration, and the spelling of the word as *Komm'nismus* makes Adenauer here the target. The satire of the consumer society is likewise achieved largely by imitating its language, as in a passage following a long list of (American) authors famous for books on various aspects of it:

all die leise und sophisticated predigenden Apostel des Verbrauchs. Wertfrei dagegen, oder sehr engagiert. Lehrend, daß schon das Kind zu einem Rekruten des Verbrauchs erzogen werde, lehrend die Manipulation des Image, Konsum: die Fortsetzung der Pro-duktion mit anderen Mitteln, Gruppendynamik. Soziometrie, Human Engineering . . .

Ridiculing the vocabulary of the advertising industry, the narrator introduces words like *Werbefeldzug*, *Trompeter des Wirtschaftswunders*, *Verschrottungspsychologie*, and the strongly Americanised jargon of the German ad-men (*Account-Exekutive, die Copy, Lay-Outer, das Research, die Publicity, der designer, public relations, brainstrust, creative staff, Campaign, Food-Konzern*). The modish assimilation of Anglo-American culture in affluent West Germany is mirrored satirically in words highlighting typical manners of expression, such as *pattern, outline, frustration*, and the verb *managen*—words widely used for their snob-value in the more exclusive circles. Frantzke, a typical upstart, proudly displays in his house a series of pictures with English titles: 'Herring's Foxhunting Scenes', 'Breaking Cover', and 'Full Cry'.

Set in an unnamed centre of West German economic resurgence on the Rhine, much of the satire is aimed at the prosperous middle class, whose predominance has led to talk about 'the new Biedermeier', a phrase that also occurs in the book: 'alles ist besser als das, was jetzt ist, denn jetzt ist Biedermeier, Buhbuh-Biedermeier'. The context of this remark, with its cabaret tone, serves as a reflection on writers who may think that by criticising this society they are avoiding identifying themselves with it, whereas they rely on its material comforts and its freedom of expression. A relationship is thus indicated between the sophisticated tastes of the upper bourgeoisie and the artistic achievements of writers, including even their rebellious reflections, as Walser elsewhere notes: 'as this literature now stands, it belongs to the upper bourgeoisie', but 'because it is no longer needed as a weapon, it has a merely ornamental function, a fate it shares with city walls, humanitarian ideals, and furniture. What is demanded is flirtation with taboos, what is allowed is jollification in the groves of culture.'

This 'flirtation with taboos' is illustrated in *Halbzeit* by Edmund, a left-wing intellectual who at a party given by the wealthy Frantzke questions his sincerity in having recently given some money to the arts. Edmund makes fundamental criticisms of the structure of society. If, he says, the social system is a good one, then the guilt for any suffering rests with those in power and they must be regarded as 'wicked fellows'. If it is bad, then they are 'really angels whose angelic virtue can take the credit for there not being more neurotics and suicides'.

Sometimes, he goes on, 'I suspect that the system is not as bad as it looks and its captains are not quite so evil as people imagine, but I don't know and, as long as I don't know, I can't applaud when one of them wants to buy his independence with ten thousand marks'. These remarks create a storm of protest, but significantly Frantzke, against whom they are directed, the representative of the upper bourgeoisie and attacked in his own house, ends the argument with a gesture of tolerance: 'and in a loud voice Frantzke joined in the noisy discussion and raised his glass: bravo, bravo, he cried, that's how I like my artists . . . the wicked capitalist thanks his prophet for the lesson. Come, my friends, drink a toast with me. It wouldn't half be a swindle if you didn't exist! Your good health!' And when Edmund replies with a toast of his own 'to the collapse of capitalism', Frantzke retorts with 'to your immortality'. In this game of repartee between the artist and the capitalist each recognises that his existence depends on the other, that only among those who can afford the leisure to cultivate refined tastes can the modern writer hope to find a public. They have wide cultural interests because they aspire to be internationally minded. This is illustrated in the description of Frau Pawel, the upper-class wife of a sales director as 'one of those subtle people who in the evening, cared for by central heating, and sipping gin and tonic in elegant chairs, talk about the latest Anouilh, Karajan's latest record, Marini's latest horse and Fellini's film (not yet syn-chronised, thank heavens), who are at the same time full of contempt for German cooking and despise German culture for having produced only the economic miracle and rich butchers, the kind of person who quite liked to be referred to as intel-lectual, and in whose ears, therefore, the word efficient sounded like a term of abuse'. It is only with hesitation, and with some irony, that the narrator concedes her the quality of being 'intellectual', but when he does so in the ensuing passage, this acknowledges her critical faculty in matters of cultural apprecia-tion and social understanding.

As to his choice of a commercial traveller as protagonist, Walser justified this by saying that it is a job of unusual import-ance in a capitalist economy, the nature of which is to produce more than is required. He has Anselm remark, about members of his profession, that they 'ought at last to realise that selling

H

merely means forcing people to buy' and 'that probably in the last ten, twelve years commercial travellers had at least as much influence as priests, doctors, lawyers, and academics'. Particularly in view of the references to 'white collar' (and 'white collar crimes') we may well be inclined to see in the novel a picture of the 'white collar man' as the 'small creature who is acted upon but who does not act . . . never talking loud, never talking back, never taking a stand'.[3] Or as illustrating the mentality sometimes attributed to the 'levelled middle class', 'constantly in a process of adapting itself to changed social situations' under pressure from 'the far-reaching effects of general social mobility', with a social mentality 'consisting primarily in the ability to adapt itself, in the indeterminacy and plasticity of its social character'.[4] It was partly this need for adjustment and readjustment in modern society that gave Hans Beumann his sense of being 'superfluous', and, with regard to *Halbzeit*, Walser said that there is no other job 'that could so forcefully make a person aware of his own superfluity as that of commercial traveller'. This 'is what makes me so sympathetic to it, it reminds me of the writer'.[5]

Accordingly Anselm Kristlein, in both respects like Beumann in the previous novel, combines a strong feeling of superfluity as outsider with an exceptionally critical response to experience, and with unusual gifts of penetrating and analytical observation. In Robbe-Grillet's *Le Voyeur*, also, the story is told from an onlooker's point of view, likewise a commercial traveller, but in the form of a series of more or less disjointed and fragmentary experiences, and with no intention of social criticism. In *Halbzeit*, on the contrary, Anselm confronts society as a whole, on which, striving to become integrated, but always retaining a certain distance, he proves to have a singularly effective focus. Edmund, a homosexual, measures society from a position of more extreme alienation, and his criticism of bourgeois society is radical, as when he tries to unmask marital love, social standing, and status symbols, as bourgeois 'substitutes for something that doesn't exist, but should exist'. At one point Edmund is in danger of losing his validity as social critic by getting too involved in a petty squabble, and then significantly it is Anselm who reminds him of his original position: 'aren't you against the whole ruling system, against capital and property, Edmund?'

Josef-Heinrich's comment is that 'Edmund is staging an act', 'playing a role to illustrate how one can live dangerously'—an argument that Anselm reacts rather coolly to, because he is aware how deeply he himself is involved in role-playing.

In a significant moment of self-reflection Anselm, in fact, depicts his life as a series of assumed disguises, enacted as in a dance: 'who led the polonaise, I don't know. I followed the pattern of the dance, changed the steps, changed women, dwelling-place, and make of cigarettes.' His wife comments that he 'was not embarrassed when I watched him playing a whole lot of roles', and in the presence of his mother he acts a different being from the one he displays with Edmund or with Josef-Heinrich, or any other of his friends, always adapting his language to the role involved, talking 'in five or six completely different languages, keeping them all quite distinct'. Obviously this demands considerable mental effort, since all the time the identity of the various roles has to be kept intact. Sometimes the actor, or 'the comedian', as his wife calls him, shows signs of exhaustion at the transformations imposed on him by the various roles expected of him by different people. These arise from the complexity of his nature, which is described in a kind of poeticised psychology. His psyche is said to have 'several floors', his mind is spoken of as being divided into isolated compartments, as if he 'has made an onion out of his brain'. Sometimes the narrative consists of debates between conflicting beings within himself, and he is able to switch his personality from one character into another. This may happen unconsciously, or as a result of premeditation, as when he is waiting for one of his girl friends: 'my role fitted me so well that what I had to guard against was complacency, against playing it too carelessly, and thus revealing that it was just a role'.

As narrator, too, Anselm is shown as a role-player, commanding three different voices. Most of the time he speaks in the first person, but sometimes we hear the voice of an informer who, taking on the role of the omniscient narrator, can step in to speak about Anselm in the third person, pronouncing on his behaviour and even claiming to have 'intimate knowledge' of him. This voice is not wholly distinct from Anselm's; it often merges with his and can become his own, and Anselm's double existence as narrator and as the object of narrative explains a statement like: 'he got out of my car in my dove-grey suit'. Another voice from within Anselm's personality is Galileo Cleverlein, 'Anselm's scientist', his imaginary dialogue-partner, acting as the voice of conscience. The intention, it must be noted, is not to portray Anselm as a schizophrenic, but to present him from three different angles—as he sees himself, as he is seen from outside, and as he struggles with his own conscience.

In fact, *Halbzeit* sets out to do no less than offer in narrative terms a model of contemporary behaviour, and in Anselm's behavioural pattern is spelt out the conduct of a man whom the environmental pressures of a pluralistic society force into a chameleon-like existence. Living in a world where everyone, consciously or unconsciously, is playing roles, he is the better able to detect it in others, as with Anna who tries to model her sexual behaviour on the parts she plays as an actress, or with Josef-Heinrich. The latter, as successful in business as with women, adjusts himself to each new fiancée, not repeating himself, but each time planning his life anew. The members of the board of the Frantzke concern, too, are depicted as multiple personalities. Seeing the transformations of one of them, Anselm, as narrator, surmises that 'there must be several Dr. Fuchs's'.

This novel lays bare by intimate observation the role-strategy of individuals in modern society and treats emotions as behavioural poses manipulated by the individual at will. When for the first time after a long spell in hospital Anselm sits down to breakfast with his wife, his efforts to find an appropriate role are described like this: 'I looked at Alissa and waited till a text occurred to me to warm our relation, and I blew on the little flame of feeling now required in order to give it more life.' Even seemingly deeper feelings are represented as gestures merely aping the expression of real emotions: 'Now I just sat there, but could not operate my well-prepared act of mimicry designed to reconcile sorrow and renunciation.' Stream of consciousness permits the reader to participate in the play-actor's role-strategy, and Walser's narrator goes so far as to translate sub-conscious and even unintentional utterances into calculated play-acting. It is in language interspersed with theatre terms that he explains how a man communicates his grief: 'and one lets one's face assume different features, it knows the expression of pain by heart, just as a pianist knows the keys to produce a bitter minor chord. It would be deceitful to show the visitors now just a fatuous jollity. In order to let them really participate in our condition . . . one must give them a repeat performance, because they could not be present at the premiere'. In another context Anselm remarks: 'in my face, in case he looked at me, I had a pitying frown all ready to use', and 'he had his lodger's face all ready in case anyone came in'.

The stress on the calculated control of behaviour does not, as we have seen in the case of Böll's *Billard um halbzehn*, mean that man is necessarily to be regarded for that reason as always a free agent. Role-playing, made necessary by the many adjustments that the individual has to make in modern society, may make him just a puppet, and so in *Halbzeit* the notion of a blind fate is allegorically introduced as 'Mieze's leaden fist', and destiny as 'whoever has his hand on the latch'. Free to choose a particular role, the individual may lose his freedom again under the determinism inherent in the role. This happens to Anselm when he dishonestly tries to persuade his wife that for the good of the family he must go to a party: 'and like a man going off to fight in a just war, but one he did not want. . . . I stood up and, at one with my role and completely convinced of what I was saying, I said: "Alissa, unfortunately I'll just have to go".'

Anselm's urge to experiment with his identity also derives from love for the artificial and the contrived. 'Hearing and smelling' the 'crude naturalness' of an uncle of his, he declares his dislike of 'hygienic illusions, deceitful stylisation', since man 'is meant to be a higher kind of creature'. Yet, recognising that 'we are chained to our identity more than to anything else', he expresses horror at the thought of changing his personality: 'to slip out of our fate, like a snake changing its skin, really to be the other person . . . no!'. All the same, he experiences individuality as incarceration, as 'being fettered always to the same root', as a 'collection of biological cells acting in my name', and this further stimulates him to experiment with possible variations. So the opening of the book describes his dejection at being forced to admit to his old identity, and, in language rich in unusual metaphors, the various stages of his waking up are followed out—a protracted process in the course of which 'face and ears . . . are deformed to look terribly like a passport photo'. The world appears as a labyrinth which he is reluctant to enter, feeling 'dragged out into the day crowded with angular objects: lurking, they welcome the captured deserter'. Identity —a name, a mode of behaviour imposed upon him by society— has willy-nilly to be accepted. Standing in front of the bathroom mirror, he addresses himself with the words: 'you must admit that that is you. What remains from yesterday and the day before yesterday. Then they still have a name for you . . you clear away the night from your teeth and sing out your identity for yet another day.' The rest of the novel then concerns the attempt to escape by means of role-playing from environmental fetters and from the illusion that one's identity is fixed like the image on a passport photo.

Anselm is well aware that putting on masks as a question of expediency may be called lying, a matter treated with great dialectic skill at various points of the novel: 'for no one can produce pure lies. When, for example, for the sake of his wife a person takes upon himself the sustained effort of lying and renounces what seems to him true, the very lying can create for her and even for him what is in fact the truth . . . A lie can be the seed of truth, just as truth can be the seed from which the artificial flower of the lie can grow organically and naturally.' Truth and falsehood can be called 'mere terms', 'useful sign-posts to the geography of the soul', and what is commonly called lying a possible way of assembling basic information: 'and most of what we regard as lying is only the result of the way things are changed in an individual consciousness, which may have a different manner from our own of assembling facts'. When the unity of selfhood is called in question, the concept of sincerity, as the virtue of being true to oneself, requires adjust-ment. 'The perfect liar believes himself entirely', which is to say that, however many different poses the role-player may adopt, he will always, provided he is a virtuoso in the art, be one with his role. For the less accomplished practitioner of role-playing the advice is more crudely that 'one can only lie if one believes at least half of one's own lie'.

Since Anselm realises that in role-playing more is involved than mere fraudulence, he can assert that 'a role is more than just a role', 'tactics is more than just tactics'. An adopted role may be contrived, but also the expression of subconscious desires. Assumed for purposes of deception, it may yet expose a truer self. So when Alissa is said to 'stage' a threat of divorce, intended to recall her husband to marital faithfulness, Anselm detects in the 'trick' a genuine wish for divorce: 'she really does want a change'. Even the foreboding of illness can appear as a 'dress rehearsal or even a final rehearsal', and words from the vocabulary of the theatre, like 'stage', 'first performance', 'actor', 'scene', 'pose', proliferate as metaphors of role-playing.

Such details of language are of paramount importance to Walser, for 'just as a liquid will only change at a certain temperature into the state we call gas, a real commercial traveller only becomes literature . . . when he is changed into the state of language', and the novel in general is a 'collection of whatever in a particular time is put into language by the author'. In *Halbzeit* extended passages of minute description co-exist with maxims, aphorisms, and philosophical pronouncements, but Walser does not limit himself to a purely literary style. He draws on contemporary jargon—of the advertiser, of the consumer society, of pseudo-intellectual women ('ich find' den Kommunismus wahnsinnig aufregend'), and of colloquial small-talk ('da hast du den Salat', 'des Menschen Wille ist sein Himmelreich'). Jargon, in particular, he exploits with telling irony, because of his fear of the 'store-cupboard of language', his sensitivity to every form of prefabricated utterance, and his conviction that 'the great conditioning machinery of language . . . has the natural tendency to dominate everyone's consciousness' with all its competing jargons ('east-west jargons, wage-struggle jargons, economic jargons, jargons in the cause of hygiene, freedom, and after-life').[6] Anselm suggests that somebody should write a dictionary of 'word-devaluation', and for the same reason Walser has declared his special interest in that 'astonishing moment when a coy noun meets an adjective known to be without any sense of shame'. Characteristic of his style are, therefore, surprising combinations of words: *diese lorbeerumstandenen Reden, terminkonzentriertes, bis zum Leid geschäftsgeplagtes Gesicht*, or (the description of an old motor-car) *ein glanzloses altes schrottplatzsüchtiges Blechgespenst*. There is also a deliberate preciousness, a playing with words, as when the semi-conscious way in which the mind can assemble images and reflections in a continuous flow is imitated in a sentence with a refrain expressing Anselm's sense of being an outsider even among his own family:

der Clown bist Du, die Idylle hat Niveau . . . taram, taram, geh auf das Dach, der Wind, der feige Lappen, verkriecht sich im Kamin, angle die Sonne und brate den Standesbeamten . . . der Clown bist Du . . . Dein Gesicht gemartert und zufrieden, Traumschrott Du . . . Sklave mit Theorien und Alpenblick . . . Monteur hübscher Schicksale . . . an den Kreuzungen warten Delegationen auf . . . grün, Zungen kreuzen Klingen klingeln Kreuzigungen . . .

It is because *Halbzeit* sets out to particularise the vision of the world as far as language will allow that detail has priority over narrative continuity: 'I maintain that when every detail fills the space allotted to it, i.e. when it has become language, then, as far as I am concerned, it can stay there. What emerges from this sum of all the details, I don't know.'[7] In this 'mammoth novel of minutiae, a gigantic microcosm',[8] important events like the plot of July 1944 against Hitler and the XXth Party Congress in the Soviet Union are embedded in a mass of detail, much of it ludicrously insignificant by conventional standards. The conception of narrative behind this obsession with detail is illuminated by Walser's remarks in an essay on Proust: 'I consider the improbable situations of everyday life—which people without interest in it call banal—to be just as important as any festival time packed with metaphysics. The wonderful thing about the exactness that Proust achieved is that it abolishes the distinction between what is important and what is not, that on the contrary he narrated in all their importance things that till then had not been noticed.' Perhaps it is 'no longer possible to portray in their totality all the conditions of human life and perhaps the only way is to select representative instances', but then 'one ought not to obscure by art and form the fact that reality cannot be seen in its totality', and so Walser praises Proust for grasping 'that reality cannot be depicted in summary abbreviation and by objectively narrating complete biographies'.[9] His own artistic practice has resulted in features that have led him to be described as 'an uncommonly acute but short-sighted observer', who 'has to get very close to the things he wants to observe', but then 'sees phenomena and details hitherto unnoticed'.[10] As a microanalyst uninterested in the generalising formula, he invites comparison in a sense with Hofmannsthal's description at the turn of the century, in a classic document of alienation, of the way 'everything seemed to me to fragment into its parts, these in their turn into other parts, and nothing could be embraced in a concept'.[11]

Since in *Halbzeit* 'epic breadth' is achieved 'by a kind of cell-division of narrative detail',[12] the result will often be grotesque, as in the description of a show-girl revue on television:

alle Beine hatten ihre Rümpfe gefunden, die Rümpfe versuchten nun, die Beine und auch die Arme wieder loszuwerden, wegwerfende Bewegungen, hastiges Abschütteln, aber es gelang nicht, die Glieder waren zu fest augewachsen. Die noch weißeren Zahnschlitze in Flimmerfleck-Gesicht blieben trotzdem offen.

It is often as if 'some little devil suddenly distorts the vision', with the result that 'whatever is received by the retina is in some curious way made to appear grotesque or unkind',[13] as when effects are isolated from causes, objects left unidentified, or the smallest gestures scrutinised in every detail. Characteristic is the account of Anselm's reflections while walking on a crowded pavement in the rush-hour:

. . . fände das alles nicht statt, wenn ich nicht da wäre? Oder bin ich beteiligt an dem Griff, der den Träger wieder unter die ärmellose Bluse schiebt? Wird das Lachen der Rothaarigen, mit knisternden Brauen, eine Spur lauter, weil ich da bin? Oder gilt das nur dem Kerl, der ihr das Netz tragen und dafür an ihr hochkläffen darf? Feuern wir einander nicht an, zwischen fünf und sechs? Zuschauer vermehren die Schönheit auf dem Trottoir.

This illustrates too how, having to adapt himself to new situations, Anselm needs to observe people he meets with extreme acuteness, for, to choose the behaviour appropriate to a situation, the role-player must assess the situation correctly: 'one has to be always asking questions, one has to be cunning . . .' 'To carry through one's role', Nietzsche wrote, 'means to have a strong will, to concentrate, to be attentive'.[14]

Since role-playing can be both adaptation to circumstances and a protection against them, there is added significance in Enzensberger's remark that prose such as Walser's 'serves to repel reality', to enable him to catch it 'in his snare'.[15] Walser in his turn has said of Enzensberger that, 'if anything is repulsive to him, he deals with it by baptising it, by giving it an appropriate name; he thus protects himself against it and makes it pay the price of having frightened him'.[16] Another German intellectual has spoken rather similarly about Robbe-Grillet: 'hence in Robbe-Grillet that reserved cavity of man's subjective consciousness which observes the world of other people from the entrenched position of its own subjectivity, picks out now this detail, now that, with its binoculars and in painful detail, and only by arranging and describing what it sees creates the sense that it, too, has a place in the world thus described.'[17] Thereby, one might say, quoting a comment about Samuel Beckett, 'he testifies to himself as a sentient being'.[18] 'I can see myself. I have succeeded in seeing myself'—the remark occurs in the interior monologue of another commercial traveller, in Martin Gregor-Dellin's novel *Einer* (1965).[19] He too, like Walser's commercial traveller, feels himself rather as an outsider, rejects the prospect of being confined in the restrictive pattern of imposed jobs and obligations, stands for 'truth against ideology' ('for what writer today has a Weltanschauung at his disposal?'[20]) and protects himself by seeking to identify himself in relation to past and present by critical observation and analysis. Walser's essay on Swift,[21] links up with several aspects of his own work,[22] with *Halbzeit*, for example, as a structure of detail protecting Anselm as narrator—to be distinguished from Anselm as the person actually involved in the situations narrated—against the direct impact of reality, from which through this structure he distances himself by and through reflection. It is in this essay that Walser makes the statement that 'to be surer of himself therefore, Swift had to attack', that 'he is only aware of himself when he has an adversary'.[23]

In both *Ehen in Philippsburg* and *Halbzeit* Walser takes up a position in the antithesis of what in Wilhelminian days went under the name of 'power and spirit', the contemporary variant of which raises problems of its own for the writer as intellectual. Enzensberger, a highly intellectual type of contemporary writer, touches on these when he speaks of 'a sceptical omni-science, doubting everything but itself', of social criticism which 'confesses before it starts, that it cannot fundamentally change anything'[24]—an observation directed actually at *Der Spiegel*, but in line with the way many people in West Germany talk about intellectuals themselves. By his very freedom, it has been argued, the intellectual 'may continue to learn more and more about modern society, but he finds the centres of political initiative less and less accessible'; 'in the world of today the more his knowledge of affairs grows, the less impact his thinking seems to have', and, 'if he grows frustrated as his knowledge increases, it seems that knowledge leads to powerlessness'.[25] In his essay *Skizze zu einem Vorwurf*,[26] published in 1960, Walser shows himself well aware of this situation, writing, on a note of irony and satire, in the first person plural to imply that he speaks for intellectuals in general. We 'sit around in Europe', 'charmed by our powers of formulation' and exhilarated by the freedom of having no public influence, but 'how embarrassed we should be if the state or society invited us to collaborate'. Our democratic society is in need of our help, but, being more or less indifferent about us, 'allows us to conceal the fact that each of us is only concerned really about himself'. A counterpart to the *Skizze zu einem Vorwurf* in narrative terms, and in parts strikingly similar in style, is the story *Eine gewöhnlich verlaufende Reise* (1966),[27] about a namesake of the protagonist of *Halbzeit*, now a writer and intellectual. His characteristics include a sense of being superfluous in the affluent society, a bad conscience about the nature of an existence in which participation in high-fallutin discussion—a form of 'show', to which he contributes largely for effect, and the language, of which is described as 'acoustic vermin'—masks the simple need to earn money, a desire despite everything to be 'absorbed into the higher priesthood of the Federal Republic', adroitness in adapting his behaviour to whatever pose circumstances may demand, and delight in sensual self-indulgence.

Anselm in *Halbzeit* is not in this way an object of satire. Formulating experience, which he is particularly good at, is one of his means of self-orientation and self-identification, and, combined, with his sensitivity of observation, a way also of keeping society at a distance. One can apply to him what Walser has said about Kafka, that, 'compelled' to be an 'observer', to observe is for him the 'first operation that leads to "self-realisation"',[28] or what has been said of the hero of Isherwood's *Down There on a Visit*, that he 'protects himself by observing' and, by so doing, helps himself 'to establish his own identity'.[29]

His identity as an individual, however, is not to be thus easily realised, and this is a central theme, with significant modifications, also in Walser's latest novel *Das Einhorn* (1966), of which, with a few additions, *Eine gewöhnlich verlaufende Reise* forms part. In addition to Anselm Kristlein, other characters in Walser's previous work are here revived. Whereas in *Halbzeit* Anselm—as object of the narrative, not as narrator—was directly exposed to the claims, expectations and pressures of the modern consumer-society, the Anselm of *Das Einhorn* stands at a greater distance from them.

As a free-lance writer and intellectual he spends a lot of time travelling around, taking part in public discussions and giving lectures, and is able only occasionally to spend short periods with his family. What is described in *Das Einhorn* is roughly a year in Anselm's life in the early nineteen-sixties. The narrator's opening introduction of himself ('I am lying down in bed') indicates a position of critical detachment in relation to the stimuli and distractions of everyday life, including his family. This withdrawal provides the possibility for him to recall, reflect upon, and write about, his experiences during this year of his life. The time during which the story is narrated is the period when Anselm is ill and is in the care of his wife and a doctor. The time to which it refers is the previous spring and summer, after the family had moved to Munich. Events of this phase include the party in Munich, the commission to write an autobiographical novel about 'love', with documentation of actual sexual experiences, the lecture tour, the stay on the Lake of Constance and the *dolce vita* of upper class society, the relations with the Dutch-Indonesian girl Orli, and finally the sudden return to Munich, at which point the two areas of time come to coincide.

At the beginning of each of the major sections we are made aware of the time in which the story is being told, as distinct from when it took place. During the action the narrator refers to the fact that he is lying in bed, and the time when the story is being told becomes, like the events themselves, an object of the narrative. Reflection on the person narrating—on Anselm, that is to say—belongs to reflection on the person—likewise Anselm —that the story is about. This is so handled as to show how the Anselm describing his experiences—the 'I—Anselm', as he is called—is acutely aware at every turn that he can never really be at one with reality as it actually was. This is not just because memory of the past is not precise, but because reality as described is necessarily other than reality as experienced at the time, narrative having quite a different type of existence from the past life that provides its material. It is a main contention of *Das Einhorn* that the language of fiction obscures this distinction, wanting to let one believe that a rediscovery of time past is possible. In criticism of Proust the psychosomatic mechanism of memory is here set in motion in order to expose it as a mechanism of illusion:

> Let someone come along and chatter to me in a consoling way about resurrecting things in memory! Just take a fistful of empty air, I would tell him, and think of all the things you have got hold of, and then tell me, what is the result? Yes, he says, it all comes back to him, the way he holds his hand reminds him of it all over again. Oh, dear old Proust. And isn't all we get from it just a haunting of the brain? Nothing but a nuisance.

The unity of *Das Einhorn*—and for all its interpolations we have to insist on its unity—is achieved by the consistent intention of revealing the unreality of memory's image of the past:

> I am lying thoughtfully in bed in order, without Clio's help, to investigate memory and, if needs be, to christen it death-mask. It will try to resist, the sentimental creature . . . in order not to be discovered to be just a cold copy, an abstract young lady. There may be a bit of a struggle. The lady is spoilt. Much wooed, little investigated.

Since 'nothing survives as such', faith in language is undermined, because words are seen as just a substitute for the past, illusions occasioned by the act of remembering: 'daß es mit Orli aus ist und vorbei, das schmiert die Sprache zu mit schlechter Vergegenwärtigung . . . ENTSINNEN, ja. Von REMEMBERN keine Spur'. Here *entsinnen* is to be understood quite literally, as progressive loss of impressions once directly experienced by the senses. Memory, the narrator says a little later, is 'only a pair of scales to weigh losses on', a 'stock exchange that daily becomes richer in its losses'.

However, life and fiction—the time narrated and the time in which the story is narrated as having taken place—can only in appearance be kept clearly distinct from each other. Memory and existence are inseparably connected. The motto of the prologue of the section entitled 'Position 1' is St. Augustin's 'I am my memory'. The title of the novel hints at this. 'Unicorn', partly a phallic symbol, is also, as a mythical creature, a symbol of the creative vitality of memory. Language and memory may be described as the 'conjuring up of the past', as the mere 'appearance' of living reality, but nevertheless it is the 'Unicorn' that the narrator allows to persuade him to write down the name Orli ('Write ORLI, says the Unicorn'), and it is this that sets the process of narrating in motion. It is not denied that memory is a part of life, but, in order not to avoid suggesting that what is written about the past is an actual reproduction of it, the fictional character of the narrator has to be constantly stressed. The narrator says of himself that he is only a 'figure', lacking 'full-dimensional reality', a 'shadow cast by something now lost'. He is thus seen as fiction, 'dressed up in words', and can declare that what language translates him into is past and dead. It is by virtue of this fictional quality that he can be the narrator of memories without creating the illusion that they are life.

Anselm, as narrator, does achieve, as he boasts, an 'identity', composed of the words he has written. Before he achieves it, he introduces himself as a multiple personality, characterised by a wide variety of reactions. As a man in society he is, like his predecessor in *Halbzeit*, a role-player; as narrator, too, he adopts many different positions, enjoying the freedom to assume a critically detached attitude to any of them. He refers to himself as 'I', 'you', 'he', and 'we'. In this part of the argument Walser may not greatly extend the scope of the previous novel, but he discovers a range of new and memorable metaphors for the multiplicity of personality: 'is one not perhaps some sort of parliament of pronouns? Anselm, that's the name of the parliament building, in it there meet the First Person, the Second Person, and the Third Person'. Belief in the idea of individuality is mocked at: 'we leave the individual to the competent authorities, that is to say, to those who manufacture suits and coats. In all other matters we beg respect for our

individuality. *Vivat Dividuum.* The thousandfold. And soon to be a
hundred-thousandfold.' As seen by Walser, unity of personality
is unthinkable: 'man is a pluralistic society Ltd.' For a brief spell
a particular intention, as one possibility among others, may be
allowed to become dominant, whereby 'many-sided man
ephemerally becomes an individual'. Anselm knows such moments from his own experience: 'he no longer knew separate
Anselms. And no single Anselm. He was a tendency, the
collaboration of a million units. He was unique. And alone.'
Right at the end of the book, adopting a position 'in the here and
now', in 'Simple Life', a position between past and future, he
believes that he has reached a degree of resolution that gives
him an identity: '. . . I cry out, ME, no longer a rattling collection of bits and pieces . . . I have . . . strangled the buzz of the
many voices and stand at the head of my own self as a compact
Anselm . . .' The self-irony of this passage, in the fuller context
of which he presents himself as a proud father of a family, shows
at the same time how impossible it is for the writer and intellectual Anselm Kristlein to find any real kind of identity beyond
his diffusive role-existence. So in a letter to *Dichten und
Trachten*, a literary brochure published by the Suhrkamp Verlag
giving news of its recent and forthcoming publications, Walser
arranges for Anselm Kristlein to write: 'I assure you once more
that I have no objection to becoming more indistinct in the new
book. Thereby the possibility increases of my having portrayed
myself correctly . . . For did you by any chance ever feel that
I wanted to establish a clear image of myself? . . . I would
gladly fade out in a pattern (*Muster*). Can you suggest one that
I could disappear in?'

In this novel an intellectual is portrayed obliterating the idea
of identity, and this helps to give it its ironic, frivolous, even
rascally, tone. In an essay written at the same time as parts of
this novel, Walser says of writers: 'because of our connection,
for which we are not so to speak responsible, with the upper
hundred thousand people in society, we are in a position to be
able to shake the whole lot of them by calling ourselves into
question. Writers as investigators of behaviour. They themselves
are the material of the inquiry'. Again: 'the writer is concerned
really only with himself, and when he has unseated himself, it
turns out that he has pulled everyone down with him. That's

utopian, certainly. But perhaps it is worthwhile to have failed in trying to bring it about'.[30] Accordingly, and consistently, Anselm is shown as one who moves in higher society, but also as one who tries, whenever possible, to escape the Darwinian law of nature and capitalist society, the struggle for self-preservation. He speaks scornfully of the 'selection by competition which in our culture is recognised as the only decent order of things'. He 'obviously lacks animal talents, Anselm does not like a struggle. Competition does not give him the slightest pleasure'. But this ranging of himself against the idea of a competitive struggle for existence is part of his own struggle to find an oppositional stance in a society where ironically 'people welcome the writer. The economy, the government, the opposition'.

In face of this situation the writer, adopting an attitude of negation, seeks to make his own position one of opposition to the powers listed in the above quotation. The acrobatics of the language characteristic of *Das Einhorn*—mixing up very long sentences, extremely short ones, passages without proper punctuation, enumeration, neologisms, Swiss German, English, Yiddish, Old High German, Middle High German, breaking-up of words, verbal distortions, and so forth—serves as an instrument with which ironically to destroy his own position in order to undermine the authority of the society he finds himself in. Such a style of formulation is a way, too, of freeing language from set patterns of thought, which are too often ideological in implication and purpose. Language, so runs Walser's line of thought, reveals itself as a vehicle of illusion through memory. Harbouring associations of the past, it can be used to consolidate the status quo. Hence the inclination of the writer to destroy language in as much as it is a means of preserving what is, and of self-defence for established authority: 'a writer, whose faith in himself as writer is undermined in the process of writing, would be an element of unrest for those engaged in the plot of conformism (*die Verabredeten*). For we are involuntarily in league with those whose authority is established as for all time, if we fail to scare language out of its grandiose relationship with a historical past claiming the right to exist into the future'.[31]

In *Das Einhorn* the acrobatics of language serve as an instrument whereby the awareness of both author and reader is so differentiated as to force it out of the rut of established modes of thought. This position of 'extreme non-conformism' makes writing comparable to 'the strategy of the partisan'.[32]

The term 'partisan' is here used not in the sense of an adherent to a party or cause, but rather of one 'trusting to a system of strongpoints', engaged in aggressive action of self-preservation between the battle lines of ideologies. ('These intellectuals of the so-called left wander about between the fronts', the conservative critic Egon Holthusen sneeringly remarks[33]). It is, therefore, of significance[34] that in 1961 Rolf Schroers published his book entitled *Der Partisan*, though its primary aim was as a 'contribution to political anthropology'. What attracted him to the theme was 'the fascination of an ultimate and extreme realisation of human existence, the majesty of the absurd'. In a situation characterised by efforts to force the world into a single political and ideological pattern, 'individuals and groups try to withdraw from the pull of circumstances and assert claims to autonomy cutting across the levelling tendencies. ... The active bearer of these struggles, the underground fighter, is the partisan'.[35]

The implications of Schroers' book, though its immediate concern was with war and politics, did not pass unnoticed in literary circles. It was much praised by Nossack, who elaborated on its relevance to the contemporary writer's situation.[36] Schroers' partisans, he said, are people 'driven by the events of war from the area they were born into. They do not belong to any of the factions conducting the war, even though they may now and again give help to one or the other and provide it with weapons'. They are not 'revolutionaries enrolled in the cause of an ideology'. What they fight for is 'something very personal against destructive abstraction', and they 'consciously choose to go underground as the last defensive position'.

In a novel on which the influence of *Halbzeit* has been suspected, in Reinhard Baumgart's *Der Löwengarten* (1961), we read: 'in talking he always seemed to be trying to escape,[37] to be fighting angry rearguard actions all the time. He did not want anyone to get too close to him'.[38] A characteristic story in Walser's early collection *Ein Flugzeug über dem Haus* begins with the words: 'when I felt the desire to lie down on my bed, I really did not know what this would lead to', and its theme is the motive behind this curious act of withdrawal, and its

I

consequences: 'I was able to confuse them all, deceive them, keep them away by my quiet kind of existence'. In the words of Kafka quoted by Walser,[39] the principle involved is that 'the limited sphere is pure'. But in another story in the same collection it is seen to be not necessarily a very effective one. An old man, living alone with his daughter in a large house in an area where all around property is being sold (and, according to his suspicions, bought up by some powerful and anonymous organisation), engages in a hopeless attempt to remain detached from the encompassing reality. He resolves to resist, to stay within his 'limited sphere', and he refuses to sell, but, as neurotically sensitive as Kafka's badger to threats from outside, he is always peering out on watch for the approach of the hostile forces. In the end, lacking the will and the means for an aggressive confrontation with reality, he is found dead in his study, hit on the head by the fall of one of his huge bound volumes of newspapers.

In *Ehen in Philippsburg* Hans Beumann disregards the principle of the 'limited sphere' and, lured away by life's seductions, he pays the price of moral ruin. Walser's play *Eiche und Angora* (1962) provides a comment on the problem as the tragi-comic picture of one who falls an easy victim of the pressures of conformism through lacking the defences of a sufficiently articulated awareness. Anselm in *Halbzeit* possesses them in an exceptional degree, and they form his main protection against forces calculated to make him, in the title of Musil's novel, a 'man without qualities'. His successor in *Das Einhorn* sees himself faced with yet more subtle pressures of society and is given a correspondingly more complete sensitivity. In other words, first-person narration assumes an important function in giving Anselm an identity. By observing himself in his diffusive role-existence he preserves a basis for self-criticism. By observing himself in relation to society he is the better able to assess its pressures on the individual. 'Anselm always knows', Walser states in a letter,[40] 'that it is *he* who is bent on survival and must survive; to attain this goal, he goes through all the transformations and roles. To have a problem of identity would seem to him a luxury. This he cannot allow himself in his struggle'. The choice of a non-heroic protagonist itself necessitates the portrayal of man as a role-player because as Walser says in the same letter, this is for Anselm the only possibility of survival in this extremely competitive modern society: 'the plan, the intention was, it is true, to describe a person more exactly than is often the case in novels. The "heroes" were mostly much too clear. One soon knows them by heart. They are mostly "poorer" than real people, but by contrast they are "greater", "more terrible", "more decisive". At any rate, they like to represent something larger than life. The more average someone is, the less "great" he is, and the more careful he has to be. He has to develop a talent for mimicry, otherwise he will not get on and he will not be able to stand up to it all. That is, I think, the main reason for Anselm's role-playing—in fact, a Darwinian sort of reason. His identity is never seriously endangered. He is chained to it as to nothing else. That is to say, he is in no sense a pathological case, in no way schizophrenic; his roles are simply the attempt by masterly adjustment to people stronger than himself to make himself appear a strong man'.

Chapter 6

Uwe Johnson

Uwe Johnson was born in Pomerania in 1934, studied at Rostock and Leipzig, and in 1959 left East Germany to settle in West Berlin. His motives in leaving East Germany were influenced by the consideration that, having arranged for *Mutmaßungen über Jakob* to be published in Frankfurt am Main,[1] he feared that 'the East German authorities would misunderstand as an attack and an accusation what in fact was just a story, an explanation', and he wanted to avoid the consequences of any such misunderstanding 'in the form of criminal proceedings against me'.[2] But that he did not 'choose freedom' quite in the usual sense of the term, and has not meanwhile been disposed to want to take sides in propaganda arguments between East and West, will become clear in the course of this chapter.

In fact, the story of *Mutmaßungen über Jakob*, which appeared in 1959, has elements in common with novels of East German 'socialist realism'.[3] Jakob would fit the pattern as the working man proudly conscious of the dignity of labour, Herr Rohlfs as the party functionary always ready to help people who run into difficulties, Dr. Jonas Blach as the vacillating intellectual, and Gesine Cresspahl as the person seduced to the West by the lures of capitalist prosperity. Jakob himself goes to the West, but he soon returns, and the novel begins with the last episode in his life, when on his return he is killed walking 'across the tracks'. Trying in a fog to avoid one train, he is killed by another, the one presumably from the East, the other from the West[4]—and the possibility is not excluded that he committed suicide. No amount of 'speculation', however, even by people who knew him well, ever settles this question, which, like much else about Jakob, remains enigmatic. Only where concrete and especially technical matters are concerned is the focus sharp and clear. 'Where reality is known only very approximately', Johnson is on record as saying, 'I would not wish to try to portray it as if it were better known than it is'.[5] The implied answer to the question, 'does anyone know Jakob?', is in the negative, if only because in modern society, and not merely in totalitarian systems, social, political, and ideological pressures will tempt the individual to hide something of himself from the public gaze, to disguise himself in one form or another. Also special difficulties will arise in trying to penetrate behind the disguise in the case of a person belonging to a society different from one's own, with other values and objectives.

The distinctive language and style of *Mutmaßungen über Jakob*, constituting much of the essence of the book, absorb these problems and uncertainties. The first two sentences begin with the word 'but', and words like 'perhaps', 'so to speak', the unconventional 'so to think', and extensive use of the subjunctive are among the devices sustaining and insisting upon the tone of reservation and doubt. Unexpected punctuation (or absence of punctuation), unfinished sentences, uncertainty as to who is talking to whom, serve to make it hard for the reader to find his bearings, and involve him with the author and his characters in probing the elusive features of human communication. The major structural elements are accordingly monologue, dialogue, and what Johnson calls 'recitation'. The first comprises 'the memories and imaginings of Rohlfs, Blach and Gesine, printed in italics. The second is organised in paragraphs and with the use of inverted commas—thus in the first and second chapter the conversation between Jöche and Blach, in the third between Blach and Gesine, in the fourth between Gesine and Rohlfs. The third consists of information provided by the narrator, who however is never identified'.[6] There is no omniscient narrator, and an authoritative authorial voice is never heard. The author withdraws behind his characters, and it is mainly on them that the reader has to rely for whatever information he can glean about Jakob. This, as one might say, democratic relationship between the author and his characters is of profound importance for the composition of the novel: 'the author cannot know everything about Jakob. There are other things that Gesine knows, and Rohlfs and Cresspahl, etc.'[7] Hence the narrative is composed of a number of opinions held by various people about Jakob, and the author functions rather as a fictional editor, collecting and arranging them.

Since what is known about the central character, and this often more tentatively than not, arises almost entirely from the observations of others, and since these (for reasons affecting both themselves and him) are not in the best position to command or communicate the whole truth, the style and structure tend to serve less to provide the final answers than to tease us into speculation.

It has been said that it is not 'clear whether our ignorance of Jakob's inner life ... is due to the conditions of life under Communism, or is fundamental to the *condition humaine*. If the latter—and the ambiguity is not resolved—Johnson's critique would seem to apply equally to other human societies rendering much of the East German background otiose'.[8] What should be said rather is that in *Mutmaßungen über Jakob* Johnson uses the East German setting in such a way as to allow him to reveal certain general problems by reference to a milieu he knew intimately. These problems, essentially the uncertainty of identity and communication, are such as to operate against symbolical interpretations making too exclusive claims.

There may, for example, be some truth in the idea that the novel is an 'allegory of the just man in an unjust time',[9] but it is too tight-fitting a concept. Jakob is described as 'thoughtful', 'thorough', 'kindly', 'serious', but, apart from an ambiguous reference at the end, never as 'just', nor are his actions of a kind to force us to think that he is. In any case, what justice should we imagine Jakob as standing for—the justice of the state he serves, or the justice he may be demanding for himself, or the justice he demands for other people? In a way these might all be possible, but there is nothing in the book to compel us to believe that he is the champion of any of these ideas. Blach, in fact, states his impression that Jakob cannot properly be described in terms of 'qualities': 'if I remember right, I immediately started to seek for words. Then I started straightaway to reject one word after the other, they all denoted qualities, and Jakob did not seem to have any'.

Problems arise, too, if, viewing Johnson as the 'legitimate heir of Kafka, carrying forward his work', Jakob is seen as one who stands 'above' the 'false contradictions between private person and the state, individual and society'.[10] To regard Jakob, however, as a figure who 'alone knows' and lives the 'inner law' of modern man's existence, is to place a mythological superstructure on the 'speculations', to treat the book as a kind of Holy Scripture offering the image of a profane Messiah. In fact, Jakob is as uncertain about the individual's position in society as most other people in his surroundings, and, as a working man of integrity, his nature is to resist the claims of ideology.

When Rohlfs tries to brainwash him into agreement with the prevailing ideology, Jakob's answer is to talk about the difficulties he has, as it is, in dispatching trains in the right order and at the right time. There is more than a suggestion that preoccupation with wider matters would only handicap him: 'I certainly have a general view. . . . And this possibility of having a general view . . . adds to the difficulties of the job'. Remaining strictly within the limits of his immediate occupation, he mentions that the 'social order only affects the occasion and the circumstances of transport in an external way', and he indicates his view that ideological considerations account for certain inefficiencies, as when trains have to be held up to allow a transport of Russian soldiers through. Jakob concludes his interview with Rohlfs by saying: 'this, my dear fellow, is what your socialism adds up to'. He does not explicitly disagree with the official ideology, but, talking about it as irrelevant to his job, implicitly criticises its claims over larger areas of life, and Rohlfs is led to wonder whether 'he really cares about anything'. Yet Rohlfs is fascinated by Jakob. Listening to him talk, he 'kept as still as a bird in a net'. For in a society whose ideology makes the working man an object of adulation, Jakob's criticism is of captivating interest to Rohlfs, the more so since Jakob is so much praised for his integrity.

The notion of integrity, however, is complicated by the suggestions throughout *Mutmaßungen über Jakob* that man is so influenced by extraneous forces, by society, politics and ideology, as to render the idea of an inherent identity of personality, necessary as it may be to the individual, illusory. So in some philosophical deliberations recounted in characteristic style as Jakob's supposed interior monologue, 'freedom' and 'identity' appear as fictitious concepts:

'Freiheit' ist eher ein Mangelbegriff, insofern: sie kommt nicht vor. Wer auf die Welt kommt redet sich an mit Ich, das ist das Wichtigste für ihn, aber er findet sich mit mehreren zusammen, und

muß sich einrichten mit seiner Wichtigkeit; niemand kann so frei
sein etwa aus der Physik auszutreten für seine Person. Als soziales
und natürliches Lebewesen (ich bin ein . . .) weitgehend fest. Da
ist wohl die Auffassung der Welt von einem Punkt Ich aus gemeint,
'dies sei aber nicht begriffen als Freiheit, solange man genau wie
die Führung des Staates den Menschen (unsere Menschen, die
Massen) beeinflußbar denke nach einem sehr schlichten Schema
von Kausalität . . .'

Despite, or because of, his awareness of forces at work on him
from outside, Jakob insists on his personal responsibility in his
job. Thereby he attains a measure of freedom and detachment,
and it is this, as much as anything else, that associates him with
the interests of humanity in the face of deterministic pressures.

This does not, however, make him a symbol of one who
'knows' and 'lives' the Law in Kafka's sense. It indicates the
general interest that attaches to him, and if our ears detect
Biblical cadences and forms of phrase in Johnson's style, this,
too, will probably make us all the more sensitive to the image of
Jakob as more than merely an efficient railway worker who
decided to sample the seductions of the West.[11]

In the same way the 'sporting hero of the people' in Johnson's
second novel *Das dritte Buch über Achim* (1961) is more than just
an East German cycling star, corresponding in some ways to the
actual figure of Gustav Adolf Schur. Nicknamed Täve by his
fans, he was the subject of a book by one Klaus Ullrich entitled
Unser Täve. Ein Buch über Gustav Adolf Schur, published in 1960
in East Berlin. This is described as the revised edition of an
earlier work entitled *Unser Weltmeister*,[12] and so in Johnson's
novel the book that Karsch, a Hamburg journalist, is trying to
write, is the third.

Karsch is interested in Achim above all as a 'mediating
figure', esteemed alike by the authorities and the people. The
public have the simple image of Achim as a star sportsman, a
respected member of the party, a member of parliament, a
model citizen, single-minded and without corruption. His
father, Karsch ascertains, had been a keen Social Democrat,
devoted enough to have listened in Nazi times illegally to
foreign broadcasting stations. This would fit the public image
well enough. But, as Karsch also finds out, Achim had been
active as a boy in the Nazi youth organisation, though also he

had had a Jewish girl friend. Also, there are reasons for believing that he had taken part in the 1953 uprising in East Germany against the government, not to mention the fact that, contravening the East German currency regulations, he had once gone into West Berlin to buy himself a three-speed gear. Karsch goes to race meetings, holds discussions with Achim, and with people who have been in contact with him, in order to get at the truth about him. In the course of these investigations, however, Achim turns out to be a figure of such complexity as to deny Karsch the certainties necessary to complete his biography.

This is mirrored in the way the subjunctive of hypothesis and hearsay comes to dominate the style, and phrases like 'it is said that from one moment to the next he left and disappeared', 'according to them Achim also might have asked him one evening . . .', 'he wanted (probably) to admit . . .', reflect the accumulating reservations and uncertainties. A simple factual statement will be made only to be quickly rectified, and much is put in parenthesis:

> Viereinhalb (und als ich erzählt habe was der Polier gesagt hat, da ließ ihr Blick los, schwamm so und dann hat sie doch gesagt daß sie in Ostpreußen wo liegt das überhaupt daß sie da eine Freundin gehabt hat, die ist nicht mitgekommen. Oder war das früher. Wie meint sie das, als ich dann stillschwieg, war sie ganz freundlich im Gesicht aber ich hab doch ach ich weiß nicht) Stunden.

Here a parenthetical statement, prolonged and gropingly unsure of itself, virtually obliterates the simple fact of the four-and-a-half hours encompassed by it. As to what Achim 'represents that is new', the answer given is 'not just victory . . . but the competition of individuals or groups for whatever you like or whatever you take it to be'. The passage omitted in this quotation is in brackets and occupies a full page. Its presence is dictated by the inadequacy of the statement that what Achim represented was 'not just victory', a generalisation evidently felt to need insight into the details and spirit of an actual race to make it meaningful, and this is what the parenthesis provides. Also having specified that what Achim 'represents' is 'the competition of individuals or groups', the narrator cannot rest content with this straightforward definition, and so resignedly contents himself with an evasive 'or whatever you like'. This time the elaboration comes not in the parenthesis but in another long and detailed description of a race viewed from inside by those taking part in it.

Sentences unfinished or with casual endings ('Wenn Karsch gelegentlich kam und ihn laden wollte zu einem Bier und allgemeinem Gespräch über die deutsche Herstellung von Zeitung, einmal so, einmal so'), a strained and often ungainly syntax, the absence of conventional punctuation, and the use of unfamiliar metaphors, provoked considerable criticism: 'his language is like someone grinding blocks of rubble and fitting the pieces together to make stones'.[13] Occasional errors may occur,[14] but the fact remains that Johnson's style opens up new possibilities of describing the uncertainties of reality, and of portraying what can be firmly established with penetrating accuracy. It is a very self-conscious style, frequently reflecting upon itself:[15] 'you see how awkwardly this second sentence is in relation to the first', 'that shouldn't be said in a relative clause', '. . . belong surely in the main sentence?' The implications and ambiguities of a word will sometimes have to be explored in order to test the truth of a statement, as in the section devoted to the meaning of 'private' (referring to the acts of sabotage by Achim's father in the Nazi aircraft industry). More extensively this is illustrated in the case of Achim's reference to the experience of his trip to West Berlin as *sonntäglich*, Sunday-like. In the ensuing discussion about this word Karsch and Achim try to agree on its meaning in the context, but without getting very far. The discussion ends in a non-committal exchange of phrases, and a few lines of interior monologue, in which the uncertainty of meaning is accepted as the only certainty:

Vielleicht so: sagte Karsch.—So eher: sagte Achim.—Vielleicht: sagte er: Irgend wie: Irgend wie (dachte Karsch) war sehr genau. Irgend wie war irgend wie vielleicht auch zu beschreiben.

To discover that one cannot be sure about meanings, even where everyday words and phrases are concerned, is a step on the way to the discovery that man may be in error in believing that he can know himself. In discussion with Karsch, Achim has a picture of himself as clear-cut as the official and public image, but this conceals, amongst other things, complicating features about his past:

er wollte nicht der sein, der roh und gern war im alten und zer-schlagenen Verband der staatlichen Jugend . . . nicht einer, den ängstigte die Rote Armee, der hätte seinen Vater verraten (für eine schlechte Sache verraten), den haben wir ja mit Gewalt hineinbringen müßen ins blaue Hemd und eingesehen hat er es doch nicht.

His inner reluctance to admit to his activities in the Hitler Youth, to his fear of the Red Army, to the fact that he had betrayed his father, and to the difficulty people had in getting him into the Communist youth organisation, all this is under-standably concealed by Achim—not necessarily by lying, because the extent to which he is now aware of it, is open to question. The position he now adopts is of one who has always been as he now is: he 'wollte gelebt haben schon wie immer jetzt und seit fünf Jahren Mitglied in der Sachwalterpartei: so endlich unterwiesen und entschieden für eine staatliche Gerechtigkeit, die ihm nicht anders denn angenehm gefiel'. Karsch's investigations uncover many inconsistencies of this kind, confirming his early doubt 'ob das Leben unter den handelsüblichen Namen wohnte'—whether, that is to say, the realities of life corresponded to the words conventionally used to describe them. This makes the job of writing his book on Achim increasingly difficult, if only because a person may without dishonesty adapt himself to people's image of him. So Karsch is led to consider what Achim stands for in the mind of the public, how to interpret their admiration for him. This brings him to realise that the people's regard for Achim as an ideal image of themselves may not be quite what in official circles it would be taken for, that it may not be unconnected with the feeling that Achim represents the ordinary man 'against the government and against the world', and that his much admired solidarity with his team could be understood as solidarity with the people against the régime.

In the case of Achim's girl friend Karin, too, it is hard for the outside observer to be sure whether she is for or against the government. Regarding recent measures of the government she declared herself 'of one mind with all people of goodwill', but according as to how one takes the phrase 'people of goodwill', this can be interpreted either as approval of Ulbricht or opposition to him, and the ensuing words ('our best wishes are with her') preserve the ambiguity. Her attitude to the compulsory collectivisation of the farms as related by the narrator have suggestions of a similar ambivalence:

manchmal sagte sie so entschlossen wie Tapferkeit aussieht: Aber Großraumwirtschaft, wie sie die werden machen können auf den zusammengelegten Feldern in der Genossenschaft, die ist doch im Vorteil, das werden sie gewiß noch einsehen, du, Karsch.

The odd opening phrase could imply that she had merely put on a brave face, as one who had persuaded herself that collectivisation is a good thing. Her comparison of East and West Germany is non-committal. West Germany, she remarks, is unjust, so, too, is East Germany, 'perhaps we shall be the first to see things in a just light'. The words, 'Yes. No. Perhaps. (If you like to look at it like that)', occurring just before the last quotation, reflect the mood of one in whom support for the régime is so interwoven with critical feelings about it that no single and simple formula could accurately catch her attitude. To Karin one could apply the remark about Achim that 'little of his life was visible', though they both lead an existence in full public view. She, too, as an actress, enjoys the applause of the masses and, with reservations, the approval of the authorities. As in the case of Achim, what she is at present cannot properly be understood in isolation from what she was, as Karsch comes to realise.

There is, for instance, a simple answer to the question 'who is Achim?': 'he was a racing cyclist, for he went cycling with others and tried to go faster than they did'. But for Karsch it is not enough to limit the description of Achim to his function as a sportsman. He sees his task as biographer like this: 'he did not want to describe every detail about Achim, but only what (in his view) distinguished him from other people and other racing cyclists'. Karsch's experience, however, teaches him that to know this you have to know virtually everything, and also that to have all the details is not necessarily to know the essentials. Thus the problem of selection arises, and it is analysed in connection with Karsch's interest in Achim's visit to West

Berlin. Karsch knows that he could have concentrated on other possible days in Achim's life. He discusses some of these only to have to dismiss them as less important, but not without the guilty feeling that to omit may be to falsify: 'unvollständig aber ist lügenhaft'. Yet the more factual information he accumulates, the more reservations he has about its validity, for the effect is to make the evidence about Achim more complex and more contradictory, to bring home to Karsch that information may only prove a 'hindrance behind which the true Achim has to be looked for'.

As a book describing the failure of a fictitious author to write the biography of a fictitious character, and a book in which analysis of itself is an integral element, one might apply to *Das dritte Buch über Achim* what Sartre said about Natalie Sarraute's *Portrait d'un Inconnu*,[16] that it is an anti-novel in which 'what happens is the process of challenging the novel as such by the practice of a particular novel, of destroying it before our eyes', demonstrating 'that we are living in an age of reflection and that the novel is engaged in reflecting upon itself'. Indeed, the title of Natalie Sarraute's novel could be transferred to *Das dritte Buch über Achim*, as a book about a man whose identity has to be established, and so could Sartre's remark about *Portrait d'un Inconnu*, to the effect that it 'reads like a detective story'. To the question in *Mutmaßungen über Jakob* 'does anyone know Jakob?', corresponds in *Das dritte Buch über Achim* the question 'who is Achim?'. About *Portrait d'un Inconnu* Sartre observes further that Natalie Sarraute introduces 'a sort of amateur detective who concentrates on a banal couple . . . spies on them and follows their tracks . . . but without ever being very clear who they are and who they are not. And he will find nothing or almost nothing'. In *Mutmaßungen über Jakob* Rohlfs is a kind of professional government detective, shadowing Jakob and reporting on his movements:[17] 'I travel around after him, I observe his daily routine'. In *Das dritte Buch über Achim* it is Karsch who acts as a sort of amateur detective, interviewing people whom Achim has been in contact with, visiting places he has been to, and interrogating Achim himself. Karsch is very much the amateur detective, too, in his reports about Karin, and her presence, for example, at the funeral is related rather with a detective's eye: 'the fresh traces of Karin's shoes could be

recognised from the sharp edges of the hole made by the heel of
her shoes and around which were the imprints of her sole, where
she had trodden the ground unsure as to what to do next'.
Ernst Bloch, under whom incidentally Johnson studied at
Leipzig, formulates the problem of the detective story thus:
'questions are asked about someone who is hidden'. This states
the central problem of Johnson's two novels, and another
observation of Bloch could be applied to them: 'there is never a
person who has a really clear image of himself. We exist in a
blind spot, unrecognisable to ourselves'. This, he goes on, is less
true of the insignificant than of the more complex person, who
is 'more deeply hidden' and 'nearer the secret of what man
truly is'.[18] *Das dritte Buch über Achim*, in fact, goes some way to
providing a positive answer to the question raised by one
critic[19] as to why on earth the detective story cannot find a more
cheerful object of enquiry than murder.[20]

The implication, especially when the environmental pressures surrounding the individual are themselves subject to rapid
change, must be to invalidate the idea of adequate biography,
and it is the impossibility of this that Johnson, in line with
Walser's thoughts on the subject,[21] exposes to full view. In one
chapter several possible ways of tackling Achim's biography are
tried, but the various attempts, listed alphabetically, peter out
when it becomes obvious that there is no limit: 'G. Or something else. H. Or not at all. I. How many letters are there in the
alphabet?' As was remarked a little while after the appearance
of *Das dritte Buch über Achim*, 'we have rather lost ... the
courage to paint a realistic portrait of a person, and our
confidence in the degree to which an individual can be described finds itself confronted with well-founded doubts about
identity as something that can hardly be demonstrated'.[22] This
is Karsch's experience when his investigations reveal Achim as
someone, for example, who has, or may have, taken an active
part in the Berlin rising of 1953, who is, or may be, a convinced
member of the Party. Information about the stages of his
metamorphosis from a member of the Hitler Youth to a
supporter of the Ulbricht régime remains equally vague,
because here, too, the evidence allows a number of different
interpretations. Does the photograph of the rising of the workers
show Achim among them, or is the person on the photograph

merely someone who looks like Achim? And, if it is Achim, what does it prove? That he was on the side of the revolutionaries against the government, or that he just happened to be there at the time? These questions are left open in the absence of proof one way or the other, and, whereas detective stories usually progress to neat solutions, the search for the true identity of Achim uncovers only possibilities.

None of Johnson's characters, in fact, are ever more than fragmentarily present at any moment, so that fullness of characterisation is the least relevant of criteria in assessing his work. The subtle ways in which people's fears of ideological commitment induce them to disguise their true selves are closely observed: 'the other was diffident and spoke mainly in a questioning tone, in the end he hesitated as if to say something, but then swallowed what he was about to say', or again: 'I'll do what you want. But if . . . Suddenly his voice faded out in the dim light. Almost every citizen was able to express himself in this vague way'. Karin, hovering between resistance to and approval of the government, has conditioned herself to act different points of view, on the stage as well as in everyday life: 'she had learned to behave in various ways. She hardly believed she was lying when she praised what was good in the régime (*am Staat des Sachwalters*) and kept silent about what you would not wish to experience. Yes. No. Perhaps. (If you care to look at it like that).' Since she is continually imitating other people's language and gestures, her true personality, it seems to Karsch, is hidden behind a mask: 'and Karsch thought that here as always (so to speak) she was standing behind herself, watching her actions and examining them to see if they were right'. This sort of detachment is also typical of Achim, whose 'person receded into a similar significant distance, when it was expressly praising the state'.

'Attitudes of omniscience', Johnson has said of the narrator of a novel, 'are suspect'. The author 'ought to admit that he invented what he tells, that his information is incomplete and imprecise', and he can do this 'by stressing the difficult quest for truth', 'by comparing or relating his own view of what has happened to that of one of his characters, by omitting what he cannot know, by not giving out as pure art what is yet another quest for truth'.[23] The narrator, nevertheless, still has in

Johnson's novels certain privileges, including a sufficiently inside view of his characters to enable him to use interior monologue. But his judgements on their situations and actions are presented as mere opinions. Now and then, talking in the first person, he may address the reader directly in the second person, as when suddenly he intrudes with the remark that 'I have already told you that . . .', and then, after commenting on a feature of Fleisg's appearance, adds that 'after two days Karsch had described how he had met Achim. It was actually the text you have read as answer to the question "who is Achim?" ' In this context occurs the observation that 'Karsch had not understood him', illustrating that the narrator will sometimes allow himself to decide whether what his characters think or say is true. So the question is allowed to arise 'whether Herr Fleisg really was as Karsch presented him or whether he (Karsch) had merely thought up a good story'. Frequently, too, the anonymous narrator allows us to see what is happening through the eyes of an outside observer, whose presence is often felt or implied. As there is no narrator in charge in the traditional sense, the story consists largely of Karsch's own account of Achim's life, of conversations between Karsch, Karin, Achim, and a number of other people. These are conversations within a conversation, for the whole story is being told to Karsch's friends back in Hamburg. The italicised heading creates the fiction of their interrupting (on behalf of the narrator) Karsch's story with questions or surprised remarks, and this helps to account for the colloquial tone of much of the book. Karsch himself is not portrayed as a person with particularly individual features, and the obscurity of the author behind Karsch as investigator represents an infinity of possible readers and witnesses, to all of whom certainty is denied.

In brief, the traditional function of the narrator is divided between Karsch, his contacts in East Germany, his friends in Hamburg, and an anonymous narrator. It is often hard to distinguish between Karsch's interior monologue, in which he refers to himself in the third person, and the voice of the narrator as such, who also speaks of Karsch in the third person. Frequent changes in the narrative perspective, ambiguities as to who is speaking to whom, and the intermingling of past and present tenses, result in a complex structure with a wide range of stylistic levels—informal conversation, formal report, interior monologue, reported speech, and interview.

The reasons why Johnson resorts to these methods have to do with matters he discussed in a lecture in America, when he referred to the problem of newspaper reporting in divided Berlin. A passenger, for example, gets on a train in East Berlin and alights in West Berlin. This, he remarked, may produce contradictory reports by newsagencies on each side of the border. Propaganda interests will interfere, biased eye-witness accounts will be unreliable, accidental errors in communication will distort the truth, and this epitomises for him the general problem that the reality in which we live is known to us largely on the basis of frequently unreliable information:

So long as a literary text . . . is concerned with truth, its subject must be checked against two contradictory tendencies of truth-finding. We know some of the sources of error in the collecting and transmitting of news: eye-witnesses who didn't look too closely, who can't say what they didn't see. They make up something that seems to round off the incident. Or they quietly arrange the situation according to their habitual points of reference, which may be private or of sectarian morality or party politics. Press, radio, television, and city gossip make additional changes in the material that has already been prepared for them. To some extent they depend on the interpretation which the first reporter gave to the incident with an adjective. They all damage reality (provided this word still applies), according to their special technical bias, by one or two dimensions. These personally or technically induced errors grow in complexity and become a rigid pattern the moment they are combined with the even more prolific source of error which political bias provides. Each side of the border has its pattern. Obviously the criteria for one cannot be applied to the other.[24]

The last sentence in this statement has, as Johnson has been at pains to demonstrate, far-reaching consequences regarding language. A passage, for instance, in *Das dritte Buch über Achim* makes its effect partly by juxtaposing the different connotations of the words *kriegerisch* ('warlike'), *ungerecht* ('unjust') and *Verrohung der Sitten* ('decline of moral habits') in East and West Germany:

die städtisch regierende Zeitung berichtete nur von der kriegerischen Rüstung des westdeutschen Staates, sprach von ungerechten

x

Gerichtsurteilen gegen Volksredner und von der zunehmenden Verrohung der Sitten . . . aber die westdeutschen Zeitungen sprachen unüberhörbar von der kriegerischen Aufrüstung des ostdeutschen Staates, von ungerechten Gerichtsurteilen gegen Volksredner und wachsender Verrohung der Sitten.

We are told about Karsch in East Germany that he was often deceived into believing in the unity of the two parts of Germany because he could still use the language he was used to in the West, but that similarity of language often only disguised underlying deviations:

die Sprache, die er verstand und mit dem er verständlich über den Tag gekommen war, redete ihn noch oft in die Täuschung von Zusammengehörigkeit hinein, wieder hielt er beide Staaten für vergleichbar, wollte in Gedanken sie reinweg zusammenlegen, da doch ein vergessenes Ladenschild oder die Sprache oder das vertraute Aussehen öffentlicher Gebäude in einem Land an das andere erinnert; dann aber gingen die Ähnlichkeiten nicht auf in einander.

He is struck at once, and throughout his stay, by these divergences. He finds it even difficult to understand the language of official newspapers, 'and this among people whose language, gestures, and faces he had had to learn from early childhood in daily contact with them'. The barrier of language is even more in evidence in *Eine Reise wegwohin* (1960), a shorter story with the same Karsch as the central figure:

selbst im umgänglichen Reden der gewöhnlichen Leute fand er sich kaum unauffällig zurecht, da ihm zehn Jahre dieser Geschichte fehlten; sie erkannten ihn ohne Mühe. Sie sprachen von Streuung. Engpaß, wo ihn nur die Worte Großhandel und Lieferschwierigkeiten zur Verfügung waren, seine Ratenzahlung nannten sie Sparkaufvertrag, und so deutlich er den Abstand bemerkte, den die Leute zu den Ausdrücken der Beamten hielten, er saß doch manchmal da und sprach sich im Kopf vor, was er sagen wollte, und hakte an beim Aussprechen.

When in this story Karsch returns to Hamburg, his own language has become so tinged with East German usage as to estrange him from old friends:

es saßen ihm aber ostdeutsche Sprachgewohnheiten noch so auf der

Zunge, daß er etwa rief, man müsse alles im Zusammenhang sehen, wenn er die Meinung eines anderen zu verworren fand, und die Blicke wandten sich ihm so befremdet zu, daß er nicht mit dem rechten Schwung erklärte, dieser offizielle Lehrausdruck der ostdeutschen Partei werde da unter den Leuten witzig verstanden, andere Druckverhältnisse vorausgesetzt.[25]

This is one reason why Johnson translates many contemporary political realities into a more detached terminology. Another is that they are thereby placed at a greater distance from the prejudice and passion of propaganda responses, as when what politicians and the press would refer to as the eastern block appears as 'die östlich benachbarten Staaten,' West Germany as 'die westdeutsche Länderunion' or 'der kapitalistisch arbeitende Teilstaat,' Ulbricht as 'der Sachwalter', the East German police as 'die Beauftragten des Sachwalters', Hitler as 'der Hausanzünder', and the National Socialist Party as 'der Verein für große Verschlechterung des Lebens'. Such terms are not necessarily without political nuances of their own, but in general the effect of such a method is to enable the contemporary reader to confront in a less instinctive way political problems poisoned by the language of ideology with its fixed and tyrannous labels: 'the positive result lies in the artistic achievement of having taken a problem of universal implications, thawed it out of the stereotyped patterns and phrases into which it had been frozen between the two fronts, and exposed it to the potential political conscience of the reader, which denotes at the same time a linguistic conscience'.[26] This adaptation of language is part of a process whereby also the particular is so formulated as to allow a more general significance. Gestures and movements can be described as isolated from and unrelated to the person to whom they belong, who thereby acquires a certain distance and anonymity. One instance would be the account of Karsch reading the paper in the tram:

morgens in den Straßenbahnen und auf seinen Reisen zu den Orten von Achims Jugend fand Karsch die Bewegung, die die Zeitungen vorbereitete zum Lesen: geübter Griff schlug das Titelblatt mit Nachricht und Ansporn und Kommentar mit dritter und vierter Seite zusammen zwischen zwei Fingern oben und unten, zog das Papier straff zwischen den Daumenballen, fünfte Seite: Sport.

Another is provided by the description of a crowd of young girls filled with rapturous enthusiasm at the sight of Achim:

> der hochatmende Ansturm junger Mädchen, die einander mit ihren Ellenbogen vordrückten zu Achim an ihn gepreßt mit Schenkeln und Busen und Haut, seine wachsame Kopfneigung inmitten all der hochgereckten duftenden Arme inmitten strahlend gläubigen Aufblicks.

In this last example Johnson concentrates into compact substantival forms what conventionally would be expressed more discursively and with greater reliance on verb-forms. Just as in the earlier example a wording like 'mit geübtem Griff schlug er das Titelblatt und die folgenden Seiten zusammen' would have conveyed a more personal and individual statement about Karsch than 'geübter Griff schlug das Titelblatt . . . zusammen, in the second the phrase 'inmitten strahlend gläubigen Aufblicks' has a more impersonal quality than the formulation 'während sie strahlend und gläubig zu ihm aufblickten'. In each case the subjective response is qualified and diminished by the focus on the noun.

While Johnson's language can thus be more condensed, it will sometimes be more expansive than the conventional usage. One example would be the reference to goods bought on hire-purchase as 'Geräte, die für teures Geld zu kaufen sind gegen den Verlauf der Zeit', where the expansion is brought about by stripping down into its constituent details a notion usually more summarily expressed. Discursive transcriptions of this sort strive for the greatest possible specificity, and at the same time they involve a greater degree of abstraction than the conventional definition. A good instance would be Johnson's version of what normal usage would be content to describe as 'berühmt als Rennfahrer', in the passage:

> fünfzehn Jahre nach dem verlorenen Kriege war Achim in Ostdeutschland berühmt für schnelles Fahren auf einer zweirädrigen Maschine, die angetrieben wurde durch die kreisende Tretbewegung seiner Beine mit Zahnrädern und Kette in die Drehung des Hinterrads übersetzt.

Inversely, abstractions can be treated as concrete realities, as when memory is talked about as a process whereby a vacant place in a person's attention is filled with a particular reality:

inzwischen nahm er sie wieder wahr, bevor er sie sah, als füllte sie eine freigelassene und nur vorläufig abgedeckte Stelle seiner Aufmerksamkeit aus mit der längst erwarteten Wirklichkeit von Schritt und Echo und langgliedriger Bewegung.

Among the characteristic features of Johnson's style[27] is a tendency to advance the verb. This technique is liable to lead to a density of adverbial phrases after the main verb as in the narrator's discussion of Karsch's original plan for a biography of Achim:

warum sollte Karsch nicht sechs Personen ehemals hinstellen in einen hartluftigen Oktoberabend unter die leise zischenden Lampen vor hupende Gepäckkarren an klappernde Biergläser und inmitten vielfältigen Lärms und Geschreis sie auch reden lassen über die Ereignisse, die Achims Aufstieg zu einer der höchsten staatsbürgerlichen Ehren vorbereiteten: oder ermöglichten: oder zumindest zeitlich davor geschahen.

His style is also marked by a greater preponderance of nouns than conventional writing would normally tolerate. Where, for example, one would expect the wording (in an observation about Karin) to run like this: 'daß sie ihre Gesichtszüge in jeder Lebenslage voll ständig in der Gewalt hatte', Johnson phrases it: 'daß sie ihr Gesicht so sich hatte und benutzen konnte für nicht zählbare Arten von Verhalten'. In the conventional version the emphasis is on the verb, on what she actually did, but with Johnson the importance of the verb is diminished by the addition of a phrase dominated by two substantives ('für nicht zählbare Arten von Verhalten') at the climax of the statement. The traditional sentence-structure, it has been said, 'expresses a sense of rounded meaning. Where this is no longer present traditional grammar is inadequate. Therefore, instead of a logical system of subsidiary clauses, Johnson prefers a paratactic sequence, a series'.[28] The inherent danger of the 'serial' sentence is obviously to reduce the style to a string of enumerations, but with Johnson the dialectic of abstraction and concretisation, of anonymity and specificity, of contraction and expansion, serves to give his writing a new and exciting tension. Since the 'serial' sentence also allows the author to view an object or problem from differing aspects, his style gains a multi-dimensional character. Keeping its distance from the language of propaganda, without forfeiting the possibility of satirising it, Johnson's style can be described as a diction of ideological disenchantment. At the same time, striving towards substantival constructions, it can reflect the situation of the modern individual encompassed by anonymous and impersonal forces. Thus many a passage, like the account in *Das dritte Buch über Achim* of Frau Liebenreuth answering the ring at the front door, yields under analysis the picture of the individual as an object among objects. But also Johnson's novels illustrate what has been singled out as a central theme in modern literature, 'the assertion of human values in everyday life and in a world of uniformity'.[29] This is evident in the way he will often, as if to take reality by surprise, grasp at the elusive moments of revealing individuality in people and things, and in those many phrases which suddenly in a word or two discover some idiosyncratic aspect—a smile, a gesture, the appearance of unattended motor-cars—transforming it into a new and startling experience.

Enzensberger spoke of Johnson's style as 'austere to the extent of being humourless and serious, solemn down to the Biblical rhythm and cadences audible in his sentences'.[30] Indeed, if one were to define the moral of his books, one might be tempted to refer to the Old Testament command: 'thou shallt make no false image'. This is used as title of a section in Max Frisch's *Tagebuch 1946–1949*, but Frisch's point is the familiar idea of the inadequacy of language to express our most essential experiences, so that we 'always talk about incidental matters which do not constitute what we really mean', and our actual experience is 'beyond the power of words'. With Frisch it is the inadequacy of language that above all hinders man when he 'feels the need to speak about a person',[31] with Johnson the point is primarily that personality itself is not stable or clear-cut enough for one to be able to have a sure knowledge of it, in oneself or in others. He sees man as necessarily always under the pressure of historical moments, local conditions, prevailing ideologies, of the need to conform, or at least to adopt the pose of conformity, in order to have a basis in social existence. Closer to Johnson is a passage in the novel *Herr Tourel* (1962) by Otto F. Walter, where he talks about the problem of communication between people and the misunderstandings that inevitably result: 'if we . . . were all to begin every sentence with the word "possibly", this would mark the beginning of peace in the world . . . I hate people who know everything about other people, their confidence gets on my nerves.'[32] What one reviewer wrote about Walter's book could just as well be applied to Johnson: 'but his distrust of the extent to which life can be narrated . . . includes a protest. It is the protest against the slick lie inherent in the totalitarian jargon of our time'.[33] A comment on Thomas Valentin's novel *Die Fahndung* (1962)[34] is relevant to the much more important work of Johnson: 'who is this person, this ego of mine? What has what I am today in common with what I was yesterday? What has what I am to A to do with what I am to B or C? Who is this single person behind all the images that people have of me: or am I any one of them?'[35]

Accordingly in one section of *Das dritte Buch über Achim* Karsch tries out Achim with a variety of possible identities in relation to a political demonstration—'for example as . . . then perhaps either it was Achim who . . . Or it may have been Achim who . . . Or an Achim who . . . Or an Achim who . . .' The same principle is at work in a passage about Karin and her life as an actress: 'Karin angrily swearing under the hands of the masseuse, Karin at the entrance to the hairdresser's saloon received by three deputies in white overalls, Karin in a whirl of rumours about the town . . . . ' It is exemplified, too, in the opening section of Reinhard Lettau's *Auftritt Manigs* (1963), where Manig is sketched from a number of different angles and in the light of a variety of different facets before we can be left with so simple a statement as 'Manig is sitting before us.' 'Each person', Lettau might be saying, 'is full of all sorts of possibilities', as Frisch puts it in *Mein Name sei Gantenbein,* whose central character exploring a set of roles, radically illustrates Johnson's dictum in *Mutmassungen über Jakob* that 'every individual is a possibility'.

So too, in a sense is *Das dritte Buch über Achim* as a novel. If in the first place it is about the problem facing a West German journalist trying to write a book about an East German cycling star, it is also about the problem of East and West and the difficulties of mutual understanding in a more than merely political sense, and about the problem of people really knowing each other in a complex, differentiated and highly organised world and, with implications about human relations of the most general kind and far beyond the fact of the division of Germany, about 'the border, the difference, the distance and the attempt to describe them'. Particular sections likewise illustrate this opening up into metaphorical possibilities. The account for example, of the night scene on the autobahn could stand in its own right as a metaphor of technically efficient and responsible driving, and beyond that of making the most of one's opportunities within the limits prescribed by the social needs of others. We glimpse this process at work in a remark about Karsch, that 'he had been led on from the portrayal of a racing cyclist to the account of a life'. Achim, an important personality in the conventional sense that he has caught the attention of politicians and the public, is more significant in that he serves to demonstrate the chameleon-like existence of modern man, who may change his identity many times in the course of his life without really noticing it himself. The identity of meaning of the novel itself can shift, its changing facets stirring our imagination to take note of new possibilities and to experiment with further hypotheses—a feature we noted also in *Die Blechtrommel*.

In one of his inner monologues Karsch is 'sure that he would never grasp anything through comparisons', and Johnson himself, asked whether he thought that East or West Germany had the better political system, answered that 'one cannot compare them. They present a fortuitous alternative, not a necessary one', it 'arose as a result of the war, and both victorious sides try now to demonstrate the value of their way of life'. Therefore 'logically this has to be regarded as chance' and the only legitimate question is 'what is of the most service to the greatest number of people'. Refusing commitment to fixed ideological programmes, Johnson's view corresponds to Enzensberger's attitude as he defined it in 1963:[36] 'we are not identical with either of these states, we cannot identify ourselves with one or the other. On the contrary, the more firmly their identity consolidates itself, the more questionable does our personal identity become'. In these words 'is defined the decisive feature that determines the relationship of the literary opposition to all-German politics. It takes up a position outside the reality of either part of Germany'.[37]

In political circles in West Germany today such an attitude is easily felt to be suspect, and it placed Johnson at one time at the centre of a heated controversy. This was sparked off by reports of a speech he had made at Milan on the occasion of the publication of the Italian translation of *Mutmaßungen über Jakob*. These proved inaccurate, but they were sufficiently trusted in influential circles for an attack to be launched against him in the Bundestag. At the Milan meeting Hermann Kesten had introduced Johnson in a speech where he spoke with rather ostentatious pathos of the epoch-making significance of the Berlin Wall. Replying, Johnson conceded that the Wall 'was an event, a real event that damages human rights'.[38] That would have been in order if he had not added the remark about these human rights that 'they were laid down in a Western agreement that the eastern block does not recognise'. Yes, he conceded, one must indeed make a choice between East and West Germany, but with understanding of the fact 'that the West German reality does not, in comparison with the East German reality, represent a genuine alternative, a national alternative. So a rational decision is not possible.' We have to understand the East Germans, he said, 'for the bravely maintained illusion of reunification demands of us that we prepare ourselves for such an understanding',[39] and so 'it would be a literary task to show that the East Germans are not, just because they build a Wall, barbarians.' In *Mutmaßungen über Jakob*, he said, his intentions had 'not been political at all', and for him the job of a writer was merely 'to tell a story,' which in this case meant 'to tell it not in such a way as to lead the reader into illusion, but to show him how the story really is.' The result to be aimed at is not to require of the reader 'that he immediately changes his views, but that he absorbs the story, thinks about it, and draws his own conclusions.' This remark sounds a Brechtian note, and many features of Johnson's novels lend themselves to comparison with Brecht's methods, by which he has clearly been influenced. Parallel to the idea of the 'epic theatre', Johnson employs the technique of breaking the narrative fiction by reflecting on it. Thus, for instance, we read in one passage of *Das dritte Buch über*

Achim that 'the economy of this conversation is not meant to give a feeling of pleasant tension', in another that 'this could be portrayed in a much more exciting way, but what's the point,' and analysis of a section like that on the theme of 'Attempt to buy a typewriter' would reveal in detail many Brechtian characteristics[40]—though Johnson had not yet appeared on the scene when Frisch, discussing Brecht's methods, wrote that 'it would be attractive to apply all these ideas to the narrative writer.'[41]

Other West German writers have published novels and stories about East Germany,[42] but Johnson alone has shaped the division of Germany into a theme of foremost literary significance. This he has done by freeing the treatment of it from the limitations of merely political discussion, and of language shackled to ideological habits of thought, and above all by raising it—in his first two novels, but not in *Zwei Ansichten* (1965)[43]—to the level of discussion of what Hans Werner Richter has called 'the modern problem of identity,'[44] which has emerged in our discussion as a central theme of the contemporary West German novel.

Conclusion

As the various chapters will have shown, the title of this book does not imply the intention to treat works of literature as if their interest lay only in the reflection of social trends, but all the same the structure and movement of the society in which these works came into being is of the greatest importance for their fuller understanding. Society provided their themes, and the whole awareness of the writers concerned was a response to its challenge and stimulus. It is the context in which, coming to grips with its problems and pressures, their imaginative activity assumed creative form, often in such a way that the relationship of the resulting fiction to the social aspects is of most compelling importance when least obvious and direct. The aesthetic qualities of these novels, including the writer's use of language, can only be appreciated, for what it intends and what it achieves, in the light of the tension between the writer and society. What this tension amounts to, and what its effects are, is the theme of every chapter. It would obviously be false to see literature as no more than the direct reflection of social data, more scientifically available anyhow to the historian and the sociologist, but we would reject, too, the other extreme of a restricted aestheticism, isolating the work from all that accrues to it from the writer's being engaged in taking issue with social experience, and tending implicitly to reject the supposed vulgarity of contemporary life by reference to an idealised image of aesthetic purity. We are, that is to say, in agreement with Böll in his hostility to any 'attempt to interpret without presuppositions a text that itself rests on presuppositions.'[1]

These considerations have, for the purposes of this book, made the fact of the affluent society of extreme importance. Since the affluent society is a pluralistic society, this term, too, is central to our discussion. By it is understood, in further extension of Tönnies's model of *Gesellschaft*, a society characterised by diversity, of individuals, groups, communities, cliques and parties. The structure of so 'opened' a society, in Andersch's sense, offers wide scope for majorities and minorities of any kind to assert their rights and intentions, which is not to say that all are represented with equal weight.[2] It is a society necessarily engaged in conflict within itself, which is something it can afford, in principle and by virtue of its material resources. Thus a leading West German sociologist has insisted on the positive importance of conflict in society.[3] and it would be characteristic of intellectuals there to regard limitation of the scope of conflict as regressive. The question of values is affected, but before one jumps to the conclusion that they do not exist, one must remember that such a society has the means, often more concealed than not, to influence the individual in given directions, to neutralise to some extent, the diversity it renders possible. Böll speaks of 'directed democracy' (*befohlene Demokratie*)[4] and Herbert Marcuse of 'subdued pluralism', in which 'the competing institutions concur in solidifying the power of the whole over the individual.[5] Koeppen's Keetenheuve, Grass's Oskar Matzerath and Böll's Hans Schnier realise this. As intellectual, picaro and clown, they particularly fear the power of ideology, to which in any case the previous stage in German history has made sensitive people exceptionally conscious.

The material prosperity associated with the pluralistic society has given rise to an enormous variety in matters of taste, so that in the arts anything can flourish, from esoteric avant-gardism to pop art, provided there is a public to regard it as worth paying for. The mass-media are the greatest patrons of an entertainment industry which has both ridiculous aspects and the virtue of furnishing unprecedented opportunities to put art on the market, but in conditions in which writers, like other producers, are subject to pressures (and not only of a simple market-kind) to outdate previous models with a new one. Yesterday's avant-garde easily becomes today's museum, as Enzensberger has noted,[6] and today's most daring experimentation with verbal structures may before long seem very much less surprising than one might imagine. The novelty of revolutionary literary techniques may be shortened to an extent that lends comparison with the production-life of many a manufactured article, whose designer quickly starts work on plans to render its appearance old-fashioned. One thing that this complex pressure for originality is coming to mean for the writer of today in terms of progress from one novel to the next—by comparison with earlier writers in slower moving societies, offering a less shifting basis to contemporary awareness—is that, like Grass, he may be accused merely of imitating himself.[7]

The fact that it is a single element in a proliferating *Kulturbetrieb* does not mean that the novel aspiring to high literary quality is lost in a mass of mediocrity. The pluralistic society necessarily increases rather than diminishes the public for it, and it is supported by many kinds of subvention, directly in the form of prizes and grants, indirectly in that this kind of society, by reason of its resources and its differentiated structure, plentifully provides forums of cultural activity, associated maybe with special publishing facilities. Also the distinction between the novel in the sphere of 'high' literature and the popular novel (of the illustrated mass-journals, for instance) is a question constantly under discussion. Certainly, by virtue partly of the increased scope of patronage, including the mass-media, and of opportunities to combine the profession of letters with at least relative affluence, the writer comes all the more under the influence of the material facilities provided by society, benefiting from it as well as harshly criticising it.

While there is no justification for Marcuse's pessimistic view that this development involves 'the liquidation of high culture,'[8] the writer is bound to feel himself to some extent superfluous in a society no longer granting metaphysical dignity to practitioners of the arts. Marie Luise Kaschnitz gives an account of a person who, having decided to give up writing, would like to take as the theme of a book a writer suddenly afflicted with doubts about the validity of art. Becoming aware of the demands and opportunities pressing on him from society, he loses the feeling of having as an artist any special function and sets out to 'find a straightforward, ordinary job'.[9] Against such a person, however, must be set those many contemporary writers anxious to assert and defend a special position in the pluralistic society, demanding from the authorities that they should be 'cultured', and complaining, like Grass in one of his election addresses, that the opposite is too much the case.[10] 'From the cabinet down to the barracks', Max Frisch has said, 'the state, as the governing power, ought to manifest culture'.[11]

Moreover, speaking thus with a sense of responsibility for man in general, as against those who for him represent particular interests (of ideologies, for instance, or political parties), the writer—one might equally in the contemporary context say the intellectual—does imply the claim to a rather special hearing amid the hubbub of voices of the pluralistic society. He may succeed in not being swamped in the buzz of conflicting argument, but at the risk of being branded a dilettante or a nuisance when he runs up against experts and men of affairs. His radicalism easily appears eccentric and, if he is allowed a hearing, it is not intended that his influence should be more than cursory. As himself providing what he says the state should manifest, namely culture, he enhances its prestige, and Böll has noted, for instance, the 'hysterical desire' of the politicians, on the occasion of the building of the Wall, to get writers to condemn it: 'when politics fails or suffers defeat . . . it is writers who are called upon to speak the persuasive word'.[12] On a cynical view one could say that, in letting the writer perform, the state does itself a service: tolerantly allowing him to indulge his critical work, society demonstrates how democratic it is. Advocating radical change, the writer to this extent consolidates the status quo. In Walser's satirical picture in *Eine gewöhnlich verlaufende Reise* of an intellectual living out the socially expected role of non-conformity, the protagonist's sense of occasion in public discussion allows him instantly to recognise when it is appropriate to shock his audience, 'in order . . . to show that with us more is allowed than one imagines'.[13]

However, it would be an oversimplification to regard contemporary West German writers merely as 'conformist rebels',[14] whose protest is ineffective. The radical non-conformity of their protest gives them, in fact, a very distinctive position. Theirs is an intellectual engagement combined with artistic sensibility, from which results an attempt to dissect society not through scientific analysis but through images of fiction.[15] Since their aim is to show, as in a model, the possibilities of human behaviour in contemporary society, they do not need naturalistic descriptions of milieu.[16] nor to keep to the laws of psychological probability. Their intention in their novels is not to mirror society realistically, but to provoke the reader into a position of detached observation from which, helped by distortion calculated to unmask hidden interests and ideologies, he can the better become aware of characteristic features too easily passed over. One consequence is a language of fiction reacting to the experience of contemporary reality both analytically and imaginatively.

While Gaiser's characters may fall fairly easily into the category of those who accept the social reality and those who do not, in the case of the other writers represented in this book, man's identity is felt as of such mobility and indeterminancy as to make the relation to society often hard to define in terms of acceptance or rejection. The very diversity of the pluralistic society may induce him to want compensation by committing himself to a binding individuality, or it may, by pressing upon him such a variety of role-expectations, make this impossible. Or he may consciously mask his individuality to preserve his freedom in conditions in which it is in the interests of modern bureaucratic and technological society that he conform to patterns of behaviour demanded by a complex system of division of labour. The state, Nossack has remarked, needs the individual to be functionalised in order 'that the organisational apparatus of society can function smoothly'. Resistance, in Nossack's phrase, can take the form of 'passive anarchy'.[17]

This is the context in which we have to see a great deal of the role-playing central to many of the novels considered in this book, consistent with the principle stated in Walser's *Halbzeit* that 'if you are one thing, you can be something else as well'. Yet, of course, metaphors of human life as a stage are of ancient, even pagan lineage, to which Christianity added the idea of God as director of the action.[18] Shakespeare's 'All the world's a stage' was already in an accepted tradition. Man could even be seen as playing many parts, but the accent was not on freedom of choice of roles such as we find in so many novels of our times. The concept of role is familiar, too, in modern sociology. Dahrendorf[19] uses a passage from Musil's *Der Mann ohne Eigenschaften* as the basis for distinguishing between man as a conglomeration of socially prescribed roles (*homo sociologicus*), as conscious of himself while governed by conscious and subconscious impulses (*homo psychologicus*), and as free—not in the sense of developing an inherently individual essence, but, in Musil's phrase as 'passive fantasy' taking possession of 'unfilled spaces'.[20] Sociologists commonly use role in the first sense, but this will not do for the novels we have been concerned with, where most frequently what is involved is a way of gaining freedom, or at any rate endeavouring to do so, and in any case role-playing in contemporary imaginative literature cannot be subsumed under a single heading. We shall have, in fact, to refer to six categories of role-playing—as an experiment with personality, as a variety of roles taken over only in the imagination, as an imposed identity, as political and ideological disengagement, as the staging of protest against society from an outsider position, and as a mechanism of social adjustment.

Role-playing as experimentation with personality is at an early stage illustrated in Elias Canetti's novel *Die Blendung* (1931), where, in contrast to Professor Peter Kien, who vainly buttresses himself against society's threat to his sense of firmly established character (the 'auto da fé' in the title of the English translation referring to its ultimate annihilation), his psychiatrist brother, assuming the identity of any patient he is treating, develops into 'a great actor', 'lives in a great number of different worlds', absorbs 'countless roles'. Experimentally, like some 'cunning Odysseus', taking over other identities, he thereby proves his superiority over other people in a society characterised 'by a mad belief in mass values'. Again in Musil's *Der Mann ohne Eigenschaften* (1941), seeing through the personalities of others as conglomerates of acquired qualities, Ulrich sets out to prevent himself degenerating into a mere personality. Encouraged by his view that what is primary is not 'qualities' but 'spirit'—the spirit of experimentation, that is to say—he sees the world as a 'laboratory'. The role-playing set in motion by this insight may foster in him the feeling of being 'broken into pieces, but it makes him 'a man full of possibilities'. The important distinction to be made here is between roles unmotivated by 'spirit', in which the individual is fettered by society to uniformity, and roles directed by 'spirit', consciously entered into, through which the individual ironically distances himself from society.

Turning to the contemporary scene, in his novel *Niembsch oder der Stillstand* (1964) the life of the nineteenth-century poet Nikolaus Lenau serves Peter Härtling as a means of projecting on to the figure of Don Juan that of his protagonist as 'experimenter', existentially exploring 'the possibility that is Don Juan'. Through this double existence Niembsch lives 'separated from himself' and, like Don Juan, without 'shamelessly . . . clinging to an existence with roots and obligations'. Existing as a figure in and through language, Don Juan appears to Niembsch as the 'echo image' of one whose life, like his own, was 'tied to language' and without words was powerless, 'saw nothing, was aware of nothing'. As a person able thus to realise his existence in role-playing (elaborated through references to Kierkegaard and Nietzsche), Niembsch is a 'comedian', always longing for the 'static' amid the experience of repetitions of love, and therefore always striving, through the roles he assumes, for the 'annihilation' of self. The counterpointing in the structure of the book of everyday realism and philosophic speculation has its justification in the dialectic, in the style of Don Juan, of zest in living and reflective melancholy. The source of the latter is the recognition that an existence lived out in a complex set of roles leaves only 'inhumanity' behind the mask, its compensation the being raised thereby into the sense of participating in, and surviving in, a general process of eternal recurrence. If 'I had not jumped into Don Juan's figure and used him as a mask, I should not have got beyond my beginning'.

The second category is illustrated in Koeppen's *Das Treibhaus*. Aside from his practical life in the everyday world, Keetenheuve fluctuates between a number of different identities. To this inner ambivalence and indeterminacy contribute the spiritual uncertainties in West Germany in the brusque transition to affluence, the alienation of the intellectual in relation to a society offering him little apparent prospect of an obvious function, the openness of the political situation, and the decline of ideological authority. In Max Frisch's *Mein Name sei Gantenbein* (1964) the roles, tersely defined in a way reminiscent of Koeppen ('Gantenbein as chess player', 'Gantenbein as host', and so forth) remain imaginary too. 'I shouldn't like to be anyone actually experiencing my stories', we read, but also 'every role has its particular guilt'. So, though every story is an 'invention',[21] their point of reference, since they indicate possibilities of existence that could materialise in hypothetical circumstances, has implications beyond the purely imaginary. The remark that 'everyone sooner or later invents a story for himself, which he comes to see as his life', raises indirectly the problem of language in so far as the reality behind the role is 'inexpressible'. What applies to Gantenbein is true of the other figures, who appear as exponents of roles assumed when the moment offers—in an imaginary present comprising past and future, which the novel accordingly fades in and out.

The third category of role-playing, as the image pressed upon the individual by society, had already been exemplified in Frisch's earlier novel *Stiller* (1954). Afraid of being forced by influences around him 'to play a role that would be very acceptable to people', Stiller's reaction is on the one hand despair in face of the apparently inescapable, on the other a longing to attempt to escape the image that society insists upon. In seeking to do so, however, and in deceitfully assuming the role of a Mr. White, he is shown as the prisoner of an arbitrary view of himself. His self-alienation in the figure of Mr. White is facilitated by the fact that in the 'age of reproduction', 'most of the things we have absorbed we . . . . have never seen directly, we see and hear and know everything from a distance (*wir sind Fernseher, Fernhörer, Fernwisser*)'. He tries to prove that he is not Stiller by means of detailed descriptions of distant parts, but the court sees through this easily enough: 'nowadays there is . . . no longer any terra incognita. So why keep telling stories—it doesn't prove that you were there.' Gradually it dawns on Stiller that, in his attempt to replace society's 'passport identity' of himself with one of his own making, he is really running away from himself.

In the fourth category belongs Böll's *Billard um halbzehn* with its portrayal, in Heinrich, Johanna and Robert Fähmel, of attempted retreat from ideological pressures into a private world, a tone of protest here combining with refusal to get involved— only Johanna is prepared to go so far as to express the need to take action. In the fifth category, where a role can serve as a means of satirically exposing society, Grass's Oskar Matzerath and Böll's Hans Schnier can assume the mask of those embodying disliked social characteristics in order thereby grotesquely to mirror them.

In the final category, represented by Johnson's *Das dritte Buch über Achim*, the stages in Achim's life from Hitler Youth to Socialist Unity Party show him adopting different roles in response to ideological demands, while using them—exactly to what extent it is impossible to know—as a facade behind which to conceal his true thoughts and feelings. In a society subjected to a succession of ideologies an individual may the more easily learn to harbour contraditions and, with the diversity of interests and pressures, the pluralistic society equally may be conducive to role-acrobatics. In *Halbzeit* Walser talks about it as a society 'in which one does not know oneself'. Anselm Kristlein's roles, however, are not just dictated by society, so he is not of the type exemplified by the Viennese satirist Helmut Qualtinger in the figure of Herr Karl,[22] always adapting himself to what circumstances demand. It is as a conscious artist in the acrobatics of role-playing that, drawing on the inner resources of a many-sided person, Anselm assumes and switches roles. He is 'richly furnished within', as someone says of him, and the 'product'—the selves he creates by self-manipulation—is 'impenetrably rich, like nature itself, for it is nature'. But Nietzsche is also right when already in *Die fröhliche Wissenschaft*, speaking of the age as one in which 'everybody is convinced of being capable of almost anything, of being up to the demands of any role', 'experiments with himself, improvises, experiments anew, experiments with pleasure', says that 'nature ceases and becomes art'.[23] Here, too, man—no longer the slave of an inherited disposition or of a particular milieu—is seen as having developed a scientific experimental attitude to himself, manipulating his existence into an artefact.

So, apart from obviously ministering to man's delight in dressing up to act a part (as with Picasso, long 'fascinated by the changes of personality that masks and disguises can bring about'[24]), role-playing can be seen as signifying a new kind of freedom. It need not be lamented as marking the dissolution of personality in the older sense, as completed, adult character. This can now present itself rather as a distortion of human nature, and already at the end of the eighteenth century Hölderlin could declare that 'only the child is free. He alone has peace. He is not at odds with himself. He is full of richness'.[25] So his Hyperion preserves a longing again to enjoy 'just a moment' of childhood's 'peace', to be 'near to nature'.[26] What is here sought in the direction of nature, the contemporary novel by contrast offers in and through society—liberation from the restrictions and obligations of personality, as something fixed and dead. The outcome may be role-playing as an aid to the business of mere adjustment to social pressures, but, (in Hölderlin's phrase) with character 'plunged into chameleon-like colours',[27] offering also the possibility of protection against them. As Adorno puts it, 'only by accommodating the objective reality within himself and . . . consciously adapting himself to it, can the individual resist it'.[28]

So, if the contemporary novel presents a satirical picture of society, this is not in order to set up against society the ideal of withdrawal to a private sphere apart. Its protagonists are made to meet the challenge of society. This confronts them, amongst other things, in its many kinds of jargon, the implications of which, as arsenals of uncritically articulated prejudice, the novel has consciously under scrutiny. In an age 'in which slogans are pasted on every wall and the newspapers disseminate their stereotyped phrases, the poet strives to reduce the catchwords and slogans in circulation to their true meaning'.[29] Recognising that everyday language has inherently the tendency to become jargon, the novelist is a lot of the time engaged in critique of jargon, himself maybe taking over its language in order to manoeuvre it into contexts calculated to force it to reveal what it would rather conceal. With the language of jargon, harnessed to the service of utility or a cause, Walser contrasts the 'free language' of the creative writer. This 'often looks as if it were useless, like the language of the spectator, and this is what it really is'. For this reason 'it never becomes blind',[30] it 'is least liable to degenerate into jargon'—or, as Böll puts it 'to have the edges knocked off' in order 'that the words can be made smooth and glib'.[31]

Walser adds that 'if it were not for this free language, jargon would have nothing to feed on. It would ossify into collections of formulae, and this is what it is'. It is because jargon is always prone to take over words and phrases originally at home in the individual language of imaginative prose that writers have an interest in fashioning language resistant to its interests—language with unusual combinations of adjectives and nouns, with long, dense sentences, esoteric imagery, and sharpness of detail, language aiming to communicate not the general and the abstract, but 'the way reality resists over-hasty interpretation'. Such language is available only to the writer whose critical, one might even say ironic, awareness recognises the alienating advantages of distance between society and himself. From this position alone, moreover, and through the medium of a language by which jargon and ideology can be measured and judged, he can in the present situation be both creative artist and engaged critic of society.

Notes

Introduction

[1] 'Zola und Daudet', in *Die Gesellschaft*, 1885, reprinted in Erich Ruprecht (ed.), *Literarische Manifeste des Naturalismus, 1880-1892*, Stuttgart, 1962, p. 58.

[2] *The Craft of Fiction*, London, 1921, pp. 172 seq.

[3] Cf. Wolfgang Kayser, 'Die Anfänge des modernen Romans im 18. Jahrhundert', in *Deutsche Vierteljahrschrift für Literaturwissenschaft und Geistesgeschichte*, XXVIII (1954).

[4] Wolfdietrich Schnurre, in the preface to his early stories (1945-47) collected and published under the title *Man sollte dagegen sein*, Olten and Freiburg i. Br., 1960.

[5] Ibid.

[6] Reprinted in Hans Werner Richter (ed.), *Almanach der Gruppe 47*, Reinbek bei Hamburg, 1962.

[7] K. A. Horst, *Das Spektrum des modernen Romans*, Munich, 1960, p. 12.

[8] Thus in 1956 it could be stated in the journal *Texte und Zeichen*, II, 4, p. 343, over the signatures of Th. W. Adorno, Max Bense, Wolfgang Koeppen, Karl Korn and Alfred Andersch that 'the word "socio-critical" seems to us identical with the word "novel"'.

[9] Addressing an audience at Marburg University, quoted by Jan Brockmann, 'Beim Blättern im Poesiealbum der Moderne', in Horst Lehner (ed.), *Zeitalter des Fragments*, Herrenalb/Schwarzwald, 1964, p. 160.

[10] The terms are here used in the sense attributed to them by René König, *Soziologische Orientierungen*, Cologne and Berlin, 1965, p. 91.

[11] *Gemeinschaft und Gesellschaft*, Leipzig, 1887, I.

[12] Deutscher Taschenbuch Verlag ed., 1962, p. 54.

[13] Peter Szondi, *Theorie des Dramas*, Frankfurt am Main, 1963, p. 83.

[14] Op. cit., III.

[15] Ed. cit., p. 20.

[16] *Aufzeichnungen 1942-1948*, Munich, 1965, pp. 8-9.

[17] Arnold Gehlen, *Anthropologische Forschung*, Reinbek bei Hamburg, 1961, pp. 133, 134.

[18] Bermann Fischer ed., Stockholm, 1948, p. 372.

[19] R. M. Rilke and Lou Andreas Salomé, Zurich and Wiesbaden, 1952, p. 126.

[20] *Gesammelte Werke in Einzelausgaben* (ed. Adolf Frisé), Hamburg, 1952, p. 665.

[21] Cf. also the motto-quotation of Ror Wolf's novel *Fortsetzung des Berichts* (1964): 'the ground on which we walk . . . is the only basis of the daily life of all of us'.

[22] *Gesammelte Schriften* (Musarion ed.), XVI, Munich, 1925, pp. 304-5.

[23] Stuttgart, 1965, p. 51.

[24] *Der Büchner-Preis. Die Reden der Preisträger 1950–62*, Heidelberg and Darmstadt, 1963, p. 126.

[25] 'Der Garten von Arles' (1920), in *Gesammelte Werke*, II, Wiesbaden, 1958, p. 90.

[26] 'Am I a German?', in *Encounter*, XXII (1964), 4, pp. 16–17. In German in *Die Zeit*, 5 June 1964.

[27] Rudolf Krämer-Badoni, 'Bankrott der doppelten Moral', in *Vorsicht, gute Menschen von links*, Gütersloh, N/D 1962, p. 20.

[28] Karlheinz Deschner, *Talente, Dichter, Dilettanten*, Wiesbaden, 1964, p. 9.

[29] Josef-Hermann Dufhues in a speech at Dortmund. Cf. Friedhelm Bankloh, 'Parteisekretarielles Mißfallen an Literaten', in *Frankfurter Hefte*, XVIII (1963), 5.

[30] 'Die Clique', in Hans Werner Richter (ed.), op. cit., pp. 22 seq.

[31] The whole speech is printed in *Der Büchner-Preis*, pp. 81 seq.

[32] Cf. ibid., pp. 63 seq.

[33] In the poem 'Landessprache', in Enzensberger's *Gedichte*, Frankfurt am Main, 1962, pp. 47 seq.

[34] *Erfahrungen und Leseerfahrungen*, Frankfurt am Main, 1965, p. 50.

[35] Max Frisch, *Tagebuch 1946–1949*, Frankfurt am Main, 1950, p. 292.

[36] Except that here the writer joins in the argument; a similar de-mythologising of the writer's authority is evident in the 'Literary Collo-quium' in Berlin. Cf. Walter Höllerer (ed.), *Prosaschreiben. Eine Dokumenta-tion des Literarischen Colloqiums*. Berlin, 1964. One consequence has been the writing within the framework of the 'Literary Colloquium' of a novel (*Das Gästehaus*, 1965) by various writers as members of a sort of team.

[37] Quoted by J. M. S. Pasley in the introduction to his edition of Kafka, *Short Stories*, Oxford, 1963, p. 16.

[38] Max Frisch, in *Der Büchner-Preis*, p. 77.

[39] Th. W. Adorno, 'Zur Dialektik des Engagements', in *Die Neue Rundschau*, 1962, pp. 93 seq.

[40] Diana Trilling on Norman Mailer, in *Claremont Essays*, London, 1965, p. 195.

[41] *Der Büchner-Preis*, p. 94.

[42] In his poem 'Ins Lesebuch für die Oberstufe', in *Gedichte*, ed. cit., p. 28.

[43] From Walser's address ('Imitation oder Realismus') to the 1964 Con-ference of Germanists in Essen, printed in full in *Germanistik in Forschung und Lehre*, Berlin, 1965 pp. 247 seq.

[44] Cf. R. F. Behrendt, *Der Mensch im Licht der Soziologie*, Stuttgart, 1962, pp. 62 seq.

[45] Michael Hamburger, *From Prophecy to Exorcism*, London, 1965, p. 96.

[46] Quoted by Victor Lange, 'Ausdruck und Erkenntnis. Zur politischen Problematik der deutschen Literatur seit dem Expressionismus', in *Die Neue Rundschau*, 1963, p. 105.

[47] Arnold Gehlen, *Die Seele im technischen Zeitalter*, Reinbek bei Hamburg, 1957, p. 12.

[48] Horst Bienek, *Werkstattgespräche mit Schriftstellern*, Munich, 1962, p. 216.

[49] From his article 'Wo Dichtung von der Naturwissenschaft lernt', in *Die Welt der Literatur*, 13 May 1963.

[50] Cf. his article 'Kleines Gnadengesuch für die Fabel', in *Die Welt*, 30 April 1965.

[51] Wiesbaden, 1964, p. 37.

[52] Alfred Andersch, *Die Blindheit des Kunstwerks und andere Aufsätze*, Frankfurt am Main, 1965, p. 30.

[53] Into this context fits, too, Walser's remark in *Erfahrungen und Leseerfahrungen*, Frankfurt am Main, 1965, p. 97; 'Wir bleiben hinter unseren Möglichkeiten zurück, wenn wir die Sprache nicht anstrengen zu solchen Experimenten des Zweifels'.

[54] Gehlen, op. cit., p. 32.

[55] Helmut Schelsky, *Ortsbestimmung der deutschen Soziologie*, Düsseldorf and Cologne, 1959, pp. 67 seq.

[56] Ed. cit., p. 280.

[57] Jürgen Becker in his introduction to Jürgen Becker and Wolf Vostel, *Happenings*, Reinbek bei Hamburg, 1965, p. 17.

[58] In this connection Martin Kessel's undistinguished novel *Lydia Faude* (1965) is of some interest, since it has the appearance of being an older version completed under contemporary conditions—its author was born in 1901. The heroine, in refined protest against this 'vulgar century' (p. 78), asserts, and sets out to live by, the principle that Benn describes as a 'swindle': 'you adapt yourselves to circumstances, I always remain the same person' (p. 258). But, in pursuit of this ideal, she is forced into an existence of role-playing, requiring a good deal of theatrical imagery, and in due course it has to be said of her that 'in fact she sometimes had not known who exactly she was' (p. 293).

[59] Cf. Egon Becker, 'Das Bild der Frau in der Illustrierten', in *Zeugnisse, Th. W. Adorno zum 60, Geburtstag*, Frankfurt am Main, 1963. Also Wolfgang Langenbucher, *Der aktuelle Unterhaltungsroman*, Bonn, 1964, and Dorothee Bayer, *Der triviale Familien- und Liebesroman im 20. Jahrhundert*, Tübingen, 1963.

[60] Dr. Gerd Bucerius, publisher of *Stern* (and also of *Die Zeit*), quoted by Hans-Albert Walter, 'Die Illustrierten. Schizophrenie als journalistisches Prinzip' (II), in *Frankfurter Hefte*, XX (1965), 4, p. 275. Cf. also (by diverse hands) *Trivialliteratur* (Berlin, 1964), pp. 23 seq.

Chapter I *Gerd Gaiser*

[1] With reference to modern literature, Ingeborg Bachmann speaks of 'a conscious weakening of names', the reduction of names to mere ciphers (*Chiffren*)' and, with special reference to Kafka, of a 'striking link between this refusal by authors to give names' and the way characters are stripped of features relating to their 'origin, milieu and individual qualities'. Cf. 'Aus den Frankfurter Vorlesungen', in her *Gedichte, Erzählungen, Hörspiel, Essays*, Munich, 1964, pp. 316, 317, 122. By this standard Gaiser would in

this instance illustrate the opposite tendency, namely the use of a character-ful, typifying name symptomatic of a person's rootedness in a community. His delight in names (cf. p. 2) might, in fact, appear as a reflection of his predominantly conservative view of life and society.

[2] Bienek, op. cit., p. 214.

[3] Cf. note 1 above.

[4] It is in part this quality of Gaiser's style that has provoked criticism from a number of intellectuals whose social and artistic ideals are dia-metrically opposed to his. In his article 'Gegen die Überschätzung Gerd Gaisers' (in *Die Zeit*, 28 November 1960) Walter Jens said: 'it really must be stated that of all post-war writers who have won fame and respect Gaiser seems to be quite the worst stylist. His German is in a word wretched'. It is true that Gaiser is open to criticism for a number of superfluous coinages, where existing words could have been used without detriment and loss of effect. Examples (in *Das Schiff im Berg*) would be *Trocknis* for *Trockenheit*, *gliß* for *gleißte*, *perlmuttrig* for *perlmuttern*. Such instances do not seriously affect his qualities in matters of style.

[5] As a portrayal of German airmen's existence, a contrast to Gaiser's novel is provided by Emil Schuster's *Die Staffel* (1958), where the rather bleak style corresponds to the sober and unheroic picture. An equivalent account of army life, apart from Böll's work, is found in Josef W. Janker's novel *Zwischen den Feuern* (1961), a little known work that Böll himself has praised. Cf. his review in *Frankfurter Hefte*, XVI (1961), 7.

[6] Ed. cit., XIII, p. 92.

[7] The dancing teachers retain their claims to be arbiters in certain matters affecting social decorum. On the occasion of the Queen's visit to West Germany, for example, it was reported in the press that 'a booklet compiled by the Etiquette Committee of the German Dancing Teachers' Association advises those who want to greet the Queen warmly but politely to clap or wave' (as opposed to shouting 'Heil'). Cf. *The Birmingham Post*, 17 April 1965.

[8] Gaiser's phrase is closely akin to Heidegger's designation, derived from Hölderlin, of the present phase of things as a *dürftige Zeit*: das Weltalter ist durch das Wegbleiben des Gottes, durch den 'Fehl Gottes' bestimmt . . . Der Fehl Gottes bedeutet, daß kein Gott mehr sichtbar und eindeutig die Menschen und die Dinge auf sich versammelt und aus solcher Versamm-lung die Weltgeschichte und den menschlichen Aufenthalt in ihr fügt . . . Die Zeit der Weltnacht ist die dürftige Zeit, weil sie immer dürftiger wird. Sie ist bereits so dürftig geworden, daß sie nicht mehr vermag, den Fehl Gottes als Fehl zu merken. Cf. 'Wozu Dichter?', in *Holzwege*, Frankfurt am Main, 1950, p. 248.

[9] Ed. cit., XVIII, p. 24.

[10] On the influence of Nietzsche in *Das Schiff im Berg*, cf. Curt Hohoff's comment (in *Gerd Gaiser, Werk und Gestalt*, Munich, 1962, p. 28) that 'Hagmann's notes sometimes sound like jottings by Nietzsche'.

[11] In his novel *Der Überläufer* (1962), Wilhelm Lehmann uses exactly the same phrase. But, unlike Gaiser, Lehmann never seems to note the ambival-ence of nature, that it creates and also destroys. The context in which this

phrase occurs in *Der Überläufer* exemplifies his one-sided, idyllic attitude to nature and also the way he draws on the language of myth to express it: 'der Lebenstraum aber bewährte allen Wesen Wohlgestalt, wie er sie trug, da er Noah in die Arche begleitete, und wie er sie morgen und übermorgen trägt, damit sie sich immer wieder in der herrlichen Endlichkeit tummeln können'. This, it is true, links up in theme and tone with an aspect of Gaiser's attitude to nature in *Das Schiff im Berg*, but, deeply aware of the destructive forces of nature, Gaiser has a much more problematical relationship to nature than Lehmann, revealing a more complex insight.

[12] Cf. Armin Mohler, *Die konservative Revolution in Deutschland 1918–1932*, Stuttgart, 1950.

[13] *Ausgewählte Werke, Prosa II*, Frankfurt am Main, 1951, pp. 321 seq.

[14] *Sein und Zeit* (1927), translated by John Macquarrie and Edward Robinson, London, 1962, p. 212.

[15] Valuable from this point of view is Fritz Stern, *The Politics of Cultural Despair*, Anchor ed., 1965, pp. 25 seq.

[16] 'Our speech has ceased to speak, it shouts; it says cute, not beautiful, colossal, not great; it cannot find the right word any more, because the word is no longer the designation of an object, but the echo of some kind of gossip about the object'. Cf. 'Die Reorganisation des Adels', in *Deutsche Schriften*, 3rd ed., Munich, 1937. First published 1878.

[17] Cf. Stern, op. cit., p. 84.

[18] 'The nation is bored: therefore individuals through smoking, reading, theatre-going, bar-loitering, home-gardening, and the addiction to magazines try to dispel their awareness that ciphers like themselves cannot stand being alone for any length of time'. Quoted by Stern, ibid., pp. 57–8.

[19] 'On the surface of the new Reich swims the *Literat* . . . This poisonous weed must be extirpated from our streams and seas, as must the political system without which this weed could not survive. (Then) the clean mirror will reflect the flowers of the shore and the stars of heaven, the ancient gods will re-emerge from the depths . . .' Quoted in ibid., p. 55n.

[20] The title of Heinz Piontek's review of Gaiser's *Gib acht in Domokosch* ('Ältere Heimat') reflects this aspect. Cf. *Zeitwende*, XXX (1959), pp. 705 seq.

[21] We put it like this to avoid going as far as the critic who describes this person as 'the representative of transcendental authorities', although he can refer to a private letter from Gaiser. Cf. Erich Hülse's analysis of *Schlußball*, in Rolf Geißler (ed.), *Möglichkeiten des modernen deutschen Romans*, Frankfurt am Main, Berlin and Bonn, 1962, pp. 180–1.

[22] A version, that is to say, of chapter 4 was published in *Das Innere Reich*, IX (1942), pp. 69 seq.

[23] As is clearly apparent in the scene between Lavinia and the narrator at the Settefontane well. Cf. original ed., Munich, 1960, p. 244.

[24] Bienek, op. cit.

[25] *Die Gegenwart*, X (1955), p. 665. Reprinted in Sieburg, *Verloren ist kein Wort*, Stuttgart, 1966, pp. 54–6.

[26] Cf. for example, his review of *Einmal und Oft*, in ibid., XI (1956), pp. 813–14.

²⁷ *Vorsicht, gute Menschen von links*, Gütersloh, N/H (1962), p. 128.

²⁸ Blöcker was one of the critics whose very positive appraisal of Gaiser it was the intention of Helmut Kreuzer to 'correct' in his essay 'Auf Gaisers Wegen. Korrektur eines Bildes', in *Frankfurter Hefte*, XV (1960), 2, pp. 128 seq.

²⁹ Cf. Marcel Reich-Ranicki, *Literarisches Leben in Deutschland*, Munich, 1965, p. 126.

³⁰ There are significant passages to this effect in his *Die neuen Wirklichkeiten*, Berlin, 1957, and *Heinrich von Kleist oder Das absolute Ich*, Berlin, 1960. The same tone is occasionally heard in his recent book of essays and reviews *Literatur als Teilhabe* (Berlin, 1966), as in the study of Jakov Lind (pp. 189 seq.).

³¹ *Kritisches Lesebuch*, Hamburg, 1962, p. 335.

³² A case in point is Soldner's attitude in *Schlußball* in the section entitled 'Eine fremde Stimme. Das Eisen ist los'.

Chapter II *Wolfgang Koeppen*

¹ Julius Deussen, 'Streiflichter und Entscheidungen', in Werner Deubel (ed.), *Deutsche Kulturrevolution. Weltbild der Jugend*, Berlin, 1931, pp. 238 seq.

² Obviously the groups here referred to correspond in certain respects to Thomas Mann's distinction between *Kultur* and *Zivilisation* (in his *Betrachtungen eines Unpolitischen*, written during World War I). For a discussion of the earlier history of these terms and equivalent categories cf. Michael Pflaum, 'Kultur und Zivilisation. Überblick über die Geschichte der beiden Wörter', in *Wirkendes Wort*, XV (1965), 5, pp. 289 seq.

³ Walter Jens, 'Der Schriftsteller und die Politik', in *Literatur und Politik*, Pfullingen, 1963, p. 10.

⁴ 'Autobiographische Skizze', appendix to Reclam edition (Stuttgart, 1961) of Koeppen's *New York*, pp. 65–6.

⁵ From Koeppen's contribution ('Ein Kaffeehaus') to *Atlas zusammengestellt von deutschen Autoren*, Berlin, 1965, p. 94.

⁶ Bienek, op. cit., p. 49.

⁷ The reference is to Moeller van den Bruck's *Das dritte Reich*, 1923.

⁸ This type of thinking is analysed by Armin Mohler, op. cit.

⁹ Cf. *Der Büchner-Preis*, Heidelberg and Darmstadt, 1963, pp. 134, 135.

¹⁰ 'Unlauterer Geschäftsbericht', in Uwe Schultz (ed.), *Das Tagebuch und der moderne Autor*, Munich, 1965, p. 13.

¹¹ Peter Rühmkorf, 'Das lyrische Weltbild der Nachkriegsdeutschen', in Hans Werner Richter (ed.), *Bestandsaufnahme. Eine deutsche Bilanz 1962*, Munich, Vienna and Basel, 1962, p. 463.

¹² Georg Lukacs, *The Meaning of Contemporary Realism*, London, 1963, p. 26.

¹³ Ernest Gellner, *Thought and Change*, London, 1964, p. 155.

¹⁴ Walter Jens, 'Melancholie und Moral. Eine Laudatio auf Wolfgang Koeppen', in *Die Zeit*, 26 October 1962.

¹⁵ Uwe Schultz (ed.), op. cit., p. 14.

¹⁶ Bienek, op. cit., p. 50.

[17] Cf. p. 69.

[18] Alfred Andersch, *Wanderungen im Norden*, Olten and Freiburg i. Br., 1962, pp. 217, 218.

[19] Erich Franzen, *Aufklärungen*, Frankfurt am Main, 1964, p. 47.

[20] From Koeppen's postscript to ibid., p. 181.

Chapter III   *Heinrich Böll*

[1] For a detailed and personal account of Böll's boyhood and youth cf. his contribution ('Raderberg, Raderthal') to *Atlas zusammengestellt von deutschen Autoren*, Berlin, 1965, pp. 191 seq.

[2] 'Hierzulande', in Böll's *Erzählungen, Hörspiele, Aufsätze*, Cologne and Berlin, 1961, pp. 429 seq.

[3] Originally in *Akzente*, 2 (1955), 1.

[4] Cf. Wolfdietrich Rasch's comment on Böll's 'resistance to the claims of compact reality', his distrust of 'what one calls reality, which, by the mere fact that it exists, exerts a sullen authority'. Cf. Rasch's essay 'Lobrede und Deutung' in the volume (by various hands) *Der Schriftsteller Heinrich Böll*, Cologne and Berlin, 1959, p. 10. A new edition appeared in 1965 with greatly extended bibliography.

[5] 'Der Zeitgenosse und die Wirklichkeit', in *Erzählungen, Hörspiele, Aufsätze*, p. 348.

[6] The theme of this play links a war-time episode of a young man sentenced to death for giving food to a Pole with that of a girl years later who dies on the eve of receiving her first communion. Her father had been a fellow-prisoner of the young man, who was secretly being prepared for his first communion (by the language of tapped signs on the cell wall), but is put to death before he can receive it.

[7] Cf. Horst Haase, 'Charakter und Funktion der zentralen Symbolik in Heinrich Bölls Roman *Billard um halbzehn*', in *Weimarer Beiträge*, 1964, 2, p. 223.

[8] Cf. J. P. Sartre, *Being and Nothingness*, translated by H. E. Barnes, New York, 1956, pp. 98–99: 'His [the café waiter's] movement is quick and forward, a little too precise, a little too rapid. He comes towards the patrons with a step a little too quick. He bends forward a little too eagerly; . . . All his behaviour seems to us a game . . . But what is he playing? We need not watch for long before we can explain it: he is playing at being a waiter in a café.

[9] In their instinctive acceptance of life, of its changes and its transitoriness, these women workers represent a sense of permanence untroubled by intellectual doubts and intellectual vanity. In case one is tempted to take the quotation as indicative not merely of Heinrich Fähmel's but also of the author's admiration for the simple people, one must be careful not to draw wrong conclusions as to Böll's idealisation of the *Volk*. His thinking is too intellectual for him not to recognise the unbridgeable gap between the position of a person like himself and those to whom, being simple and intellectually undemanding, integration presents no problem at all. His admiration on the one hand and his awareness of being different on the

other emerge in his introduction to a volume of illustrations of Cologne (*Unter Kranenbäumen—Bilder aus einer Straße*, Cologne, 1958): 'these streets can only live in their totality, not in their isolated features. They are like colonies of plants nourished by secret roots. In them the simple *Volk* is still alive—ancient, proud, unapproachable, and true to its own laws'.

[10] 'Vom deutschen Snob', in *Die Zeit*, 8 September 1961.

[11] These aspects are obviously connected with the sense of unreality, or waning reality, that pervades the book from the start. They stand in sharp contrast to the 'life in the street' as sketched in through a chain of nouns in the passage: 'lorries, apprentices, nuns; life in the street, boxes in front of green-grocers' shops: oranges, tomatoes, cabbage'. The vital phrase ('life in the street') is repeated in a number of variations throughout the narrative to accentuate the extent to which the Fähmels, particularly Robert, have taken up a position remote and detached from ordinary life.

[12] 'Leiden und Größe Richard Wagners', in *Adel des Geistes*, ed. cit., p. 398.

[13] 'Freud und die Zukunft', ed. cit., p. 579.

[14] *Kritisches Lesebuch*, Hamburg, 1962, p. 288.

[15] Ed. cit., III, p. 46.

[16] 'Die Sprache als Hort der Freiheit', in *Erzählungen, Hörspiele, Aufsätze*, Cologne and Berlin, 1961, pp. 442–3.

[17] Rudolf Walter Leonhardt, 'German Parallels', in *The Guardian*, 4 July, 1963.

[18] Marcel Reich-Ranicki, in his review in *Die Zeit*, 10 May 1963.

[19] Cf. in this connection Böll's reference in his *Frankfurter Vorlesungen* (Cologne and Berlin, 1966, p. 108) to Jean Paul's comment about humour, that its concern is not with 'any single foolishness, any particular fools', but with 'foolishness and a crazy world'.

[20] 'Potemkin am Rhein', in *Die Zeit*, 14 June 1963.

[21] The dangers of the other approach are illustrated, for example, in Paul Schallück's *Engelbert Reineke* (1959). The moral idealism of the book, turning on the principle that 'everything we now do is connected with what lies behind us' and involving the question whether one can make 'a fresh start, without the past, without sorrow, revenge and ressentiment', is obvious enough, and the cause the novel pleads is a worthy one. But it relies too easily on what are basically propaganda statements and it is too fond of opposing jargon attitudes of one kind by ready-made attitudes of another. Just as Schallück confronts his schoolmaster-hero with representatives of the older generation in the staff room, in *Anfrage* (1960) Christian Geißler has his hero seek out protagonists of the attitudes he abhors (for equally worthy reasons) and argues with them. The result, however, as K. A. Horst observed in *Jahresring 60/61*, p. 354, has rather the character of polemical journalism. The hero of *Anfrage* is—like Hans Schnier for that matter—in revolt against 'the whole magic world of demagogic half-truths', but one may be forgiven for not taking too kindly to the element of demagogy in his own crusade and the way his convictions, like Engelbert Reineke's, tend, as so often with self-righteous virtue, towards stereotyped and cliché positions.

[22] Peter Rühmkorf, *Kunststücke*, Reinbek bei Hamburg, 1962, p. 116.
[23] Cf. p. 103.
[24] Joachim Kaiser, reviewing *Ansichten eines Clowns* in *Die Zeit*, 31 May 1963.
[25] H. A. Grunewald (ed.), *Salinger. A Critical and Personal Portrait*, London, 1964, p. xiv.
[26] *Der Fänger im Roggen* and *Franny und Zooey*, Cologne and Berlin, 1963.
[27] Op. cit., pp. 56, 49.
[28] Reinhard Baumgart, reviewing *Ansichten eines Clowns* in *Die Zeit*, 21 June 1963.
[29] Tristan Rémy, *Clownnummern*, Cologne and Berlin, 1964, p. 276—a translation of Rémy's *Entrées Clownesques*.
[30] 'Der Intellektuelle und die Gesellschaft', in *Die Zeit*, 29 March, 1963.
[31] H. M. Enzensberger's poem 'Schwierige Arbeit' (dedicated to Adorno) in *Blindenschrift*, Frankfurt am Main, 1964, p. 58.
[32] *Die Blindheit des Kunstwerks und andere Aufsätze*, Frankfurt am Main, 1965, p. 2 n.
[33] *Der Mensch ohne Alternative*, Munich, 1961, p. 276.
[34] 'Links in der Bundesrepublik?', in Horst Krüger (ed.), *Was ist heute Links?*, Munich, 1963, pp. 35 seq.
[35] *Schreibtisch unter freiem Himmel*, Olten and Freiburg i. Br., 1964, p. 229.
[36] 'Personal Responsibility under Dictatorship', in *The Listener*, 6 August 1964.
[37] *Encounter*, August 1964, pp. 54, 55.
[38] 'Polemik eines Verärgerten', in *Was ist heute Links?* pp. 43 seq.
[39] Cf. for example Josef Beuys, in Jürgen Becker and Wolf Vostell (ed.), *Happenings, Fluxus, Pop Art, Nouveau Réalisme. Eine Dokumentation*, Reinbek, 1965, p. 327: 'Die Absicht: Das heilsame Chaos, heilsame Amorphisierung in eine gewußte Richtung, die bewußt eine erkaltete, erstarrte Vergangenheitsform, gesellschaftliche Konvention durch Auflösung erwärmt und zukünflige Gestalt erst möglich macht'.
[40] Op. cit., p. 107.

Chapter IV *Günter Grass*

[1] Quoted by H. M.-Brockmann, *Dichter und Richter. Die Gruppe 47 und ihre Gäste*, Munich, 1962, p. 120.
[2] Published in *Die Zeit*, 16 February 1962.
[3] Cf. Grass's letter to Anna Seghers in ibid., 18 August 1961.
[4] 'Grass als Redner', in ibid., 24 September 1965.
[5] Since the Dreyfus affair brought the term into the vocabulary, Cf. Victor Brombert, *The Intellectual Hero. Studies in the French Novel 1880–1955*. London, 1960, pp. 21–2.
[6] Michael Hamburger, in *Die Zeit*, 19 October 1962.
[7] Robert Alter, *Rogue's Progress, Studies in the Picaresque Novel*, Cambridge, Mass., 1964, p. 107.
[8] Ibid., p. 107.
[9] Rudolf Krämer-Badoni's *In der großen Drift* (1949) did not make enough impact to contribute, as did *Die Blechtrommel*, decisively towards

reviving the picaresque tradition in the post-war German novel. A revised edition appeared in 1961.

[10] *Der Zeitpuls fliegt. Chansons, Gedichte, Prosa*, Reinbek bei Hamburg, 1958, pp. 77–8.

[11] Ibid., p. 78.

[12] 'Einige Notizen zuvor', foreword to the novel, Deutscher Taschenbuch Verlag ed., p. 7.

[13] Review by Wolfgang Maier, in *Sprache im technischen Zeitalter*, I (1961), pp. 68–71.

[14] Frank Kermode, in the Third Programme.

[15] Walter Jens, *Deutsche Literatur der Gegenwart*, Munich, 1961, and Grass, 'Ohrenbeichte', in *Sprache im technischen Zeitalter*, II (1962), p. 170.

[16] Cf. p. 26.

[17] For a short discussion of this novel, cf. Hans Mayer's essay in the symposium *Walter Jens. Eine Einführung*, Munich, 1965, pp. 88 seq.

[18] Walter Jens, 'Eine Kumpanei zur Verhinderung von Unfug. Fünfzehn Jahre Gruppe 47', in *Die Zeit*, 21 September 1962.

[19] 'Vom Kinderreim zur heutigen Lyrik', in ibid., 25 August 1961.

[20] Munich, 1963, pp. 17, 18, 61.

[21] Günter Blöcker reviewing *Hundejahre* in the *Frankfurter Allgemeine Zeitung*, 14 September 1963.

[22] Klaus Wagenbach on *Hundejahre* in his review in *Die Zeit*, 20 September 1963.

[23] Roland Barthes, 'Littérature Objective', in *Critique*, X (1954), p. 585.

[24] H. T. Levin, *The Gates of Horn*, New York, 1963, p. 453, referring to Robbe-Grillet's *La Jalousie*.

[25] *La Modification*, Paris, 1957, p. 196.

[26] Roland Barthes, op. cit., p. 591.

[27] Review of *Die Blechtrommel* in *Frankfurter Hefte*, XIV (1959), II.

[28] Cf. p. 101.

[29] Hans Egon Holthusen, *Avantgardismus und die Zukunft der modernen Kunst*, Munich, 1964, p. 56.

[30] C. G. Jung, *Symbols of Transformation, Collected Works*, V, London, 1956, pp. 218, 219.

[31] *Der Spiegel*, 17 September 1962, p. 77.

[32] To this criticism of a particular feature of the translation of *The Tin Drum* by Ralph Manheim (London, 1961) we should like to add the comment that in our view the translation is in general strikingly successful.

[33] In his review ('Trommelt weiter') of *Katz und Maus* in Frankfurter Hefte, XVI (1965), 12.

[34] The phrase is in Blöcker's review of *Hundejahre* in the *Frankfurter Allgemeine Zeitung*, 14 September 1963, reprinted (with many other of Blöcker's reviews) in his *Literatur als Teilhabe*, Berlin, 1966.

Chapter V *Martin Walser*

[1] In his postscript to the first volume of *Einzelheiten* (edition suhrkamp, 1965, p. 207), Enzensberger quotes the same statement from Aby Warburg,

the art historian, with the comment: 'I personally would not go so far as that. But it does seem to me advisable to get closer to phenomena and not to be afraid of the resistance that the particular and the specific may offer. We have been often enough and all too hastily informed about beauty and truth, about humanism, or about the broad connections and the background of things'.

[2] Bienek, op. cit., pp. 193–4.

[3] C. Wright Mills, *White Collar*, published in 1951, republished in the Galaxy Book series, New York and Oxford, 1956, p. xii.

[4] Helmut Schelsky, *Wandlungen der deutschen Familie in der Gegenwart*, 4th ed., Stuttgart, 1960, p. 230.

[5] Bienek, op. cit., p. 195. In a later work, in fact, he emerges as a writer. Cf. p. 103.

[6] *Erfahrungen und Leseerfahrungen*, 1965, p. 66.

[7] Bienek, op. cit., p. 198.

[8] Marcel Reich-Ranicki, 'Der wackere Provokateur Martin Walser', in *Die Zeit*, 27 September 1963.

[9] *Erfahrungen und Leseerfahrungen*, pp. 124 seq.

[10] Reich-Ranicki, op. cit.

[11] 'Ein Brief', in *Prosa II*, ed. cit., p. 14.

[12] Enzensberger, 'Ein sanfter Wüterich', in *Die Zeit*, 29 September 1961.

[13] Wilfried Berghahn, reviewing *Halbzeit* in *Frankfurter Hefte*, XVI (1961), 2.

[14] Ed. cit., XVI, p. 307.

[15] Op. cit.

[16] 'Einer der auszog, das Fürchten zu verlernen', in *Die Zeit*, 15 September 1961.

[17] Günther Zehm, in *Die Welt*, 7 December 1963.

[18] F. H. Hoffman, *Samuel Beckett. The Language of Self*, Carbondale, 1962, p. 8.

[19] Olten and Freiburg i. Br., 1965, p. 216.

[20] Ibid., p. 78.

[21] Walser's introductory essay to *Jonathan Swift, Satiren*, Frankfurt am Main, 1965.

[22] The remark, for example, about Swift's 'need to be accepted by other people' connects Walser's argument with Hans Beumann's problems. The way Walser seeks to relate the fact that Swift 'did not learn how to find himself confirmed as a stable person through continuity of contact with a firm social reality', and the need and ability he attributes to him to assume masks and roles, is in line with essential features of *Halbzeit*.

[23] Ibid., pp. 34, 30.

[24] *Einzelheiten*, I, ed. cit., p. 75.

[25] Wright Mills, op. cit., p. 157.

[26] Printed both in Wolfgang Weyrauch (ed.), *Ich lebe in der Bundesrepublik*, Munich, N/D, pp. 110 seq., and Walser, *Erfahrungen und Leseerfahrungen*, 1965, pp. 29 seq.

[27] In Enzensberger (ed.), *Kursbuch*, 4, 1966.

[28] *Beschreibung einer Form*, Munich, 1961, pp. 12, 13.

²⁹ *Encounter*, 110, 1962, p. 88.
³⁰ *Erfahrungen und Leseerfahrungen*, p. 98.
³¹ Ibid., p. 98.
³² Werner Riegel, *Gedichte und Prosa*, Wiesbaden, 1961, pp. 42 seq.
³³ *Ja und Nein. Neue kritische Versuche*, Munich, 1954, p. 217.
³⁴ In addition to the references that follow, mention should be made of the novel *Der Partisan* (1961) by Hans Joachim Sell. It is the story of one who asserts his desire for independence—epitomised in his motor car, in which he travels restlessly from place to place, striking roots nowhere—by resisting any kind of human relationship that would bind him to the demands and conventions of society, and by cultivating an aristocratic detachment of a kind curiously attractive to people he comes in contact with. As to the definition of 'partisan' in this book, there is the statement: 'what matters to him is always the moral stand, the assertion of an attitude. And if he does not find antagonists, he leads an existence apart until some appear.'
³⁵ p. 17.
³⁶ 'Der Mensch in der heutigen Literatur', in *Jahresring 62/63*, Stuttgart, 1962, pp. 44 seq.
³⁷ The 'partisan' image, of course, has a certain relation to the 'deserter', and, as we have seen (cf. p. 98), this too creeps into *Halbzeit*. The 'deserter' motif figures, for instance, in the title of Peter Weiss's *Fluchtpunkt* (1962) and prominently in the work of Alfred Andersch, notably in *Sansibar oder Der letzte Grund* (1957) and *Die Rote* (1961).
³⁸ Olten and Freiburg i. Br., 1961, p. 163. All the same, Leo in *Der Löwengarten* is more a satirical picture of the intellectual who has renounced ideology, by contrast with those 'ideologists' who 'used to throw bombs at the structure of the existing order of things'. He is a person 'who is no longer concerned with the world as a whole'.
³⁹ *Beschreibung einer Form*, p. 22.
⁴⁰ Walser in a letter to Melvyn Dorman, 1967.

Chapter VI *Uwe Johnson*

¹ Johnson's first novel, written between 1953 and 1955, never appeared because the East Berlin Aufbau Verlag demanded alterations of a political kind; 'to make the changes, I should have had to alter my way of looking at things, and I could not do this. So I withdrew the manuscript.' Cf. Bienek, op. cit., p. 105. *Mutmaßungen über Jakob* is thus really Johnson's second novel, but his first published one.
² Ibid., p. 88.
³ As noted by Marcel Reich-Ranicki, 'Der Mensch zwischen den Gleisen', in *Die Welt*, 21 September 1963.
⁴ There is inevitably a strong temptation to read this as a symbol. Gotthard Wunberg's sensitive interpretation of the episode, however, is too restrictive when he says ('Struktur und Symbolik in Uwe Johnson's Roman *Mutmaßungen über Jakob*', in *Neue Sammlung*, II, p. 448): 'Jakob, so to speak, deliberately places himself at cross-purposes with this link between East and

West. In crossing the lines, he retraces the line of the frontier'. This would be acceptable if it were put forward as a single 'speculation' among other possible ones.

[5] In an interview with *Konkret*, January 1962, p. 19.

[6] Johnson in a letter to W. van der Will.

[7] Günther Rühle, 'Notiert nach einem Gespräch', in *Neue Presse*, 24 October 1959.

[8] John Mander, in *Encounter*, 110, 1962, p. 80.

[9] Marcel Reich-Ranicki, op. cit.

[10] Wilhelm Emrich, *Geist und Widergeist*, Frankfurt am Main, 1965, p. 64.

[11] One experiment in 'speculation' suggests itself if one recalls, for instance, that Jacob's name is traditionally associated with a pilgrim's staff ('with my staff I passed over Jordan'). The context (in *Genesis*, XXXII, 10) then becomes curiously suggestive—Jacob had 'sojourned in Leban and stayed there until now', he 'divided the people that was with him . . . into two bands', the Lord said to him, 'return unto thy country and thy kindred', and he said to the Lord, 'deliver me, I pray Thee, from the hand of my brother'.

[12] Cf. Karl Pestalozzi, 'Achim als Täve', in *Sprache im technischen Zeitalter*, VI (1963), pp. 479 seq.

[13] A reviewer in the *Schwäbische Donauzeitung*. For some very good comments on the language, particularly as regards sentence-structure, cf. Karl Migner, *Uwe Johnson, Das dritte Buch über Achim*, Munich, 1966.

[14] One must, however, be careful to distinguish between errors and avant-garde usage—as Karlheinz Deschner fails to do in his review sarcastically entitled 'Johnson auf der Schwelle der Meisterschaft', in *Rhein-Neckar-Zeitung*, 2–3 June 1962.

[15] Cf. Conclusion, note 21.

[16] Paris, 1956, p. 8.

[17] In his novel *Der Mann, der nicht alt werden wollte* (1955) Walter Jens had applied certain features of the detective story in the account of a person's efforts to reconstruct another's biography.

[18] 'Die Form der Detektivgeschichte und die Philosophie', in *Die Neue Rundschau*, 1960, p. 665. Bloch's comment is quoted by K. A. Horst, *Kritischer Führer durch die deutsche Literatur der Gegenwart*, Munich, 1962, p. 444.

[19] Richard Alewyn, 'Das Rätsel des Detektivromans', in Adolf Frisé (ed.), *Definitionen, Essays zur Literatur*, Frankfurt am Main, 1963, pp. 177 seq.

[20] A further instance of the way present-day writers seem sometimes to like to adopt the airs of a detective story is provided by the first novel of a young Swiss writer living in West Germany, *Im Sommer des Hasen*, by Adolf Muschg (Berlin, 1965), in which a group of young writers is under scrutiny by a firm anxious to select the right man to work in its publicity department. The narrator, telling the story in the form of a report, says: 'for I don't want to throw away what these pages, about the choice of a suitable person, have in common with a detective story by wilfully excluding a suspected person—if it is not a Whodunit, it is at any rate a Who-will-do-it' (p. 52). In the last sentence, emphasising the tone of the detective story, the English term ('Whodunit') is taken over.

²¹ Cf. p. 100. How far views have changed in the past thirty or forty years is incidentally reflected in the case of Joseph Roth's novel *Der stumme Prophet*, in which the 'attempt at a biography' is carried through with a confidence uninhibited by any comparable misgivings. Completed probably in the late 'twenties, this novel was published (Cologne and Berlin) in 1966.

²² Peter Rühmkorf, 'Ein Rücktritt als Auftakt', in Hans Werner Richter (ed.), *Plädoyer für eine neue Regierung oder Keine Alternative*, Reinbek bei Hamburg, 1965, p. 23.

²³ In an address at Wayne State University, printed in *Evergreen Review*, XXI, November–December 1961, pp. 29–30.

²⁴ Ibid., pp. 21–2.

²⁵ *Eine Reise wegwohin, 1960* appeared in a collection of short texts by Johnson entitled *Karsch und andere Prosa*, Frankfurt am Main, 1964. Compared with *Das dritte Buch über Achim* the story, which is a variation of the novel, shows a tendency towards a strengthened position of the anonymous third-person narrator. Karsch has been transformed from an agent to an object of the narrative. He is not allowed to give his own accounts of a situation. He now is himself the object of the story. We learn, for example, that Karsch is fat and that he is suffering from an illness with symptoms that could indicate epilepsy. Such close-ups of his person could never have been permitted in the novel, where he is the medium through whose information we get to know the events. Already in the sketch *Boykott der Berliner Stadtbahn*, published in *Die Zeit*, 10 January 1964, pp. 9–10, the author no longer tolerates a narrative which, through the employment of a number of narrators, becomes a search for possibilities, of understanding and interpreting facts from various points of view. Although still writing in the detached style developed in his earlier novels, and despite the cool tone of his language, the author is heavily committed to demonstrating the absurdities of Western policies in Berlin. As a focus for his narrative he chooses the boycott by West-Berliners of the 'Stadtbahn', which is run by the railway authorities in East-Berlin and which maintains stations in both parts of the city. In his novel *Zwei Ansichten*, Frankfurt am Main, 1965, Johnson confirmed this tendency towards conventional third-person narration. Except in minor and incidental respects the style is fairly orthodox, and of the two main protagonists the East German representative is a more living and plausible person than her opposite number from the West. A section originally destined to form part of this novel was published separately under the title 'Eine Kneipe geht verloren' in *Kursbuch*, 1, 1965, edited by Enzensberger. That this was separated off may be significant, since its style is more characteristic of the author of *Mutmaßungen über Jakob* and *Das dritte Buch über Achim*.

²⁶ H. P. Piwitt, 'Chronik und Protokoll', in *Sprache im technischen Zeitalter*, 1, 1961, p. 86.

²⁷ The question as to the influence of this on other writers is still a very open one. There are, for instance, features in Jürg Federspiel's *Massaker im Mond* (1963) and Peter Faecke's *Die Brandstifter* (1963) that justify at least a reference in this context, but the evidence is not substantial and, as regards Faecke, his subsequent novel, *Der rote Milan* (1965) adds nothing

to confirm the hypothesis. When in Rolf Dieter Brinkmann's *Raupenbahn* (1966) one comes across a phrase like '. . . dazwischen Sätze, halbe Sätze und Satzfetzen, die nah herankamen und, plötzlich zu verstehen waren für drei, vier Worte . . . one is bound to suspect Johnson's influence.

[28] Karl Korn in the *Frankfurter Allgemeine Zeitung*, 4 April 1964.

[29] Walter Jens, 'Der Schriftsteller und die Politik', in *Literatur und Politik*, Pfullingen, 1963, p. 20.

[30] In his review of *Mutmaßungen über Jakob* in *Frankfurter Hefte*, XIV 1959), 12.

[31] *Tagebuch 1946–1949*, Frankfurt am Main, 1950, p. 31.

[32] Munich, 1962, p. 168.

[33] *Neue Züricher Zeitung*, 1 September 1962.

[34] *Die Fahndung* concerns the search by an investigator for the identity of a person who is described as one of those people who keep making a fresh start and want every year to discard their past.

[35] Rino Sanders, 'Schnitzeljagd aufs Ich', in *Die Zeit*, 30 November 1962.

[36] In his Büchner Prize speech, in *Die Zeit*, 25 October 1965.

[37] Karl Sontheimer, 'Die unbequemen Mahner', in *Die Zeit*, 19 June 1964.

[38] On 8 December 1961 *Die Zeit* published extracts from Johnson's speech side by side with Kesten's account, a tape-recording having been made. The whole episode and related matters are briefly described by Reich-Ranicki, *Literarisches Leben in Deutschland*, Munich, 1963, pp. 45 seq.

[39] It is just such 'understanding' that Enzensberger seeks to foster in his 'Katechismus zur deutschen Frage' (in *Kursbuch* 4, 1966), to which, for example, Günther Zehm replied, in his article 'Reaktionärer Katechismus', in *Die Welt*, 26 March 1966.

[40] Brecht, of course, is not the only writer who should be mentioned in this context. In an interview with Günther Rühler (op. cit.) Johnson mentioned Musil, Joyce, Hemingway and Faulkner, as well as Brecht. It would be tempting to add to this list Barlach and Döblin, and also Gide who, notably in *Les Faux-Monnayeurs*, operated with a story within a story. In this novel, too, as in *Das dritte Buch über Achim*, the method is to have a fictitious author assemble the material.

[41] Op. cit., p. 294.

[42] Cf. Gerhard Zwerenz, *Aufs Rad geflochten* (1959), *Die Liebe der toten Männer*(1959); Eckhart Kroneberg, *Der Grenzgänger* (1960); Martin Gregor-Dellin, *Jakob Haferglanz* (1963—first published in East Germany, 1956), *Der Kandelaber* (1962).

[43] Our misgivings about this novel are very similar to those stated by Marcel Reich-Raniki in his review in *Die Zeit*, 24 September 1965.

[44] In discussing the problem facing a modern author in trying to keep a diary. The fuller context is: 'if I were to sit down to write a diary, doubts would immediately arise. Is the person thus writing his own life—my ego, namely—identical with himself? The modern question of identity could not be avoided, and the whole thing would then collapse'. Cf. Uwe Schultz (ed.), op. cit., p. 109.

Conclusion

1 *Frankfurter Vorlesungen*, Cologne and Berlin, 1966, p. 29.

2 Cf. C. Wright Mills, *The Power Elite*, New York, 1959, pp. 243 seq. First published 1956.

3 Cf. R. Dahrendorf, *Gesellschaft und Demokratie in Deutschland*, Munich, 1965, pp. 161 seq.

4 Op. cit., p. 42.

5 *One-Dimensional Man. Studies in the Ideology of Advanced Industrial Society*, London, 1964, p. 50.

6 Cf. Introduction to his *Museum der modernen Poesie*, Frankfurt am Main, 1960.

7 Walter Jens, '*Das Pandämonium des Günter Grass*', in *Die Zeit*, 6 September 1963.

8 Cf. Marcuse, op. cit., p. 70: 'the liquidation of high culture is a by-product of the conquest of nature, and of the progressing conquest of scarcity'.

9 'Der Schriftsteller', in *Die Neue Rundschau*, 1965, p. 572.

10 'We notice with horror that we have delegated the responsibility of government to men whose love of power is vast and unscrupulous, but whose degree of culture ought to make the nation blush with shame'. Cf. *Ich klage an*, Neuwied and Berlin, 1965, p. 13.

11 'Der Autor und das Theater', in *Die Neue Rundschau*, 1965, p. 36.

12 Op. cit., p. 18.

13 Cf. p. 103.

14 Cf. Erich Franzen's essay 'Die angespaßten Rebellen', in *Aufklärungen*, Frankfurt am Main, 1964, originally in the *Süddeutsche Zeitung*, 5/6 November 1960.

15 What can be meant by this is well illustrated by Walter Höllerer's comments about the novel *Das Gästehaus*, written by a number of collaborators, including himself (cf. p. 146): 'the main theme, as is hardly surprising in the case of a contemporary novel adhering closely to the social reality, is the individual in the group, his deviating from convention and his adhering to it in the larger unity of society with its division of labour. Significant symptoms of contemporary life find expression—the mechanisation of agriculture (making the town appear by contrast something of an idyll), an atmosphere of rationality and technology pushing religion more into the background, the "healthy commonsense" of the pragmatist, with its associated excesses of drug-taking and adventure, the primary importance of economic conditions, the effect of astrology and public relations on the individual existence. Neuroses and a militarist cult of order come into conflict. No, all this is not just irresponsible fantasy!' Cf. *Das Gästehaus*, Berlin, 1965, p. 232.

16 Reinhard Baumgart, however, treating them as if they were nineteenth-century realists, mistakenly supposes that Grass, Böll and Johnson 'would like faithfully to reproduce the contemporary reality, especially the social milieu'. Accordingly he criticises them on the grounds that all they depict is 'characters' instead of 'models of behaviour' (*Verhaltensmuster*),

that they restrict themselves to 'the petty-bourgeois milieu', which means that what they present is the social reality of the 'twenties and 'thirties, but not 'what seems contemporary in our society today'. Borrowing a phrase from Adorno, he speaks here of a 'realism derived from loss of reality'. It is true that in many of these novels petty-bourgeois attitudes play an important part, but not because these authors share them, but because they are dealing with a society in which they are very marked. In any case, the novels of Grass, Böll and Johnson include between them the technological world, the effects of extreme social mobility, and the sphere of the upstart and upper bourgeoisie. Cf. 'Kleinbürgertum und Realismus', in *Die Neue Rundschau*, 1964, pp. 650 seq. Cf. also Kurt Batt, 'Zwischen Idylle und Metropole', in *Sinn und Form*, XVIII, 3, pp. 1001 seq.

[17] 'Stimme und Verstummen', in *Jahresring 65/66*, Stuttgart, 1965, p. 239.

[18] Cf. E. R. Curtius, *Europäische Literatur und lateinisches Mittelalter*, Berne, 1958, pp. 146 seq.

[19] *Homo Sociologicus*, Cologne and Opladen, 1964, pp. 62 seq. First published 1958.

[20] *Der Mann ohne Eigenschaften*, Hamburg, 1952, p. 35.

[21] The technique whereby the narrator keeps interrupting the narrative by statements of his own in order to draw attention to the fictitiousness of his story is very much in evidence here. It is characteristic of some of Johnson's work too. More recent authors like the Swiss writer Peter Bichsel in his contribution to *Das Gästehaus*, and the Austrian Peter Handke in *Die Hornissen* (Frankfurt am Main, 1966) have obviously in this respect been influenced by Johnson and Frisch.

[22] *Der Herr Karl* (record), Lebendiges Wort (Austria), text by Carl Merz and Helmut Qualtinger in *Der Herr Karl und weiteres Heiteres*, München, 1959.

[23] *Die fröhliche Wissenschaft*, 5th Book ('Wir Furchtlosen'), 1886, ed. cit., XII, pp. 282–3.

[24] *The Sunday Times Magazine*, 25 April 1965, quoting from Roland Penrose, *Picasso at Work*, London, 1965.

[25] *Sämtliche Werke*, ed. Hellingrath, Seebass and Pigenot, 3rd ed., Berlin, 1943, II, p. 93.

[26] Ibid., p. 289.

[27] Ibid., p. 93.

[28] 'Glosse zur Persönlichkeit', in *Neue Deutsche Hefte*, 109, 1966, p. 52. Cf. also Arnold Gehlen, 'Das Ende der Persönlichkeit?' (1956), in his *Studien zur Anthropologie und Soziologie*, Neuwied and Berlin, 1963.

[29] Walter Jens, *Deutsche Literatur der Gegenwart*, Munich, 1961, p. 20.

[30] 'Einheimische Kentauren oder Was ist besonders an der deutschen Sprache', in *Die Zeit*, 20 November 1964.

[31] Op. cit., p. 28.

Chronological list of works

Koeppen, Wolfgang	*Eine unglückliche Liebe*	Berlin	1934
		republished	
		Stuttgart	1960
Koeppen	*Die Mauer schwankt*	Berlin	1935
Gaiser, Gerd	*Zwischenland*	Munich	1949
Böll, Heinrich	*Der Zug war pünktlich*	Opladen	1949
Gaiser	*Eine Stimme hebt an*	Munich	1950
Koeppen	*Tauben im Gras*	Stuttgart &	
		Hamburg	1951
Böll	*Wo warst du, Adam?*	Opladen	1951
Böll	*Und sagte kein einziges Wort*	Cologne &	
		Berlin	1953
Koeppen	*Das Treibhaus*	Stuttgart	1953
Gaiser	*Die sterbende Jagd*	Munich	1953
Koeppen	*Der Tod in Rom*	Stuttgart	1954
Böll	*Haus ohne Hüter*	Cologne &	
		Berlin	1954
Gaiser	*Das Schiff im Berg*	Munich	1955
Böll	*Das Brot der frühen Jahre*	Cologne &	
		Berlin	1955
Walser, Martin	*Ein Flugzeug über dem Haus und andere Geschichten*	Frankfurt a. M.	1955
Gaiser	*Einmal und Oft*	Munich	1956
Grass, Günter	*Die Vorzüge der Windhühner*	Neuwied &	
		Berlin	1956
Gaiser	*Gianna aus dem Schatten*	Munich	1957
Walser	*Ehen in Philippsburg*	Frankfurt a. M.	1957
Gaiser	*Schlußball*	Munich	1958
Koeppen	*Nach Rußland und anderswohin*	Stuttgart	1958
Böll	*Doktor Murkes gesammeltes Schweigen und andere Satiren*	Cologne & Berlin	1958
Gaiser	*Gib acht in Domokosch*	Munich	1959
Gaiser	*Sizilianische Notizen*	Munich	1959
Koeppen	*Amerikafahrt*	Stuttgart	1959
Böll	*Billard um halbzehn*	Cologne &	
		Berlin	1959

Grass	*Die Blechtrommel*	Darmstadt, Berlin & Neuwied	1959
Johnson, Uwe	*Mutmaßungen über Jakob*	Frankfurt a. M.	1959
Gaiser	*Am Paß Nascondo*	Munich	1960
Grass	*Gleisdreieck*	Darmstadt, Berlin & Neuwied	1960
Walser	*Halbzeit*	Frankfurt a. M.	1960
Koeppen	*Reisen nach Frankreich*	Stuttgart	1961
Böll	*Erzählungen, Hörspiele, Aufsätze*	Cologne & Berlin	1961
Grass	*Katz und Maus*	Neuwied & Berlin	1961
Walser	*Beschreibung einer Form*	Munich	1961
Johnson	*Das dritte Buch über Achim*	Frankfurt a. M.	1961
Walser	*Eiche und Angora*	Frankfurt a. M.	1962
Böll	*Ansichten eines Clowns*	Cologne & Berlin	1963
Grass	*Hundejahre*	Neuwied & Berlin	1963
Böll	*Entfernung von der Truppe*	Cologne & Berlin	1964
Johnson	*Karsch und andere Prosa*	Frankfurt a. M.	1964
Walser	*Erfahrungen und Leseerfahrungen*	Frankfurt a. M.	1965
Grass	*Ich klage an*	Neuwied & Berlin	1965
Johnson	*Zwei Ansichten*	Frankfurt a. M.	1965
Böll	*Frankfurter Vorlesungen*	Cologne & Berlin	1966
Walser	*Eine gewöhnlich verlaufende Reise* (in *Kursbuch*, 4, ed. Enzensberger)	Frankfurt a. M.	1966
Walser	*Das Einhorn*	Frankfurt a. M.	1966
Böll	*Ende einer Dienstfahrt*	Cologne & Berlin	1966

Index